Education in Early Childhood

First Things First

Edited by
Sue Robson and Sue Smedley

David Fulton Publishers
in Association with
THE ROEHAMPTON INSTITUTE

David Fulton Publishers Ltd
2 Barbon Close, London WC1N 3JX

First published in Great Britain by David Fulton Publishers 1996

British Library Cataloguing in Publication Data

A catalogue record for this book is available from the British Library

ISBN 1-85346-385-X

Typeset by The Harrington Consultancy Ltd. London N1 6DL
Printed in Great Britain by the Cromwell Press Ltd, Melksham

Contents

Contributors

Lynne Bartholomew is a senior lecturer in education at Roehampton Institute London and coordinator of Redford House Nursery, situated at Froebel Institute College. She was previously deputy head of a nursery school in Southall, West London, and is co-author, with Tina Bruce, of *Getting to Know You: a guide to record-keeping in early childhood education and care.*

Jane Devereux is a principal lecturer at Roehampton Institute London with responsibility for the Postgraduate Certificate of Education Primary Programme. She has a particular interest in science education and early years. Her other main area of interest is observation, and its place in teaching and learning, which includes research and shared publication with colleagues in Roehampton and a local education authority in London, of *Profiling, Recording and Observing: a resource pack for the early years.*

Pat Gura is a research associate at Froebel Institute College, Roehampton Institute London. She is deeply committed to collaborative action research with practitioners in the field of early childhood education and care, and the rights of children, parents and educators. She has served in both the voluntary and the maintained sectors as nursery nurse, playleader and nursery teacher. The editor of *Exploring Learning: young children and blockplay*, she is currently researching self-assessment in three–five year olds.

Peter Long is a senior lecturer in education at Roehampton Institute London. He has a particular interest in supporting student teachers and experienced early years practitioners in developing appropriate curricula and practice against a background of increasing legislative and external demands. Formerly an infant school headteacher, he is also a nursery and primary phase OFSTED accredited inspector of schools undertaking research on the impact OFSTED inspectors are having on early years practice.

Shirley Maxwell is currently the coordinator of Early Childhood Teaching Studies at Roehampton Institute London. She is involved in teaching across a wide range of courses and is particularly interested in INSET work with early years practitioners. Her past research interests have included investigation into language development and social integration, and she is currently involved in a study of practice and provision in reception classrooms.

Sue Robson is a senior lecturer in education at Roehampton Institute London, working on the Primary PGCE and MA programmes as well as INSET courses. She has worked in infant and nursery schools in West London, as teacher in charge of the nursery and as the deputy head of an infant and nursery school. Her main interests are home and school relationships and research into children's conceptions of play and work.

Sue Smedley is a senior lecturer in education at Roehampton Institute London, working on initial teacher education courses as well as INSET and education studies programmes. Her main areas of interest are early years teachers' culture and work, equality issues and language and literacy. Prior to joining Roehampton she worked as a teacher in primary schools in London.

Preface

Education in Early Childhood is a book for the present and the future – of children and those who teach them, and thus of us all. For children, their needs cannot wait, yet as professionals we must consider both the present and the future. This book looks at the immediate needs of children and the adults who work with them, as well as supporting longer term reflection and critical evaluation. It brings together aspects of working with young children, as seen by tutors in the Early Childhood Centre at Froebel College, Roehampton Institute London. The themes addressed are underpinned by a Position Statement compiled collaboratively by Early Childhood tutors which describes the priorities and aims of the Centre. Its themes are returned to and emphasised in different ways in each chapter.

The first three of these principles present a view of the child as a 'meaning maker' (Wells, 1986) and a 'going concern' (Winnicott, 1964), whose understandings arise from and are embedded in a social context. Wells' research led him to conclude

Figure 0.1

EARLY CHILDHOOD CENTRE
ROEHAMPTON INSTITUTE LONDON

POSITION STATEMENT

The purpose of the centre is to promote and foster early childhood philosophy, practice and profile, through enquiry and dialogue based upon the following principles:

- The child is a 'going concern'
- The child is a 'meaning maker'
- The child's understandings arise from and are embedded in a social context
- A distinction is made between education for understanding which is transferable; and education as the acquisition of inert bodies of knowledge
- The way that we teach children influences their present attitudes to learning and their future learning
- Equality of opportunity is not just an interesting option: it is an imperative
- Teaching is most effective when it is based upon informed observation of children and recognises that:
  - parents and other professionals concerned with the care and education of young children have important insights and contributions to make to learning and development
  - education and care interpenetrate in early childhood

that children are meaning makers, and the term conveys his view, shared by the Early Childhood team, that 'children are active constructors of their own knowledge' (Wells, 1986, p.65). This is exemplified by Shirley Maxwell's plea in Chapter 7 for professionals to take notice of children, to 'really look them in the eye' (p.87). Central to these principles is the imperative of taking children seriously.

Such a view carries with it implications for our role as teachers and for the ways in which we teach. In Chapter 2 Sue Smedley looks at what it means to be an early years teacher, challenging some traditional assumptions. Shirley Maxwell in Chapter 1 and Pat Gura in Chapter 3 look at the interconnectedness of teaching and learning, and some of the ways in which teachers influence the attitudes of children to their own learning, both present and future. Those attitudes will, to some extent, be shaped by the organisation of the environment in which adults and young children live and work, a theme considered by Sue Robson in Chapter 11.

The Position Statement draws attention to a distinction which can be made between education for understanding, and education as the acquisition of knowledge. This in turn has implications for the range of priorities we might choose to have for the education and care of young children, and for the nature of the curriculum. Pat Gura, in Chapter 10, argues for a particular view of that curriculum, based upon a moral rather than a legalistic view of entitlement. Sue Smedley in Chapter 8 considers the centrality of equality and equity as guiding principles, a theme further elaborated by Peter Long in Chapter 9, in his discussion of special educational needs. All three are underscored by the principle that equality of opportunity is an imperative and not just an interesting option.

Teachers do not work in isolation, and the principle that parents and other professionals concerned with the care and education of young children have important insights and contributions to make to learning and development forms a central theme of this book. Lynne Bartholomew, in Chapter 4 looks at this in relation to the nursery team, and the roles of professionals concerned with the education and care of young children. In Chapter 5 Sue Robson looks at this from the perspective of parents, stressing the need for a partnership between homes and schools based upon shared understanding and mutual respect. This theme is further taken up in Chapter 6, where Jane Devereux looks at the ways in which informed observations of children contribute to the effectiveness of teachers, as well as providing opportunities for a shared dialogue between homes and schools.

The suggestions for further reflection and activities included in many of the chapters can be considered by individuals or shared by colleagues. They are intended to focus thinking and to support critical reflection on early years' philosophy and practice. Above all, *Education in Early Childhood* emphasises the integration of action and ideas and the need for both in the work of professionals. Philosophy without action is no more useful than action without philosophy, and a consideration, both of what we do and of our beliefs, is central to the development of practice of a kind which remains open to reflection and scrutiny.

Sue Robson and Sue Smedley
March 1996

Chapter 1

Coming to know about children's learning

Shirley Maxwell

Introduction

The 1988 Education Act laid down a child's entitlement to receive the National Curriculum. It is apparent in the mid 1990s that this has resulted in an emphasis on *what* children must learn, the curriculum content, possibly at the cost of attending to the *ways* in which children learn.

In recent years OFSTED reports have been mainly positive about work in early years classrooms. There have, however, been research studies which do not show a good match between teacher-directed tasks and children's competence, needs and understandings. Bennett and Kell (1989), Wells (1986), and Tizard and Hughes (1984) have all produced evidence to indicate that this match is difficult to implement. The research of Stevenson (1987) showed four-year-old children actively engaged in classroom activity, constructing, estimating and measuring their buildings in collaboration with their peers while their teacher appeared unaware of the nature of their task and of the sophisticated nature of their discussion.

Could it be that practitioners were not clear as to the development of the children, the stage they were at? Could it be a lack of knowledge about pedagogy which persuaded them to employ a less than effective teaching strategy? Was it a lack of clarity of the purpose of tasks which allowed confusion in the focus? At least one matter is clear: that what the teachers intended was not always what the children perceived as their task. The children did not deem what they were asked to do to be valuable nor did it appear to be meaningful to them. As professionals we are becoming more accustomed to asking such questions of our practice.

An HMI report of 1988 suggested there was too much emphasis on formal reading and writing tasks by four year olds in reception classes and that children needed many opportunities for practical involvement. The OFSTED report *First Class* (1994) commented that the implementation of play as a tool for learning was not always well understood, and OFSTED reports from school inspections mention the need for challenging activity for the youngest children in school.

Understanding aspects of children's developmental growth and the ways they develop skills in interactive strategies is necessary for professional competence. Gaining confidence in one's knowledge of pedagogy is essential to the effective implementation of a curriculum if children are to experience learning that is both interesting and meaningful. I suggest three phases through which our understandings might progress, but, as with all conceptual understandings, there cannot be real divisions into separate entities and they will usually intertwine in reality.

The first phase is virtually inevitable. We have our own theories, formed from our own cultural background and affected by the people and situations we have met and the nature of the professional development we have experienced. Many who come in to teaching would say they like children, and that they have had particular experiences with them. However, there is usually a wide gulf between the knowledge acquired through these experiences and the complexities of knowing about the development of children and the professional role of working with them. Also, while it *is* important to recognise what our views are, and to start from where we are at, this can be difficult when we know so little of the whole. The second phase, though not separated from the first, might be a looking outward to other people's theories and practices. What literature do you turn to, and what journals do you read to become informed? What do you really know about what has been written, and how up to date are you with published research? What effect does it have on your practice? The third phase might be to turn to exploratory thinking about the nature of learning. This is where we take the theories of others or the viewpoints from our reading and begin to test them out for ourselves, in a genuine attempt to understand something more of children's learning. In order to do this we notice and focus on changes in the children and implement this knowledge through developments in professional practice.

Consider your own theories

Where do theories come from? It is certain that we all have them for this is the way we make our lives coherent for ourselves. Our own view of young children, and what they should become, is culturally determined by our own early experiences, in the first instance by our own childhood and later from the experiences which shape our lives. It is a useful exercise to draw up a time line of your life, from birth onwards, and to mark the important influences that have affected your development and made you the person you are with the beliefs you have.

Everyone has had the personal experience of being a child and of going to school, the result is that most people hold strong theories about the ways they think children should grow up, the best places to learn and the manner in which learning takes place. When we consider our theories we should take account of the following factors.

Cultural influences

Patrick, two years old and with nothing covering him but his bare skin, jumps high into the air, drops of water falling back into the sea as he does so. To western culture his whole body suggests movement and full involvement, freedom and the joy of living. There is developing physical control, personal action and sensory awareness of space and time. However, if we had been brought up in a country with strong religious beliefs pertaining to certain faiths, it could be that such a picture is offensive. Our mother may be the only person to have seen our body, and a child-centred culture of activity and individual freedom would not apply.

Atkin (1991) draws attention to some effective ways of considering our own cultural growth and awareness. She suggests that our idiosyncratic ways of looking at the world and our personal views of learning are deeply entrenched in our own cultural background, and that we draw from the ways those around us behaved, their sense of humour, and what they played out and enjoyed with us.

Children's learning in an early years setting must build upon what children bring to it if it is to be effective. Children must be able to 'make links in various ways with the everyday activities and special events of their families, their local communities and cultures' (Ministry of Education, 1993). This document was written in New Zealand, a country which has made a serious attempt to recognise the needs of people with differing cultural understandings.

A gap between personal understandings and the lives of the children and their families in early childhood settings is, to some extent, inevitable. However, to make the most of the environment for children's learning, practitioners need an awareness of their own thinking, alongside a knowledge of children's backgrounds, if they are to get close to providing a school situation where children's different experiences and cultural understandings, interests and competences on entry to school are recognised and valued.

Home and school

The unconsidered belief that children only start to learn when they go to school is a hard one to shift. Although research from Wells (1986), Tizard and Hughes (1984) and Heath (1983) has gone a long way to show the value and quality of learning that goes on at home, there are still many who hold a view that school is the place for learning how to read, write and do sums and that this will begin to show soon after entry, irrespective of whether children are four, five or six.

Historically, research into learning at school and at home has shown positive developments in both environments. The belief, prevalent in the 1960s and 1970s, that school was there to offset the deficiency of the home, was gradually eroded by powerful descriptions of the competence of children from developmental psychologists and the effective nature of interaction between parents and children in the home. By the 1980s the view was more prevalent that schools were the problem, with their lack of understanding of the richness of the home setting. A subtle change took place in the form of strengthened links between home and school and through such partnerships grew an understanding of the saying

'Learning does not begin at nine in the morning nor finish at three in the afternoon.' Parents became more consciously aware that children are learning everywhere and all the time. What we must question is what exactly it is they are learning, and whether it bears any resemblance to what we might have intended that they come to understand. Young children in a gallery class at the turn of the century were probably learning that the seats were very hard and the day very long, that teachers were to be feared and that remembering was difficult.

To extend children's learning in all facets of their lives, adults must feel comfortable with children. They will then be able to take notice of the sorts of things that children notice; they will know the sorts of things they enjoy, and the ways they are likely to respond. The more they know about children, the more confident they will feel in their presence and the more time and mental space they will then have to consider what they are doing with them. Concerns about controlling children will diminish and they will see evidence of how much children learn from their surroundings and their interactions with others.

Interest begets learning

The recent focus on providing interesting experiences for young children through the development of hands-on exhibits in museums and art galleries, might bring greater awareness to all families in the UK about the way young children's interest can be gained and their learning extended. Adults have a strong propensity to overload children with more information than they can manage and to overestimate their need to remember facts, at the same time underestimating the considerable intellectual capabilities of the young child: to question, explore and find out for themselves. Research would suggest this does not happen so often at home, but is prevalent in school learning. The following example, taken at news time in a reception class might illustrate the point. A young child tells the class that she went on a pony ride, and her teacher asks 'What colour were the ponies? Did they have names?' Another child, telling about the experience of playing on a bouncy castle is asked 'What shape was the bouncy castle?' This urge to monitor and vet the factual correctness of what children say is not often useful for extending children's thinking and can persuade them that it is better to keep silent. When teachers sterilise children's experiences in this way, they may be turning what was an interesting and emotionally rewarding account into a meaningless lesson. They are also assuming the right to test the child on his own experience, to define for the child which elements of that experience are to be valued.

Three, four and five year olds, at the stage when they move to a school setting, will still be the same children as they were in the home, but with a little more experience of their world. They will be learning to make transitions from the safety of people they know to people and places outside and beyond family life. It is likely that they will still be intensely interested in all they notice, feel and think about the world; that they will not yet know enough to care about the norm; and that the opportunities they experience and enjoy will depend to a large extent on the adults around them. They will still need adults to help them understand and make sense of all they do, but they can gradually do many more things for themselves with growing independence, and they are gradually becoming more interested in what others are doing and enjoy joining in as they do it.

It may be worthwhile to consider your own case:

- How did you come to know some of the things you already know and in what ways might you have come to know them?
- You are reading this book so can probably consider that you were a successful learner – why was that? Was it intelligence, a good school, your own or your parents' expectations, hard work?
- What is something you learned very quickly or something you learned very slowly? Were these practical skills or the development of concepts?

Consider other people's theories

Evans (1995) states 'nursery education in Britain is underpinned by a formative discourse which embeds the thinking of recognised pioneers in an essentially middle class values system, engages a narrative on psychological growth which is selectively constructivist, and reifies the action orientation of children's play'. The tone of this statement is one of criticism. If practice can indeed be described in this way, then it is important to ask if such practice arises by design or ignorance. Is there in fact a 'hole at the heart of early childhood belief', a 'vacuum caused by sitting at the feet of the gods for too long' as suggested by Drummond (1993)? The current view of young children in today's western culture means it is reasonably common that those who become engaged in work with young children fairly quickly adapt their thinking to accept child-centred philosophies. It can mean that they value the necessity for the children to be active in their learning but are unsure and confused as to where this leaves them as teachers. Does a commitment to child centredness mean allowing children to do much of their own thing? Is the adult role, as a rule, to stand back and only intervene with caution? How are decisions made as to where and when to intervene? How does one determine what is appropriate for each child if they are to be seen as individuals?

Just such a dilemma was well illustrated by a mature student, Ginny, during her post-graduate training. At the time of this example she was trying to work with a class of four-year-old children which included one child who refused to sit anywhere but under the table in the classroom. Ginny's intuition and sketchy understandings of child psychology persuaded her that she must be sensitive and not force the child, that the child's rights were important and her attitudes and emotional state possibly vulnerable. Yet, in her role as teacher, she knew there were parameters she must expect of children's behaviour and things they must learn at school. She was undecided whether to leave the child there or coax her out, and meanwhile was concerned in case all the other children decided to follow her example and sit under the table too. Impressions of a whole class of small children out of control came to the fore. Ginny did not have the means, at that point, to know what her action should be. Her knowledge of theories of child development and pedagogy were not sufficient to support the dilemmas she met in her practice.

Similarly demands in the 1990s for children to achieve levels on National Curriculum attainment targets can result in anxious teaching to the test. Critical thinking on how children learn best and holding one's nerve in the face of constant demand for change do not allow time or mental space for proper reflection on what theories underpin professional practice, nor even bring out the confidence truly to consider what one has already studied about learning. In the most negative scenario, teachers for whatever reason may be working only from received wisdom, that 'consensus' which Van der Eyken *et al.* (1984) describe. Sampling classroom practice they saw that sand and water play, painting and fantasy play were evident in most early years settings but these activities appeared to be more about occupying than stimulating. As a result Van der Eyken *et al.* questioned the value of the sand and water play they saw, suggesting it was a responsibility of students and teachers that they personally understand the nature of what they offered and its purpose better, if they were to provide effective learning opportunities. When work becomes merely customary and goals pragmatic there is the danger of taking practice for granted. Yet 'no practice is neutral or without values' (Tamburrini, 1981, p.161).

In the sections that follow I have chosen factors from well-known theoretical writings to highlight theories which are, in my view, relevant and important to current work with young children. However, these are not meant to be exhaustive nor the only important issues. What I do consider important is that professionals commit themselves to investigate and interrogate the things that interest them in their work. Like McAuley and Jackson (1992), I accept that the study of all human development is a legitimate and important area for research and repeat their statement that 'uncertainty is built into knowledge, and that is why the quality of judgement is so important and reflectiveness so prized'.

Early learning: a scientific view

Scientific evidence is said to have shown the remarkable plasticity of the human brain, especially before the age of five when 90 per cent of brain growth takes place (Brierley, 1987). This evidence would suggest that the years from 0–6 are fundamentally important in developmental growth. By three or four, a child's curiosity, critical sense, logic and imagination are well advanced, and their use of language, understanding and powers of thinking are all developing at a very fast rate. The branching of nerve networks in the brain and their possible responsiveness to their environment, Brierley believes, make it vital that children have new and challenging experiences which offer opportunities to use these connections. If this period is neglected, this optimum time for the acquisition of important skills and attitudes might pass by. They may never be so easily learned again and apart from anything else, children may learn to be passive and not feel responsible for their own thinking.

Early learning: recognising children's ability to take on perspectives

Donaldson (1978) demonstrated the vital significance to children's learning of the contextual features within which that learning is taking place. Many studies build upon this premise, including the Froebel Early Education project reported by Athey (1990). Athey highlights that 'visits increased the "stuff" of mind in project children'. What seemed important was the *involvement of parents, extensive preparation, shared experience* and afterwards the *opportunity for representational practice.*

Reports of shared reading and number schemes bear witness to this same factor, the spin-offs gained from the affective sharing in a learning experience. In other words, children who engage in reading projects with their parents gain as much in an affective way from the communal nature of the exercise as they do in perceived developments in their reading progress. The Reggio Emilia region of Italy, fast becoming world-renowned for innovative early childhood professional practices, is also cognisant of findings concerning the significance for learning of children's perspectives, fostering intellectual development through intensive project study, with a systematic focus on symbolic representation (Edwards *et al.*, 1995).

Dunn's findings from her many studies of interaction within the family concern a child's growing understanding of the feelings and wishes of other people (1988, 1993). It is of crucial importance that such evidence is considered by practitioners who work with children and their families in early years settings. The long-term ethnographic study reported by Brice Heath in which she said 'it is the interactions across living, eating, sleeping, worshipping, using space and filling time which ... was all part of the milieu in which their [children's] learning took place' (Heath, 1983, p.3) similarly provides a useful resource for looking at children's awareness of the perspective and attitudes of others.

Fantasy is part of the learning process

Cohen and MacKeith (1991) suggest that there has been a positive attitude to play, fantasy and the imagination since the 1970s and that American psychologists see these as rich skills in the learning process. Earlier researchers Singer and Singer (1979) would have us believe that children's concentration and pleasure in their learning were heightened by fantasy play. For many people fantasy play and the development of the imagination, is not a supplementary activity for young children but is one of the basics.

Meek (1985a, p.44) talks of the importance of first time feelings and suggests that, whatever else it might be, imagination involves the simultaneous experience of thought and feeling, cognition and effect. Playing with language and sound, the understanding of jokes and the opportunities for rituals all allow for affective and imaginative engagement. Such subjects are not always valued or given a high focus in research projects.

It may be worthwhile once again to consider your own case:

- How will the developing understandings which you are gaining as a questioner of theoretical principles show in your work?
- If you believe children to be competent:
  - are you giving them enough responsibility?
  - do you respect their ideas?
  - do you believe in their ability to succeed?

- If you believe learning to be a process:
  - do you welcome children's own attempts?
  - do you expect drafts to be untidy and errors interesting?
- If you see children as individuals:
  - how do you deal with idiosyncratic behaviour?
  - do you accept all children?
  - are you confident about working with individuals within groups?

Actively address your practice

Reports that twice as much can be learned in one classroom as in another do not surprise us and, although there might be many factors contributing to this, research would show that the work of the teacher is the most significant.

I have already tried to show that the theories we adopt develop over time and experience. It has become more and more evident since the onset of the practitioner-as-researcher model that this is a most rewarding and probably the most effective means by which teachers can come to new understandings about children's learning. Active researchers might consider the findings of two very recent studies, the first concerning children's activity and the second children's perspectives. The first relates again to the mismatch between what teachers plan for children and what the children actually do with the provision.

Objectives: whose agenda?

Bennett *et al.* (1995) cite the instance of a shop set up in the classroom, promoted so that the children could practice playing out the rituals of shopping, and with an aim that they particularly learn the value of money as they practised buying the goods. However, this was not the game the children in fact played. Instead, their time was taken up with chasing robbers, being security guards and stopping thieves who were taking the stock. Such evidence of children's play creates some interesting and fundamental questions which the teacher must ask. Was the shop play building on what children knew? Indeed do they ever go shopping or does access to the television set mean they are more familiar with a robber's role? There is an interesting dilemma here for the practitioner, who must decide how to act: to explore the children's ideas and develop the study of security in shops (the child's possible agenda) or to force the children to carry out the business of buying and selling goods (the adult agenda)?

There is an interesting point to be made here which is reiterated in Chapter 7. We cannot wholly claim to be starting from the knowledge of the child if we are dictating what is and is not permissible. Child centredness which only takes notice of what the adults vet as suitable, can hardly be worthy of its name. A theory of learning which offers answers to such knotty problems arises best when the practitioner knows as much as possible about what is going on. This can only be achieved by gaining insights through on-the-spot observational research.

Objectives: do they make sense?

The second example is taken from Bridges' (1995) study. Bridges posed three fundamental questions: what do pupils perceive of the purpose of the provision they experience in a school setting? What do the pupils make of the adult's curriculum planning? And, to what extent do these same adults evaluate their planning in the light of pupil understanding?

The Year 2, Year 3 and Year 6 children whom Bridges interviewed showed that they recalled nursery experiences which were memorable to them, the digging of a pond, a rainbow in the water, the adoption of a stray cat, the birth of her kittens and the death of one of them. Such times apparently offered much that was exciting and amazing, the sort of stimulating environment which early childhood practitioners value. Yet what was less obvious to these children was what use these experiences were for them, what links they could make to other areas of learning and which ways to think about what they had learned.

There is scope in both these examples for teacher intervention which might extend and enrich children's learning experiences as a result of what has been seen from the focuses taken in the research. There is also heightened interest and energy created for the teacher within the dynamics of working with the children.

Conclusion

It seems that it is sometimes politically expedient to represent teachers as unthinking people following trendy theories and dogma, and that this has brought poor standards to classrooms. It was noted in the Leeds Primary Project that 'Over the last few decades the progress of primary pupils has been hampered by the influence of highly questionable dogmas which have led to excessively complex practices and devalued the place of subjects in the curriculum' (Alexander, 1993, p.1).

Teachers do need to be clear about the thinking that underpins their practice. Theory that has been extensively explored and tested by the rigours of practice, can hardly be dogma.

I have suggested that cultural perspectives will play a significant part in the way tasks are perceived and undertaken by children and this requires specific knowledge on the part of the teacher. Theories of learning can be less specific and slower to come to know and measure. Knowledge of children's growth and development comes about best by being an avid watcher of children and questioner of why they think and act as they do.

Hughes (1989) suggests that the gap between the theories of the developmental psychologists and the practice of early educators is a wide chasm. He cites a study by Gulliver which showed that although research may have been putting forward evidence of young children as intellectually competent and the home as a powerful learning environment, the teachers who were observed focused more on the children's deficiencies and the shortcomings of the home.

Isaacs' classroom in the 1930s saw a heavy emphasis on observation in order that practitioners might know about children and what they were doing, and, in turn, be informed of what they might introduce next. Such methodology meant that adults learned about children in general, as well as children in particular. It is to be regretted that such practices do not seem to have remained consistent in early years classrooms, despite their worldwide acclaim in Isaacs' time.

What were the theories of children's learning that the people in these two examples were drawing upon? Gulliver's study seems to show a determination to stick with personal theory despite the contrary ideas in research writing and literature. The Isaacs example suggests that the practitioners were coming to their understandings by practical application and interrogation of their underlying theory.

Purposes matter a lot in teaching. They come from within and often reflect a teacher's passion. Students who decide to become early years practitioners probably admire the happiness, keen interest, energy, spontaneity, and direct and honest approach which young children frequently bring to their tasks. Children's enthusiasm is not strongly tinged with preconceptions or assumptions, and their behaviour is blessed with a fetching lack of inhibitions. This is also one of the alarming things about managing them in a classroom setting. It is easy, if you are not an experienced knower of children, to be anxious and unsure of how to respond to what seems like unpredictable behaviour, frequent distraction and quick loss of interest. 'They can be there one minute and seem interested, then just run away' said one young student. 'Where is my starting point? How can I make them share?' 'How do I know when to interact and when to leave well alone?' 'When do I give them correct information. They do not seem to want to know about it!'

In a world which offers much rhetoric about starting from where the child is at and the importance of children being active in their own learning, it is important that teachers can go very much beyond their own personal views in their justification of their work. Through a consideration of their own thinking, the thinking of others and their own practice they may come to know more about children's learning. Children need 'adults who are determined to try out ideas for themselves, who think deeply and are convinced slowly, who are prepared to read more widely when in doubt and who wish to influence outcomes from an informed conviction which they have tested in their own experience' (Holdaway, 1979).

Chapter 2

Personality, professionalism and politics: what does it mean to be an early years teacher?

Sue Smedley

Introduction

Watching young children playing 'teachers' can be a rather puzzling, and sometimes salutary, experience. The girls (usually) line up the dolls or some other children and conduct lessons in the style of a mixture of Joyce Grenfell and Mary Poppins. The atmosphere is often one of tolerance and benign discipline. Some teachers would not like to be told they look and act 'just like a teacher'. Why not? Because the stereotype of early years teachers and what they do, is this: nice, cooperative or compliant, eager to please, devoted, ever-smiling, not a high flier academically and very sensible. And eternally patient of course.

This image is not one early years teachers themselves are immune from – it can help to shape the way teachers see themselves and the work they do. As a stereotype it clouds the more real picture of what it means to be an early years teacher. The stereotypes which persist and seem to prevail detract from the serious yet stimulating, intellectual, political and professional work that teachers do. Being an early years teacher (in fact any teacher) *is* very much about personality, but not just in terms of personal characteristics – it involves personal ideology and understanding, informed by study, practice and reflection. It is work which is inextricably tied in with the 'teacher as a person' (Fullan and Hargreaves, 1994,. p.67) and work which has implications and importance both within and beyond the parameters of the classroom and school.

Here are three things teachers, I hope, will not become:

- technicians trained to deliver the curriculum,
- neutral in outlook and not involved,
- instrumental and dogmatic;

and three things being an early years teacher must always be about:

- personality – if taken in the sense of identity (gender, race and class), ideology, knowledge and understanding, priorities and principles
- professionalism – for example, taking children seriously, teacher collaboration and autonomy, reflection and development
- politics – not party politics, but about social ideals and change.

Being an early years teacher is part of who you are; it is not like a hat put on in the morning and taken off in the evening, though in the early stages individuals might feel they are 'trying on' their identity as teachers, as they construct it. McLean (1991) talks of student teachers being 'desperate to try on the shoes of the teacher' (p.231), but her whole premise is that becoming a teacher involves personal engagement and growth; to risk taking the analogy too far, the hat and shoes must become old favourites moulded to and by the wearer!

My proposition is that being an early years teacher is about personality, professionalism and politics – all three aspects should interrelate fluidly as elements of an early years teacher's identity and work. It is work to take seriously, to enjoy and to be proud of, and it is work that should never be boring. I am not arguing that there are no elements of routine, frustration and grind in working with young children – experience tells me there are; I am not trying to idealise the early years teacher's work either. Rather I am saying that it is crucially important for teachers in all stages of their teaching careers, to discuss and reflect on what it really means to be a teacher, in order to construct, reconstruct and refresh understanding. Here I intend to explore some of the ideas and images that perhaps haunt early years teachers, to expose the assumptions, to explore the social, historical and cultural contexts, and in the process to help teachers themselves refresh their *own* versions of what it means to be an early years teacher.

Reflecting on personality, professionalism and politics involves standing back from the business of the nursery or classroom and taking the time to ask questions about teaching, about aims and beliefs and about yourself. This chapter aims to support that constructive reflective process.

Personality

Patience – not the only virtue

'You must be very patient.' This seems to be the stock response to informing others that you are an early years teacher. Some seem to imagine that being an early years teacher is all about patience. Indeed it is an important attribute, but of course only a small part of the picture. Summarising and encapsulating the attributes of the good early years teacher in the word 'patience' is a caricature. It implies that if you are patient you will make a good early years teacher. You will be able to 'put up with' all the demands of very young children. This is a very limited view, reflecting a simplistic notion of what it means to be an early years teacher. It does not recognise that a teacher's theoretical position, her thinking and understanding, even her view of the world underpin the kind of teacher she will be and the ways she will choose to work with young children.

Patience is highlighted by prospective student teachers and frequently mentioned in applications for Initial Teacher Education courses. It is part of the way we are used to talking about teaching young children – part of the discourse. Of 271 questionnaires completed by Year 1 BA(QTS) students at Roehampton Institute London in 1994, 134 identified patience as an important strength for a primary teacher. No other single attribute was mentioned so frequently.

References for applicants for Initial Teacher Education courses repeatedly describe the students as having 'a pleasant personality' or a 'cheerful disposition'. Those lacking in analytical powers could make up for it by being able to 'brighten your day'! Many are described as, 'polite and cooperative'. And a neat and tidy appearance would complete the outward manifestation of inner teacherliness (Smedley, 1992, p.37).

Such personal characteristics are commendable, but the dilemma is twofold:

1 One aspect of the dilemma lies in what these descriptions of early years teachers seem *not* to emphasise, for example about critical and intellectual abilities and about aspects of professional and political strengths and insights. There is lurking here still, a myth about the incompatibility of academic rigour and teaching young children (which we will consider later).

   The predominant descriptions of the personal qualities of teachers of young children highlight certain personal characteristics, which, important though they are, omit the more reflective and outward-looking aspects of the 'teacher's personhood' (McLean, 1991, p.x), such as her personal ideology, aims and ideals. This intersects with important professional and political dimensions, which are also omitted from the descriptions I have cited, such as intellectualism, social and cultural awareness and aims, developing ideology and theoretical stance, and vision. These are historically rooted descriptions which can seem patronising and are inadequate.

2 The other main aspect of the dilemma lies in the tendency to have extraordinarily high expectations of teachers in terms of their personalities and abilities. Such expectations also have a history and were a focus of Nathan Isaacs' lecture entitled 'What is required of the nursery-infant teacher in this country today?' (1967). Isaacs claims the nursery-infant teacher needs 'a superhuman assemblage of personal qualities', plus the ability to respond to the 'intellectual demands of the training' (p.7). A tall order indeed!

Trawling the Hadow Report, 1933, and the Plowden Report, 1967, Walkerdine (1989) compiles a 'formidable list' of ideal qualities for the teacher of young children, which includes: the right temperament; patience; tender care; the capacity to lead from behind (p.73). McLean (1991) reviewing early childhood texts of the 1970s and 1980s lists recurring personal qualities, for example, patient, friendly, compassionate, empathetic, happy, sense of humour... (p.8). The identification of these characteristics has a particularity because most early years teachers are women, so this can be seen an expression of expectations of how women should behave. Male student teachers are also working within this context and will experience a range of tensions and dilemmas, as a result of the stereotypes and assumptions made of early years teachers.

Cockburn (1992) argues that the skills of an early years teacher are not 'peculiarly masculine or feminine' (p.82), but the significance of gender in relation to teachers' identity and work cannot be denied. Current constructs of masculine and feminine do impact upon decisions to work as a teacher. Perhaps what is necessary is a reworking of the constructs, as it may also be the case that there are tensions between predominant views of masculinity and predominant views of what it means to be an early years teacher, which may be limiting to women and to men (*see* Skelton, 1994).

Reflecting on personality relates very closely to the decision-making involved in choosing to work as a teacher of young children. In what ways is that decision made? What are the characteristics people have that make them think they could work as early years teachers? What influences and informs these choices? For student teachers and teachers working with young children, the decision to teach and to focus on this age group will have been informed by a whole range of varied influences and ambitions. I will consider some of the issues here, with a view to helping early years teachers reflect on their own decision-making, and subsequently their identity and perceptions of themselves as teachers.

'I always wanted to be a teacher'

There are many different reasons for choosing to become an early years teacher and these have been explored, for example, by Evetts (1990) and Nias (1989). In general, themes and commonalities emerge which are interesting to note. Many people choose to teach because they have enjoyed school and can imagine themselves as teachers – 'I always wanted to be a teacher.'[1] For others, through childhood and adolescence, certain teaching qualities have been recognised in them and reinforced. These usually tend to be, for example, patience, caring, reliability, sensitivity, calmness and a sense of responsibility for others, 'I love children and I had a lot of experience baby-sitting, play-schemes and so on.' Girls in particular may have played schools or taken on the role of teacher's helper in school. This is also reflected in comments made by students at Froebel Institute College, during the 1930s. For example, 'I didn't choose teaching as a career, my mother thought it would suit me as I used to play "schools" as a child' (Rosemary Mann, at Froebel Institute College 1938–41).[2]

Teaching young children is generally perceived as a traditionally acceptable and suitable job for women. As a career choice it seldom provokes surprise; it is positively reinforced, expected even. But men also choose to work as early years teachers and in so-doing are making what could be described as a non-traditional choice. In choosing to become early years teachers, men are positioned in a context which is numerically (though not in terms of hierarchical power) dominated by women. The teacher's role is often defined and discussed based on the assumption that early years teachers are women. There are tensions for women and perhaps differently for men. Areas such as leadership, management and accounting, traditionally male-dominated, are increasingly being seen as important in a business-oriented educational world. This is a double-bind for women, who are expected to demonstrate what Maher and Rathbone describe as 'contradictory qualities of nurturance and authoritarianism' (1986, p.227). Male early years teachers may feel they experience difficulties, individually, being inducted into a 'predominantly female culture' (Annan, 1993, p.100). They may also expect or be expected to make speedy career progress, which may create tensions, as well as being potentially advantageous.

Being an early years teacher may be experienced differently by men; assumptions and perceptions may shift. But it is not helpful to make generalisations about 'all men', and differences are subtle and complex rather than distinct. Assumptions, for example, about authority, commitment, care or career development take on a different guise for early years teachers who are men, although it is important to remember that not all men, or all women, will straightforwardly experience the effect of those assumptions in the same way.[3]

People choose to become teachers for positive and forward-looking reasons. Talking with teachers and student teachers, statements are often made about wanting to do something worthwhile, to help children, provide children with a good start in their life at school, make the world a better place. Comments include: 'make a real contribution', 'help people', 'be someone the children will remember', 'rewarding'. Such ideals are to be valued; wide-ranging aims such as these should form part of every teacher's philosophy. But, ironically, such altruism is open to accusations of an inflated ego and to being disparaged. Steedman reflects on her teaching, 'I don't care any more about sounding pretentious, so now I tell people who ask at parties why I did it for such a long time, that it did seem a way of being a socialist in every day life' (1987, p.126).

There may also be a process of elimination in the way choices about teaching are made, what Ball and Goodson describe as 'a negative decision or series of non-decisions' (1985, p.21). Teaching may be chosen because other options do not appeal: individuals may reject office-bound work, for example, or be reviewing a restricted range of possibilities. This is echoed by earlier generations of teachers: 'I didn't think I was good enough at games to be a PT mistress and a Matron was out, as I can't sew, so I said I would rather do teacher training' (Daphne Groves, at Froebel Institute College 1938–41, p.40).[4]

The historical background to these ways of perceiving early years teachers and women's move into teaching young children in the nineteenth century is relevant here as it provides a backdrop to the context within which teachers work today. As such, it has a bearing on current perceptions of early years teachers and their perceptions of themselves. There are connections and recurring patterns and themes between past and present, although of course there are also differences.

It is interesting to note that there has been a shift in the numbers of men and women in the teaching profession. In the early nineteenth century the majority of teachers of infants were male; in the 1870s, the numbers of men and women teaching in elementary schools were roughly equal; by 1914 women made up about 70 per cent of the teaching force (Steedman, 1987, p.120). Statistics for January 1994 show women making up just under 98 per cent (19,767 women) of qualified teachers working full-time in infant schools, and 425 men making up just over 2 per cent (DfE, 1994b).

In the latter part of the nineteenth century many middle-class single women in England were in need of paid work. They longed to move beyond family duties, but also knew that after the death of their parents, they would need an independent income. The way forward for them was to enter the world of the school or hospital. This provided work for them which did not challenge the existing social order as it was seen as 'carrying the domestic world into the public' (Vicinus, 1985, p.15). This was an extension of the woman's role as carer of the young or sick, as a public servant, and as such was seen to employ women's natural abilities. Although this move into teaching offered women independence, it was also problematic in that it was tied in with an unintellectual view of the work and a view of teaching as essentially a domestic task.

So, there were and are contradictions and complexities in the decision to become a teacher. In the past women teachers saw teaching as a positive means to earn an independent income, but teaching was also seen as low status work with young children; it also dictated that women lived by certain restrictions, such as the marriage bar and considerable responsibilities and duties.[5] This historical background is echoed in some current perceptions of teachers, for example, teacher as public servant.

The idea of choice is caught up with complicity in the notion of teachers as duty-bound servants working for small financial rewards in a caring profession. The idea of the teacher as being *in loco parentis* and the tremendous responsibility on teachers can be seen in this broader historical context of teacher as public servant, 'married to the job'. On the one hand this sense of responsibility is something to take pride in, but equally it can have tinges of being tied; as one student teacher commented, 'Every morning these children are there and however you feel you can't go and have a coffee, you've got to be enthusiastic and ready for the children' (Smedley, 1992).[6]

The choices we make are not completely free, however, but are contained within what we see as possibilities. And this seemed also to be the case nearly 60 years ago.

> Everyone assumed I would 'take up' teaching, and perhaps because I felt my life was being planned and manipulated for me from outside, I began flirting with other possibilities...[but] in the end I knew a Froebel training was what I always wanted anyway.[7]
>
> (Margaret Barrow, Froebel Institute College, 1938–41, p.9)

Decisions may seem to be free choices, but in fact are strongly influenced by our past experiences and the encouragement, feedback and reinforcement received from others. In each case, as Weiler explains, choices are made 'within a kind of logic of existing social structures and ideology' (Weiler, 1988, p.89).

'Mummy – I mean Miss!'

Children sometimes make a mistake and call their teachers 'Mummy', although this may be deliberate and said in jest, the result of children's awareness of irony. Male teachers may also be called 'Mummy' – 'Mummy, I mean Miss – I mean, Sir!'. Again, this may be by mistake or on purpose, but in either case, it confirms, 'teacher as mother' as one of the pervading images of the early years teacher.

It is interesting that some children seem to persist in calling their teachers 'Miss' or 'Sir', sometimes in spite of teachers asking children to use first names (setting aside for the moment important debates about Ms, Miss and Mrs and the implied status of 'Sir'). This can be seen as a recognition of the authority the teacher holds, a complex position in reality. Teachers weave together authority and democracy; as Salmon reflects, 'these seemingly contradictory stances, if they can be integrated, may lead in the end to unusual kinds of insights' (Salmon, 1988, p.45). In reflecting on this integration of authority and democracy in practice, teachers learn more about teaching, children and what it means to be a teacher.

Thinking about how children address teachers is a significant aspect of the nature of the relationship between teachers and children. Part of the context of this relationship is created by the metaphor, 'teacher as mother'.

Here are two comments, suggesting that the perceived qualities of an early years teacher have changed little during this century:

> 'She is unselfish and altogether devoted to children ... Her manner is delightful.'
> (Esther Lawrence, Principal of Froebel College, 1929)[8]

> 'Charming, polite, co-operative, sincere and well-balanced with a cheerful disposition.'
> (Comment noted in Smedley, 1992, p.42)

In particular these comments suggest a melting together of the biological, the natural and the social, which results in a version of 'teacher as mother'. Positioned as mothers, teachers operate within a pastoral, supportive, responsible and self-sacrificing role – attributes which do not convey the whole of the teacher's job.

'Teacher as mother' acts as a metaphor. Metaphors call up discourses that tap into value-laden webs of cultural understandings. These metaphors are significant in that they have an impact on the way teachers can experience and describe their work. They create an unavoidable context, which has a history. One of the most powerful metaphors in relation to teachers of young children is teacher as mother.[9] It has the potential to shape the identity of both men and women as teachers, in some positive, but more negative ways.

Metaphors can extend thinking in the way they refresh perceptions, and they can also influence more subtly by tapping into wider networks of social and cultural understandings. These influences may not always be positive. Being positioned as mothers, teachers are subjected to the same assumptions about it being an exclusively pastoral, supporting role. Casey (1990) describes how teachers in North Carolina resist such stereotyping and see the nurturing aspect of their teaching as a 'form of political responsibility, not domestic duty' (p.306).

Teacher as mother is problematic because it refers metaphorically to a particular version of mother; she is not the mother who is too busy to play, or who, worse still, loses her temper – she is the faultless mother of the soap-powder advertisements. The idealised mother and the idealised teacher are not images that encourage understanding of the complexity and the compromise involved in both. McLean (1991) urges us to, 'go beyond the idealized images of early childhood teachers facilitating children's development in fictitiously aseptic environments' (p.1). It is important to recognise that teaching can be quite a messy business in practice, philosophically and emotionally.

Weber and Mitchell (1995) investigate a range of cultural images and stereotypes of teachers in their fascinating and entertaining book, 'That's funny, you don't look like a teacher.' They describe different scholars' schemes for classifying metaphors, for example, that of Fischer and Kiefer (1994), who propose two groupings of metaphoric images:

> those referring to the teaching self (for example, teacher as interpreter, teacher as presence);
>
> and those referring to relationships between teacher and students (for example, teacher as advocate, teacher as therapist, teacher as parent, teacher as companion.
>
> (cited in Weber and Mitchell, 1995, p.22)

Thinking about the range of possible metaphors that shape a teacher's philosophy and practice, and perhaps looking for metaphors for the future is a constructive way of shaping the discourse about teaching young children.

There is a fundamental interrelationship between the teacher and the culture of teaching, and its wider social and cultural contexts, which underpins this view of discourse and development; this requires a little more consideration and is explored in the following section.

The individual in society: 'the context and the person are interconnected' (McLean, 1991, p.6)

An individual is born into a society with its attendant cultures, traditions and language. In continually learning about these complex aspects of society, the individual can also act upon the structures and traditions that form that culture. So, a teacher is inducted into the culture of early years teaching, but also acts upon that culture, and in so doing is continually constructing and developing a sense of identity as a teacher and an individual.

Vygotsky's conception is that, 'the true direction of the development of thinking is not from the individual to the social, but from the social to the individual' (1986, p.45) and this urges us to see the formation of individuals (their ideas and practices) as embedded in society, history and culture. Alongside this I would place Weiler's explanation of the dialectical relationship between the individual and society. Weiler (1988) recognises students and teachers as 'historically situated subjects' (p.125) who need to reflect on and to explore their positions in order to develop professionally. Goodson (1992) describes reflection as the telling of 'the life story and the life history' (p.6) and urges students and teachers to reflect upon and explore their own positions in work, society and history. Such reflection or autobiographical critique is not an indulgent or sentimental pastime, but creates opportunities to connect personal experiences with wider themes and perspectives, and, most importantly, to consider opportunities for action (Smedley, 1995).

Professionalism and politics

In reflecting on what it means to be an early years teacher, both professional identity and political identity are also significant features alongside personality. In this section I want to begin to discuss the factors which influence early years teachers' perceptions of their professionalism.[10] Again, the context within which they work will have a strong influence on this. I also want to consider the political aspects of early years teachers' work, not in a party-political sense, but in relation to a wider conception of aims for the kind of nursery or classroom, community, and, one could argue, by implication, world, teachers may be trying to create. It is political in its demand for reflection on fundamental issues such as equality, rights and responsibilities. This involves early years teachers, on a day-to-day basis, in social and moral dilemmas which may not be easy to resolve, but to which teachers must practically respond. And this inevitably leads to compromise: compromise which perhaps should not be viewed as failure, rather the reality of creating a working community.

I see two strands as relevant here – one is an apparent polarity between theory and practice and the other is anti-intellectualism.

Theory and practice – poles apart?

According to some publications in the media, theory is something that college tutors brainwash students with: it is an orthodoxy and significantly in opposition to practice. Such a view is stated, for example, in the *Daily Mail*'s headline – 'Forget the theory, just teach us to teach!' (Ray Massey, 30 April 1991). Tutors must apparently put drops of theory onto sugar cubes of practice. This view is reinforced by Sheila Lawlor who provides a good example of the rhetoric surrounding issues of theory and practice. 'Teaching theory has subverted teaching practice' (1990, p.21) and, 'the theorists will see it as their job to infiltrate theory into classroom practice' (Sheila Lawlor, *The Times*, 6 January 1992).

Such a view of theory as a separate and unhelpful thing is patronising and undermining. Theory is seen as a diversion and at the expense of practice. But without theoretical frameworks to help understand and inform teaching, teachers will find it difficult to move forward professionally; they are more likely to feel personally inadequate and stay in a rut; professional development then becomes unlikely.

I am not just arguing pro-theory, but for a particular conceptualisation of theory and practice – one which allows each to inform the other and is not driven by opposition and polarity.[11] The current and unhelpful polarity can be seen to have historical roots in concerns about women's involvement in intellectual matters and in education, and works alongside a populist notion that spending time on theory is at the expense of developing practical teaching ability. This reflects an overly pragmatic view of teaching, based on short-term survival over and above, and to the detriment of, longer term development, on the part of the children and the teachers. Similar themes emerge in considering teaching as intellectual work.

Teaching as intellectual work

'Self development, a relatively novel idea for dutiful daughters, collided with deeply ingrained beliefs about family obligations' (Vicinus, 1985, p.172). At the turn of the century it was not easy for women to move into academic pursuits or training. This was compounded by the strong links between what was perceived as women's natural abilities and the nature of the professions they entered, which in turn worked against arguments for special training or education and against intellectualising that work.

The first teacher training colleges in the 1840s offered, 'a narrowly based vocational training rather than an education from which a girl might in some sense better herself' (Miller, 1992, p.2). The regime at colleges for women included domestic duties and little time for reflection or choice – an emphasis that is not unfamiliar in its demands for utilitarian relevance and shaping of characters: in the late 19th century, students over 25 years of age were not admitted to teacher training college, as it was seen to be too late to shape their character. At Whitelands College, in the early 1900s, time was spent in ordered physical exercise and also in needlework (against the clock!).[12] As Miller concludes, 'The training of teachers ... was designed to maintain order rather than to expand minds or possibilities' (Miller, 1992, p.4).

The public view in the late 19th and early 20th centuries, connected ill-health with colleges. When Eliza Furnace died of rapid consumption at Whitelands College in 1853, there was concern for the reputation of the college, as well as about women's ability to cope with the pressures of the training. Indeed, a doctor regularly gave the women medical check-ups to ensure they were not suffering from the demands of their training. Women at teacher training colleges were dislocated from intellectual endeavour and this, plus the view that teaching was an extension of domestic and natural duties for women, reinforced arguments that teaching young children did not warrant theorising or have an intellectual dimension.

But teachers' intellectual understanding, and ideas and construct of an early years teacher, will also inform and be informed by practice. This is what enables the teacher to work, and continue to work, towards worthwhile goals for children.

Not everyone would agree, however. It depends on the underlying view of what a teacher's job is. A view of the teacher as someone who simply has to be good at keeping the children quiet, obedient and busy would result in a very different view of the part theory and informed reflection play in the teacher's work. It would reduce the teacher's job to a narrow, very mechanistic and basic task, perhaps reflected in the connotations of talking of the 'delivery' of the curriculum and this would be quite inadequate.

Thinking through what it means to work as a teacher of young children must be an ongoing task. There must be time to think about professional roles and understanding, as a teacher, in order to do the job well. Meek (1985b) summarises this view: 'Contrary to popular belief, teachers are made not born. They become experts as other experts do, by a progressive understanding of what they are about' (p.27).

And there are many early childhood pioneers and scholars who famously have progressed the theoretical and intellectual dimensions of early years teaching, as well as very clearly the practical. Bruce (1987) mentions women such as Margaret McMillan, Susan Isaacs in the UK and Pattie Smith Hill in the USA, and considers the work of three most influential pioneers in forming the bedrock of the early childhood tradition: Friedrich Wilhelm Froebel (1782–1852), Maria Montessori (1869–1952) and Rudolf Steiner (1861–1925). As Bruce points out, 'All were skilled practitioners as well as being educational theorists. Each was concerned, amongst other things, with world citizenship, respect for persons' individual needs, poverty and the concept of community' (Bruce, 1987, p.9). It warrants reflection that the work of early years teachers is this far-reaching and fundamental in its aims. It is in this sense that it is political. It is about the art of government and the nature of citizenship, about the policies which will determine the rights and responsibilities of citizens – for the early years teacher, of children. To be reminded of the intellectual and pedagogical strength of educational pioneers and teachers of previous generations, can be a source of inspiration in the present day.

In thinking about the politics of early years teaching, it is perhaps worthwhile to pause briefly to consider child-centred pedagogy, as it has such a deep-seated influence on the culture of early years teachers and teaching.

Child-centred pedagogy

'Child centred' is a particularly slippery term and a frequently taken-for-granted position in education. The nature of the child and the centrality of the individual child in the education process was encapsulated in the Plowden Report (CACE, 1967) with its inherent position that early years teachers teach children rather than subjects. Child-centredness becomes an unquestioned starting point. 'Its power lies in its status as incontrovertible fact' (Walkerdine, 1983, p.80); and yet, there are contradictions and tensions here. Expectations that teachers should regulate behaviour and maintain order, clash with notions of the individual and democracy. A wider context of measurement and monitoring children's development and interest in child studies in the late 19th and early 20th centuries reinforced 'the general understanding of childhood growth as a natural unfolding of a preordained sequence' (Steedman, 1990, p.97). The work of Piaget in the 1920s provided a scientific and therefore valued rationale for the natural development and maturation of the child. As Walkerdine (1989) argues, 'Teachers are responsible for the normal development of all children ... This impossible task is likely to produce considerable guilt at inevitable failure. It has particular gendered consequences for women teachers' (p.78).

This provides a significant background to the arguments here, as child-centredness can impact upon teachers' own perceptions and interpretations of their work. It is part of early years culture, but it is important for teachers to discuss and decide for themselves what child-centredness means; the concept needs to be reflected upon and reworked, not routinely accepted as a dogma.[13] Treating girls and boys the same, and letting children, as individuals, make choices for themselves, may be one interpretation of child-centred thinking. Commendable in one sense perhaps, but this apparently liberal and democratic approach can lead to a failure to acknowledge and address inequality. Well-intentioned attempts to create equality by avoidance are in one sense highly political pedagogical moves. As an early years teacher, a neutral stance is not an option. Early years teachers are continually having to take a stand in relation to principles, whether those are explicitly known or implicit. As such it is a challenging, theoretically informed professional task. To quote Siraj-Blatchford, 'teaching is a moral as well as a practical and intellectual endeavour' (Siraj-Blatchford, 1993b, p.404). Early years teachers are professionals and are political, and need to find their own professional voice.

Language and learning

But how is this to be done? How does the discourse evolve and how is a professional voice developed? Words and meanings are not fixed or finite. Student teachers and early years teachers need to take on and develop their professional voice, the discourse of teacherliness, in a conscious and critical way. This requires exploration of words and their meanings through talk and writing. This could encourage teachers to rewrite and redescribe their work in new ways, creating new metaphors. Vygotsky tells us that, 'The word is a direct expression of the historical nature of human consciousness' (1986, p.256). He is drawing our attention to the historical and cultural background and context to language. Words are not merely words; they mean more than they say, because of their history and the connotations they already carry. These meanings themselves will be different for different people and in different contexts. Language changes, and individuals and groups can shape the discourse and change the dominant metaphors. The professional voice is not static. But change requires early years teachers to be aware of their history as professionals, to be reflective and to be bold.

So, language is never neutral; it shapes thinking and perceptions and is shaped by them. Language and inequality are closely connected, although language is not responsible for inequality – nor does it simply hold the key for equality. As Cameron explains, 'The use of linguistics and metalinguistic resources to oppress others should not be ignored; but we must acknowledge the limitation of theories of oppression that do not go beyond the linguistic' (1992, p.171).

Difference can be recognised and discussed and can throw into sharp relief assumptions and taken-for-granted practices. It is not necessarily an advantage to move quickly to consensus among teachers or with children, as this usually means difference and inequality are being masked. Gussin Paley's *Kwanzaa and Me* (1995) explores integration and multiculturalism in fascinating and reflective detail, as she tries to find out about individual's experiences of school culture. These are fundamentally important issues for teachers to reflect upon in relation to personal, professional and political aims.

The work of French feminist, Hélène Cixous, interpreted as a clear pedagogy by Sellers (1989), presents ways to work with students that could also be of interest to teachers working with young children. The basis for the pedagogy more readily allows difference to be considered, for example, considering the student–teacher hierarchy, giving students time, and listening without judgement. These are significant practical principles for working with young children, which lead into a consideration, more widely, of aims and ideals in early years teaching.

Democracy and vision

To reflect on what it means to be an early years teacher involves a consideration of ideals, aims and a wide range of complex philosophical questions, for example, what are schools for? Schools are frequently seen as 'other worlds' or 'ivory towers' and teachers are criticised for not getting it right or achieving their ideals. But schools and colleges are part of society, 'Reforms that limit their focus to specific school problems or the politics of instruction ignore the ways in which public education is shaped, bent, and moved by wider economic, political, and social concerns' (Giroux, 1989, p.183).

Notions of democracy and vision can be disparaged as idealistic and unattainable. Visions of what teachers might work towards should not be within a context that idealises teachers and what they can do, but not one that ridicules them either. Teachers of young children are belittled as unintellectual; teaching is praised for being a worthwhile and fulfilling vocation.

Teachers should be 'transformative intellectuals' (Giroux, 1989, p.108) who understand how classrooms are socially constructed, historically determined and can be reproduced by institutional relationships of race, gender and class. It is that understanding and awareness that enables and stimulates change and the reshaping of how early years teachers perceive themselves, and how they work. As Katz (1987) explains, 'Professions identify the goals of their work with the good of humanity at large, placing strong emphasis on social ends' (p.4). Teaching young children is a huge responsibility; there will be some drudgery no doubt, some mundane aspects, and a genuine need for a considerable amount of patience too. But it is also professionally demanding and politically profoundly important; there should be a strong sense of shared intellectual endeavour, between teachers and with children. 'What happens in classrooms is living' (McLean, 1991, p.175).

Developing political professionalism

Professionalism is not a simple package of skills or ideas to be acquired. The purpose of reflecting on active professionalism is not to provide labels or to decide who is professional and who is not. Nor to add to the guilt teachers seem skilled at feeling.[14] Developing professionalism is an ongoing process and has all the complexities of learning itself. In looking for ways forward professionally, it may be helpful to think of professionalism as a developing continuum.

Figure 2.1, 'Political professionalism in practice – a continuum', provides a representation of aspects of political professionalism and general ways in which they might be experienced in practice. The elements of practice identified are intended to serve as a tool for critical reflection, a frame of reference, not a shopping list. The ongoing development of mature professionalism in practice is a developmental one and professionalism is not quantitative, like ticking off targets in an I-Spy book.

Figure 2.1: Political professionalism in practice – a continuum

Professionalism undeveloped ◄——►	**Developed and active professionalism**
Sharing of knowledge and skills infrequent	Genuine collaboration; support given and accepted
Little contact with parents, or other professional bodies	Partnership with parents and close liaison with professional bodies
Interactions with children too friendly or too strict	Reflective authority based on trust and consultation
Decision-making the preserve of the teacher	Collaborative decision-making that respects children while recognising the knowledge and experience of the teacher. Children taken seriously.
Personal growth, learning and development not a high priority	Recognition that personal learning and reflection are central to developing practice
Tends to be overdependent on others in the team	Independent with a responsibility to others in the team. Aware of boundaries.
Little awareness of the wider social and cultural dimensions in the classroom	Critically reflective on the culture of the classroom and active in involving the children in creating that culture
Passive in response to issues of equality and equity	Equality and equity are principles that are practically and actively followed
Ideals exist but constraints prevent their realisation. Disillusion may result in less activity	Ideals exist and are pursued rigorously; constraints result in compromise and continued activity
Limited awareness of educational debates, past or current	Involvement and voice in educational debates e.g. through professional associations

Katz (1984) talks of non-professional responses and unprofessional responses, as well as professional ones. She makes the distinction thus:

- professional: the use of judgement based on advanced knowledge and the adoption of standards;
- non-professional: personal predilection and common-sense wisdom, rather than professionally accrued knowledge and practice. Katz is referring to people without professional education or training;
- unprofessional: unethical behaviour e.g. giving in to the temptations of the situation at hand (Katz, 1984, p.41).

Katz explores a specific dilemma: there are two tricycles among 20 four year olds. She emphasises the 'professional question' (p.39), that is, what does it (i.e. a teacher's response) teach?, and considers the range of possible teacher responses in thought-provoking and practical, helpful ways. Her argument suggests that those who respond only to the 'here and now', whose priority is, for example, to simply stop an argument between children, are non-professional. They miss an opportunity to teach, and 'teaching is the professional's commitment' (p.38). A professional would look for ways to teach children how to solve their problems, to negotiate or to think about what is just. The aims are more long term. This is a distinction that can stimulate critical reflection.

But it is complex. As McLean (1991) points out, the lived classroom is complex and a teacher's responses are guided and informed by personal perspectives and wider contexts – and because teachers are human, not superhuman! Teachers have professional expectations of themselves, but realistically will not always meet them. There is always a subtle interplay between ideals and realities, so part of teaching *is* sometimes about coping and surviving, for and with the children. Where compromises occur, and less satisfactory situations result or real problems emerge, as teachers and as professionals there is a basic and important process of critical reflection and forward planning to follow.

Teaching is about ideals and aspirations, compromise and complexity; it is work carried out by people, with people, in context.

Summary and conclusions

The main purpose of this chapter has been to inform and support reflection on what it means to be an early years teacher and to explore the personal, professional and political dimensions of teachers' identity and work. The culture of early years teaching and teachers is rooted in a history which helps to create the context of some of the assumptions and expectations made today.

Here is a summary of the main points:

1. Being an early years teachers is about personality, but it is not just about being 'nice'.
2. Deciding to be a teacher of young children is a decision made by individuals,

but within a social context which has a historical dimension.

3 'Teacher as mother' acts as a powerful metaphor in shaping perceptions of early years teachers' work.
4 Teachers' sense of identity is shaped by the culture of which it is a part; teachers (individually and collaboratively) can shape and change the culture of early years teaching.
5 Theory and practice are integral aspects of early years teachers' work.
6 Teaching young children is intellectually, as well as physically and morally, demanding work. It is political, in the sense that it is work that demands reflection on wide-ranging, fundamental issues, such as children's rights and responsibilities.
7 'Child centred' is an influential pedagogical concept and significant part of early years culture. It warrants critical reflection and interpretation, rather than acceptance or rejection.
8 The ways teachers talk about their work is not a fixed, but a changing discourse; all teachers have a part to play in developing a professional voice, which expresses and conveys the character of early years teaching.
9 Being an early years teacher is about more than the 'here and now'; it involves working for valued aims and ideals.
10 Developing professionalism is an ongoing process, which involves setting priorities and working with compromise.

Recognising that being an early years teacher means being part of a wide culture of traditions and history is important. This contextualising provides a basis of understanding, and an informed perspective, from which to think about what it means to be an early years teacher. Like learning itself, that process is an ongoing one.

Notes

1 Comments here and elsewhere in this chapter were made by BA(QTS) students at Roehampton Institute London in response to questionnaires and interviews, as part of research carried out by Sue Smedley and Sandy Pepperell.
2 Comment is taken from *The Froebel Touch, Roehampton Students Reminisce*, edited by Frankie Hancock, 1985. This is available for reference in The Early Childhood Collection, Froebel Institute College, Roehampton Institute London.
3 See Seifert (1988), Skelton (1991), Coulter and McNay (1993), Weber and Mitchell (1995) for further discussion of male early years teachers.
4 See Note 2.
5 *I'm Not Complaining* by Ruth Adam is a novel written in 1938, which brings to life many aspects of a school teacher's work. It was published by Virago in 1983, but unfortunately is currently out of print. For a good historical background, see *Lessons for Life. The schooling of girls and women 1850–1950* edited by Felicity Hunt (1987).
6 See Steedman (1987) for a reflection on the burden of responsibilities involved in being a primary teacher.
7 See Note 2.

8 Reference for a teacher, written by Esther Lawrence, Principal of Froebel College, 1929, Early Childhood Collection, Froebel Institute College, Roehampton Institute London.
9 See Steedman (1985). Burgess and Carter (1992) build on Steedman's discussion of 'the mother made conscious' and discuss what they describe as the 'mumsy' aspects of the primary teacher's role.
10 Pollard *et al.* (1994) provide a significant analysis of the impact of the Education Reform Act at Key Stage 1, in particular considering autonomy and accountability.
11 This argument is developed further in Smedley (1994).
12 The Whitelands College Archives, Roehampton Institute London, contain a wealth of records and evidence relating to teacher training.
13 See Walkerdine (1989). Although the focus of the book is girls and mathematics, the chapters on nursery and infant teaching are of particular interest here.
14 See Hargreaves (1994) for an exploration of guilt in teaching.

Activities

Activity 2.1

Complete the following:

- I chose to be an early years teacher because...
- As an early years teacher I see myself as...
- I hope the children I work with think I am...
- I hope the parents I work with think I am...
- The early years teachers I most respect can ... or have ...
- As an early years teacher I can see myself as responsible for...
- The main thing I would like to change about my teaching is...
- I would be a better teacher if...
- My main aim as an early years teacher is...

Think about what you have written. Do any connections emerge with what you have read about in this chapter or elsewhere? Can you identify any themes? Think about what the children's expectations might be of you – as well as vice versa – for example, fairness, interest, organisation, challenge, support, new experiences. What can you say about what it means to be an early years teacher?

- Do any particular words or ideas recur?
- How do you perceive your role? Is it in terms of the social (e.g. developing children's relationships), maternal or domestic (e.g. seeing the children as a family, creating a happy environment) or is it more political (e.g. working for equality)? Is it a combination or can you identify other groupings? Do you prioritise the affective or the cognitive or both? What models exist and what metaphors would you choose (e.g. mother, public servant, gardener, police officer, manager...)?
- Do any questions or tensions emerge (e.g. conflicts such as, on the one hand being a friend and an equal, and on the other, being in charge and being a teacher)?

Activity 2.2

Using Figure 2.1, think about each statement and think about where you would place yourself approximately (this is not a scientific exercise!) on the continuum. This will involve reflecting on your own teaching and workplace. Remember Figure 2.1 is not intended as a checklist, but as a frame of reference for thinking about developing professionalism.

Reflect on the statements themselves. Perhaps there are other statements you want to add. Consider specifically how you could develop your professionalism, identifying aspects of thinking and practice.

You may wish to think about these statements, alongside the statements in Figure 2.1:

- A teacher is never off duty.
- Consistency with colleagues and children is a reasonable expectation.
- Teachers must be 100 per cent reliable.
- Early years teachers must be independent but also part of a team.
- Children have rights and responsibilities.

Compile a personal action plan: select an area that is important to you and write a list, under two headings, 'Do' and 'Don't', to clarify what it means to be a professional, and to identify ways forward. For example, you might focus on decision-making. Your list might include – Do involve children in decision-making; Don't assume adults will always have better solutions to problems than children – or Do tell children what is happening; Don't talk about children, within earshot, or as if they don't exist.

Some of your statements might well involve Do, but... or Don't , but... or you might prefer Do more... Avoid... It is not necessarily cut and dried, although you may identify aspects about which you will not compromise.

- Think about implications throughout and principles. For whom might your decisions and practice present tensions? Ask questions about what you have written down; think explicitly about your own ideas, practice and workplace.
- Think about compromises you make and why. What are the constraints and opportunities; what changes are desirable and can be made. Take control of your professional development, realistically yet with ambitions for your teaching and for the children.

Chapter 3

Roles and relationships

Pat Gura

Introduction

The most baffling aspect of early childhood education for me in the early months of becoming a student nursery nurse, was adult/child roles and relationships. My perceptions were confused by relationships just relinquished with my own teachers. They decided what was worth knowing and doing, where and when and for how long, on behalf of the adolescents in their charge. In the nursery, no one ever seemed to organise the three, four and five year olds as we had been.

There was no public address system for the announcement of storytime, milktime, lunchtime. No bells or whistles signalled times for starting and stopping. Events flowed one into another, effortlessly, it seemed. Between regular events, children, for the most part, organised themselves in play.

What was my role, as an adult? Just as I had been schooled to do, I needed someone to tell me. Sensing this was one place where this would not happen, I set about what is proving to be a lifelong task: unravelling the mystery of how to teach without seeming to.

The very lack of compulsion appeared to enable children to challenge themselves, to persist, to invent and create. Research indicates that children identify play with choice and lack of choice with work. Play is for the self, work is done at the request of others (Adelman, 1989; Barrett, 1989b; Robson, 1993). Being told by the teacher that 'It is your turn to be the shopkeeper today, Kirsty' may have a different effect on Kirsty to when she chooses this for herself. If, given a free choice, she chooses to play 'being at school' with her friends, she will play at working: she will write letters and numbers and do drawings for the pretend teacher.

When responding to worries that we may not be 'fully exploiting the educational potential of play',[1] the significance of choice is worth reflecting on.

Alison Stallibrass uses the metaphor of a 'caterer' in describing the role of the adult who: 'obtains the "food"... places it on the table [and] makes it possible for the children to digest the mental and emotional nourishment that they need if their basic and essential faculties are to grow' (1974, p.222). Adopting her metaphor, the menu was buffet style rather than a set meal. Like all good caterers, she was not above making the occasional serving suggestion which the diners were free to decline, about the use of a piece of equipment.

Stallibrass represents the thoughtful, reflective adaptation to practice, of Piagetian cognitive developmental theory, aimed at liberating children's thinking. Psychodynamic theory also informed her role in helping children deal with their feelings about self and others (Isaacs, 1951; Tudor Hart, 1963; Winnicott, 1964). Her work deserves to be read with this in mind. Where practitioner understandings remain at the surface level of theory, the result may be children 'learning any old thing by doing any old thing' (Wall, 1975, p.204).

From a Piagetian perspective, learning is seen as resulting from the *independent* cognitive activity of the *individual* 'child', who need do little more than interact with the environment to learn. Adults provide companionship, encouragement and an environment rich in opportunities for autonomous learning. On paper, Piaget's 'child' is an individual without personal, social or cultural history. It is not an *actual* child, nor even an *actual* mind but what has been termed 'a pure cognitive system' (Bradley, 1989, p.151).

Piaget underplayed the role of others in the learning of individuals. This was reflected in the approach of my earliest colleagues who, like Stallibrass, tended to understate the role of adults, while stressing the importance of peer interaction. In this respect, the influence was psychodynamic theory, which focuses on emotional/social development (Isaacs, 1951; Tudor Hart, 1963; Winnicott, 1964). The aim is to help children come to terms with conflicting feelings about self and others, so that as individuals they may become increasingly strong and 'together' within themselves. This involves recognition of the rights and feelings of others and through this a sense of relatedness to others. The growth of competence in all aspects of living is a key concept, in the development of a strong self.

Piagetian and psychodynamic theory complement each other very well, in terms of the whole child, but the emphasis rests on 'the child'. Learning is primarily by and for the self. Interaction is between *independent* entities (Gordon, 1966).

An alternative view, the subject of this chapter, emphasises the *merging* of entities. From this perspective it is difficult to tell where one person ends and another begins. Each new life is seen not so much as a beginning, as a continuation. We are born with a history: of humankind; of society; of our culture, community and family. From birth we engage with our history and in our turn we become makers of history.[2]

The social context

Post-Piagetian understandings of what is 'developmentally appropriate' experience in early childhood education has been greatly assisted by the insights gained into the informal teaching and learning which goes on within home and family settings.

It is now widely recognised that the family and home play a central role in the education of young children by providing them with their earliest and most powerful reference points for interpreting and relating to the wider world.

Studies of young children as they actively participate in the bustle of home and family life have contributed to a recognition of their strengths, rather than their failings. They are described as skilled social operators who actively use *other people* to learn (Bruner and Haste, 1987b). They observe, listen, question, argue, agree, negotiate, manipulate, ask for help, join in.

Our outer and inner selves

According to Vygotsky (1978) learning takes place in two contexts:

- out in the open as dialogue *between* people;
- within each of the participants, as *inner* dialogue with the self.

These outer and inner dialogues continually inform and *transform* each other.

The difference between adults and children is viewed as quantitative, rather than qualitative:

- adults have a greater range and depth of experience;
- adults can handle more information simultaneously.

Because of the head-start they have on children, Malaguzzi suggests adults owe it to them to make them 'small loans' when they are struggling to understand or achieve something which is just out of their reach (1995, pp.79–80).

The narrowness of the gap and the smallness of the 'loan' are critical. A large gap cannot be bridged with a large loan. It must be reduced little by little. The term 'loan' is used deliberately to emphasise the expectation that it will be paid back, with interest, in terms of the child's increased power as a *contributor* to the social context. The idea of 'loans' is Malaguzzi's adaptation of Vygotskyan theory about the conditions for successful teaching and learning (Vygotsky, 1978). From this view, the individual mind is part of the larger collective whole.

In this context, children's different experiences outside school, their personal, social and cultural backgrounds, gender and any special characteristics they may have, together with their teachers' histories and characteristics, are valued as important elements in the shaping of learning situations.

Changing roles and relationships

Due to our developing awareness of young children as competent social operators and the significance of the social world for learning, there has been a noticeable change in early childhood education in terms of adult–child roles and relationships.

From being 'child centred', i.e., viewed entirely from children's perspectives on the basis that learning is an individual/internal affair, there is movement towards the adoption of a flexible repertoire of roles and relationships for children and adults. In addition to the 'responding' adult role of the child-centred tradition, we now find early childhood educators advocating *play-partnering*, in which play is mutually directed by children and adults. Aspects of playing with children are dealt with more fully later in the chapter.[3]

Tutorial partnering, in which children are viewed as apprentices[1] is another developing trend. This picks up the idea of adult 'loans' and a further idea adapted by Bruner from Vygotskian theory: that of being alongside children in their striving for independence and understanding, sharing control of a task, sometimes making a small loan, then pulling back until another is needed.

Bruner termed this process 'scaffolding'. It is one which parents engage in all the time: at first they hold the hand of the baby which has the spoon in it and guide it to the mouth; they let go for a moment, nodding and smiling encouragement, waiting to see how the baby copes. Maybe they will go back to holding for the next move or maybe the baby will make it instead.

To scaffold a situation successfully, adults have to juggle continuously with several pieces of information simultaneously:

- the child's constantly changing level of understanding and know-how;
- the goal;
- what the next move might be in bringing child and goal ever closer together.

The goal might be anything from holding a conversation, learning to read, doing a jigsaw puzzle, or rolling out pastry. The next move sometimes involves going back a step.

Practitioners as people

A contemporary focus in educational research is the critical part which educators play *as people*. In this capacity they act as human, social, cultural and personal role models. Children need to see the adults they meet in nurseries, playgroups and schools as rounded people, who care about a whole range of issues. As early childhood educators, we need to do more than simply exude a generalised warmth towards everyone and everything, suggests Katz (1977). Letting children know what matters to us and putting them in touch with each other's concerns, beliefs, wishes and feelings, is an essential aspect of our work (McLean, 1991).

Practitioners as agents of change

Sensitive adult *leadership* is also valued. If we are concerned about change as well as development, decisions about worthwhile and appropriate experience cannot always be made entirely from children's perspectives.[5] Children cannot, any more than adults, consider and develop ideas they may never have, if left to chance. The valuing of diversity and equality of opportunity to participate in the making of history, often requires positive action by families and schools. When we do take the initiative, we need to be able to justify our decisions on a principled basis. We also need to reflect carefully on how to scaffold the process of extending and elaborating on presently held beliefs and understandings about each other.

Practitioners as researchers

Throughout the present chapter reference will be made to the case study narratives of Vivien Paley, an early childhood classroom teacher/researcher. Her work illustrates the role of practitioners in researching their own classrooms. Stenhouse (1975) suggests that it is only by adopting a critical, questioning approach towards the way things are in our classrooms, can we make them better places for learning. Paley makes sense of her own practice through the stories she weaves out of the continuities and discontinuities of everyday living in her classroom. She also encourages the use of storytelling by children in helping them make sense of theirs. The later sections of the present chapter deal more fully with storytelling as a universally accessible context for reflection and learning and with the work of Vivien Paley.

In practice, roles and relationships are not separated out as they have been presented here, but interpenetrate each other, influencing our actions from moment to moment.

Power relations

If adults and children/children and children are to be seen as a collective force for learning, some understanding of existing adult–child and child–child power relationships is needed. In general, in our society, children are not as free as adults to speak, or remain silent, on any subject, on any occasion. The younger the children, the less power they tend to have in this respect, in relation to adults.

The hierarchical positioning of children within different social contexts significantly affects not only whether they are allowed to speak but also the kind of contribution that can be offered. In schools as elsewhere there are conventions about who may and may not lead, who can change the subject or close it, what can and cannot be discussed and turn-taking procedures. A lapse in the application of the rules may be more serious than an error of fact or logic (Cazden, 1988; Walkerdine and Sinha, 1981; Willes, 1983):

> When a child laughed out loud in assembly at a word which had tickled his funnybone, an attack of 'group glee' broke out.[6] The initial giggle spread contagiously from child to child until it had the entire child population of the school in its grip. If the headteacher was amused, she did not show it. Calm was eventually restored, whereupon the head informed the children: 'That was not funny.' A hand went up and a voice called out: 'It was really.' She was five and had been at school barely half a term. The glee of a few moments before became a collective shudder.[7]

This story demonstrates something of the complexity of power relationships and the *meanings* of the conventions which maintain them: raising the hand does not permit the speaker to speak but merely indicates a desire to; adults are not required to make sense if it is their game; rights to the 'last word' tend to be distributed in favour of adults. What I find humbling and often worrying, is that more children do not say what is on their mind, more frequently in school. The fact that they do not can make dissenters seem deviant. Often they are saying something we need to hear (Cousins, 1990; Paley, 1990).

Peer play

Hierarchical power relations exist between children as much as between adults and children. Peer social play may seem anarchic to the outsider, but is as rule governed as any adult–child encounter. Some rules are flexible and negotiable, others non-negotiable. Recognising which is which takes time. As indicated in Figure 3.1, there are children who may need help.

Figure 3.1: Further reflection – access to peer play

A consistent research finding is the high level of solitary play and observer behaviour of three-year-old entrants to nursery groups, often persisting into the second term. Such social contact as does occur is more likely to be with children than adults.

- To what extent might this be regarded as developmental and inevitable?
- Is it adaptive, i.e., survival behaviour?
- Do they have any choice in the matter?
- How do you interpret the low incidence of contact with adults?
- Could/should adults 'scaffold' the entry of newcomers to peer play? (Why? and if so, how?)

Research on entry behaviour: Blatchford *et al.*, 1982; Hutt *et al.*, 1984; Garvey, 1991, pp.123–43, offer insights on the processes of learning to play with others.

Negotiating and renegotiating the rules of play goes on *throughout* play episodes (Adelman, 1989). This makes access to play in progress a complex business.

Children who are ignorant of, or choose to ignore, the local rules for gaining access to child initiated group play, will in their turn, either be ignored or openly rebuffed.

Attempted adult entry is likely to disrupt play, if the conventions are not strictly observed. Instead of being the children's game it becomes the adult's and may no longer be seen by them as play.

Jones and Reynolds describe an incident in which a teacher spontaneously joined in the children's 'kitty' play. For several days the children had been developing a game involving kittens and their owners. One day, the teacher entered, dropped to her knees and started behaving like a kitten. She was promptly told: 'You can't be a cat ... You're a teacher. You have to sit in that chair.' The conclusion drawn by these writers is: 'The appropriate role for an adult in children's play is defined by children; they expect the adult to play their game, not her own' (1992, pp.43–6).

Bullying

In our leadership role we need to be able to deal with power relations between children which verge on and sometimes become bullying. There is not scope in the present chapter to develop this important topic fully. Vivien Paley's method of dealing with children's power to exclude others from play is discussed later in the chapter and some useful references can be found in the notes at the end.[8]

We need also to stand back from our own practice to consider the ways in which we use our much greater power in school. A framework for reflecting on this is offered in Figure 3.2.

Figure 3.2: Further reflection

Jones and Reynolds identify three ways in which adults exercise their considerable power in schools:

(a) on children
(b) for children
(c) with children
(1992, pp.74–9)

- On balance, how is power distributed in your relations with children in school/out of school? Are they different and if so, why?
- How do you exercise power in relation to play in school?
- On what grounds might you enter children's play? Would this tend to be an exercise of power on, for or with children?
- What do you make of the suggestion that we structure play too little and structure work too much? (see Note 1). What are the implications in terms of power relations?
- In dealing with the children's refusal to pick up the playdough was Paley using power on, for or with the children? (this chapter: 'Power play')
- How powerful or powerless do you feel in determining the distribution of power in your own practice?

Power play

As a protective device, aimed at safeguarding the identity and status of people within and between groups, rules of engagement create barriers to communication with non-members.

One reason adults often have difficulty in communicating with children, is to insist on using their own terms of reference. Children, on the other hand continually have to try to make sense of adult roles, rules and conventions.

Paley offers a salutary example of children turning the tables, by responding to her in the language of fantasy play: the children are unwilling to clear up the playdough, which they have deliberately thrown around and are blaming on 'Mr Nobody'. The last time she had been confronted with this situation by the same children, she had responded by pulling rank and souring adult–child relationships. This time she goes along with the fantasy, by persuading the children to treat the problem as if it were imaginary and could be solved by applying imaginary rules.

According to the children:

- Mr Nobody is invisible;
- he can see only that which is also invisible;
- the playdough is visible, therefore he cannot see it.

The mutually agreed solution is:

- to pretend everything is invisible, including the playdough;
- to pretend everybody is invisible, like Mr Nobody.

By this means the playdough was visible, allowing children and teacher to clear the room together (Paley, 1988, pp.100–1).

What is a 'child' to children?

Children's concepts of 'childness' (Gumpertz, 1991) offer a useful illustration of the processes of social differentiation and the positioning of children relative to others. Gumpertz uses the term 'childness' to refer to children's 'self-generated social categorisations' (p.28). Analysis of references to self and others suggests that children do not define themselves in universalistic terms, but in relation to the people with whom they are involved. Opposing categories are common: adult–child; big–small; girl–boy; brother–sister; big girl/boy baby; younger–older. These categorisations, according to Gumpertz denote the child's grasp of social difference and power relations, e.g., 'big–small' may symbolically define the social difference between adult and child: 'After a meeting in the street with a neighbour and her "new baby boy" Mark (age three) asked: "When I was a new baby, was I a little bit boyly?"' (personal observation). Having established that this was a question about gender and not temperature, its meaning became apparent. He was puzzled to know how a new baby could be a boy. To accommodate the idea of a baby boy he was wondering about the possibility of a developmental continuum of boyness from 'a little bit' for newborns to his present state.

Gumpertz describes the active struggle of children to assign a male researcher, who had adopted the role of adult playmate, to a social category. Having decided as a result of questioning him, that he was not a teacher or parent, but recognising him as an adult and a playmate, the children after several weeks began to refer to him as 'Big Bill' (p.251).

This solution seems to demonstrate that the children were able to transform the basic categorisations they already had of adults and peers, into a new category which would enable them to engage in a reciprocal relationship with the researcher. What Gumpertz suggests in effect is that children are continually reconstituting themselves and others according to their relationship to the person or people with whom they are engaged at any given moment. Sometimes they are in a subordinate role, at other times they are superior or see themselves as equals. The constantly shifting nature of roles and relationships is illustrated in Figure 3.3.

Children explore aspects of their childness through social play. They take the part of another who is bigger or smaller, stronger or weaker: a baby; brother or sister; mother or father. Superhero roles are often appropriated and super-human powers adapted to the local situation. Superheroes are symbolic of powerful adults.

Figure 3.3: Further reflection

What effect might it have on a child's perception of roles and relationships between self and a member of school, nursery or playgroup staff who:

- is a family friend or relative
- makes a home visit
- is met while shopping in the local supermarket
- horses around in the Christmas panto with other staff and parents?

By behaving 'as if' they are someone else, children gain some understanding of both the self and others, in a way not possible in everyday interaction. In play, according to Vygotsky: 'the child always behaves beyond his average age, above his daily behaviour. In play, it is as if he were a head taller than himself' (1978, p.102).

Events and scripts

In much the same way as the rules of traditional games are passed on to children, so they acquire the rules of behaviour which apply in various other social situations. Here is one example overheard in the doctor's waiting room: 'Now when the doctor asks what's wrong with you, don't go all quiet. She hasn't got all day ... and what are you going to do if she asks to see your tongue? That's it ... right out ... Good.'

Nelson (1986) and Nelson and Seidman (1984) suggest that children remember their experiences in terms of 'events' they have been involved in, particularly regular events: visiting the doctor, going to the shops, hospital, school, a bus ride or special events like a birthday or wedding. Each event has detail particular to it, including its own 'script': who says what to whom, in which order. Children use scripts from familiar events in trying to make sense of unfamiliar ones.

Role or 'script' knowledge helps support the process by which in their social make-believe play, children explore together ideas about the social world. It works by providing a generalised format, which can adapt itself to new content and is open to continuous revision.

Induction

A major task for children in the early years is making sense of the conventions of social interaction and forms of speech which apply at different times and in different situations, in relation to different people in school. We should not underestimate the scale of the task and the importance of these understandings in terms of children's feelings about themselves and others and their competence as *pupils*. Settling in is a gradual and lengthy process of adjustment. Failure to allow for this may disadvantage and alienate many children (Barrett, 1986, 1989a).

Social make-believe play along with stories, offers one means by which children can think about themselves and others away from the pressures of the actual world. They are likely to have a particular need for this, when starting school. In addition to their own, multidimensional role of 'pupil' there are many other people to be accounted for. When we add to this, the newness of many of the topics they have to deal with, often at a symbolic level, involving listening to adults and printed forms of communication, we can appreciate their need for the 'space' afforded by play to integrate their experiences, as they go along.

In play, ideas and 'scripts' merge and may become detached from their original meaning, developing a new life and possibilities. Reifel and Yeatman (1991) describe how the class topic of 'pets' was transformed during play as it was woven together with themes from television as well as everyday roles, events and scripts.

Making history together

Our human past is encoded symbolically in rituals, conventions, rules, myths, legends, personal narratives, literature and bodies of knowledge. Each generation of a society or culture, in turn, takes from and transforms history, achieving in the process continuity, progression and change.

Family and classroom life both represent this historical process at a micro level. The history which is made and shared by adults and children in school plays a significant part in the business of making sense together. Memories can be recalled with the help of someone who knows what has gone before. This kind of knowledge makes possible the 'scaffolding' of children's striving for independence and understanding (Tizard and Hughes, 1984).

Mixed age groups are rich in potential for children to recall their past and anticipate their future. This may be used to help them understand the feelings and concerns of others. Adults have the critical role of helping children make connections from person to person, across the day, from day to day and term to term. In the final section of the chapter, we shall see how one practitioner tries to achieve this. No two groups of children are alike and we ourselves change over time as a result of experience. Each new intake of children brings with it the opportunity to reflect on roles, rules, rituals and conventions. It may take some time before children feel safe enough to question what we take for granted. An example is offered in Figure 3.4.

The peer group

The peer group has a special significance in terms of historymaking, as many children can expect to be with the same group of children for several years. It can provide a sense of continuity in the midst of change.

Figure 3.4: Further reflection

Research indicates that newcomers to nurseries often have difficulty in coping with compulsory grouptimes and find registration particularly tedious (Blatchford *et al.*, 1982).

- What value can you see in compulsory group activity in the nursery? Should new children be excused?

A six year old who was eager to get on with his plans was grumbling about having to hang about whilst the register was taken: 'Why don't you just look round to see who is missing?, he suggested to the teacher. He scanned the circle, naming absent friends. Others joined in. The noise level rose. Registration took even longer than usual. They shrugged when asked what they thought was the purpose of registration. The teacher explained the safety reasons. They then saw why registration had to be dealt with at the beginning of each session (personal, non-participant observation).

- Put yourself: (a) in the shoes of six year olds; (b) in the shoes of the adult – do you like the system of formal registration; why do you? why don't you?
- Find out what children think is the purpose of registration
- If you think there is room for improvement, can you do this within the legal requirement; could this six year old's suggestion be developed?

According to Corsaro and Schwartz (1991) nursery teachers are called upon by children for help, as interpreters of peer behaviour, far more often than teachers of older children, as a result of younger children's limited experience of peer relationships. Thus adults are deeply implicated in the formation of children's perceptions of the peer group and the relationship of this to adults. Differences were found when the practice of an American and Italian nursery school teacher were compared. The importance of the individual within the group was characteristic of the American teacher, while her Italian counterpart was found to emphasise the importance of participative group membership. Both teachers acknowledged and valued the peer culture, using their insights to help children reflect on their behaviour by reference to the effects on peers.

In their studies of children in the family, Dunn (1988) and Brown and Dunn (1991) have shown that children show greater understanding of and sensitivity to others, where parents have referred to feelings in their interactions with them: expressing their own feelings; asking about the child's feelings; offering interpretations of the feelings of the child and others.

Childhood has its own distinctive cultures. Sometimes these are interpreted as 'counter-cultures', with children portrayed as having opposite interests to authority figures like parents, teachers and the established order (Davies, 1982; Holt, 1984; Pollard, 1985, 1987b). One study found that in a situation allowing freedom of movement and choice of activity in nursery schools, 'working-class' boys spent most of their time in rough and tumble play with each other, rather than interacting with teachers (Tizard *et al.*, 1982). Peers are seen as exerting a strong counterclaim on the child's attention when first starting school, and nursery staff are advised to act 'quickly' if they are not to lose out to peer influence (Blatchford *et al.*, 1982). Similarly, HMI (1989) deal with the settling in period for children starting school in terms of: 'ensuring that young children feel secure in their new circumstances and *quickly* [my emphasis] learn to co-operate and respond positively to others' (p.7). While accepting the importance of teachers actively pursuing partnership with, as well as between children, the suggestion that it can be done quickly, contradicts everything which has been discussed so far in this chapter.

Small-group learning

Small groups of children who know each other are a potentially powerful context for learning. It is important to be aware, however, that conflict and disagreement are always possible consequences of encouraging children to consult each other. Adults, in their turn, need to accept that the conclusions and decisions reached by children as a result of putting their heads together may be at odds with their own. This can happen due to the diversity represented within any group of people. In addition to working together in small groups, regular dialogue is needed between adults and children in order that differences can be resolved, or the legitimacy of different views acknowledged.

Meetings

Despite much unfavourable reporting on small groups as a context for learning, serious attempts are being made to understand successful small group dynamics.

Teachers sometimes like to set aside a time each day for a group meeting. Adults and children come together to discuss matters of mutual interest and concern. Meetings or 'circletime' offer the chance for adults to model the processes of listening, negotiating meanings, and turntaking (Drummond, 1993, pp.62–9; Mosely, 1993; Rowe and Newton, 1994; Stamford and Stoate, 1990; Thacker *et al.*, 1992).

The most important meaning-making principle in the social context of learning is that of *reciprocity*.

Reciprocity

In order to collaborate with others we need to be on the same wavelength. Reciprocity involves:

- individual awareness of and respect for the fact that other minds may have different contents to our own: I do not necessarily know what you know, believe, want or intend and vice versa;
- taking turns at speaking and listening;
- negotiation of meanings and intentions;
- listening with care to each other for the meanings and intentions underlying our words and actions;
- seeking clarification: if puzzled, we might ask 'do you mean...?' or 'are you trying to...?';
- using what has just been said or done as the basis for deciding whether to go back a step, continue in the same vein or try a different tack.

Where the transaction involves an adult and child, the onus is on the adult to support the child's turns and be aware of the need to make the occasional 'small loan' to use Malaguzzi's phrase. The principle of reciprocity is at the heart of the 'scaffolding' process, described in an earlier section.

The more we share experience, the more we create the shared wavelengths which allow us to learn from and with each other.

Traditional games

Snakes and ladders, hopscotch, skipping, circle games, singing, movement and finger plays are part of our cultural inheritance. They provide adults and children with a common repertoire of pre-scripted contexts for shared enjoyment and learning. These game-like contexts pose different sets of constraints and offer different opportunities to those of open-ended, child-initiated group play. They offer the 'bounded freedom' suggested by Bird (1991) which allows room for manoeuvre, within narrower limits. They also offer contexts in which an adult can participate as a co-player more readily perhaps than in make-believe play, helping to guide and support inexperienced players. In a game, adults and children are partners in mutually directed activity.

Traditional games belong to everyone. All have an equal right to play, although this may involve waiting for a turn. Once in the game everyone has equal playing rights. Changes in the rules cannot be arbitrarily imposed but have to be negotiated between players. The bounded nature of traditional games make them more accessible to newcomers and others who might be having difficulty in gaining entry to more open forms of social activity.

Mutually directed activity

In addition to games, there are many opportunities in nurseries and schools for adults and children to engage in mutually directed activity (Henry, 1990). General housekeeping tasks, like washing up and packing away the blocks are rich in possibilities for learning when done with an adult. Projects, too, provide contexts for joint ventures.[9] Mutually directed activity is, by definition, dependent for its success on *reciprocity*.

Sharing control

Where the general climate within the group is trusting and supportive, disagreement is a catalyst for reflection and shifts in thinking. If children are to be as committed as teachers to their classroom experiences, they must be allowed to share control of the contents and contexts of the curriculum. Research by Nias (1989) into teachers' perspectives on teaching suggests we are not against sharing control but overcautious about completely losing it.

Paley (1984) writes of her discomfort when the noise levels rose in her classroom, as a result of her decision to trust more in the children's own ability to regulate their behaviour. Instead of having her classroom door standing ajar as formerly, so that people passing by felt free to drop in, she closed it, concerned about the construction her colleagues might put on the increased noise. After a few weeks, despite the noise, she re-opened her door. Sharing control of classroom interactions needs teachers who have confidence not only in children but also in themselves.

Narrative

Narrative, or story, is central to the history-making process. A favourite story in one nursery is about a missing milk-label:

> The children use a special label bearing their name to reserve their daily bottle of milk. To lose this milk-label is to lose part of oneself and one day Natalie lost hers.
>
> With love, a camera and the cooperation of the local council refuse collection department, Jean Ainsworth-Smith, her teacher, recreated the last journey of Natalie's milk-label to its final destination: 'a huge hole' in the gloriously named landfill site of Mucking beside the River Thames. Having mourned it and laid it to rest, with the help of the story, Natalie was free to accept the offer of a new milk-label.[10]

Natalie is no longer at the nursery but her story lives on, speaking to all the children on the important themes of identity, sadness, loss, time and space, chaos and order, renewal and love. A sequel has been written about a missing drawing and a recycling scheme has developed around these stories. The past is continually updated, offering promise of future stories.

Stories, role play, dramatic play have been an important feature of this chapter. They all come under the general umbrella of *narrative*, which is claimed by many sources as the primary 'act of meaning'.[11] We all tell stories and we know when a story is being told. We tend to relate events in the form of stories, not only to entertain, although we may have that effect, but also as a way of making sense of our lives. Life recounted in strict chronological order seldom makes sense.

The story form allows for events separated in time and space to be ordered and reordered until they do make sense to us, as in the tale of Natalie's milk-label: a seemingly random happening makes sense when it is seen as part of a larger event. Before falling asleep, very young children may assemble and reassemble the events of the day, in what are referred to as 'sleep narratives' (Whitehead, 1990).

In relating, listening to or weaving stories, our consciousness shifts from the reality of here and now, to a position outside this, so that in effect we become onlookers. Children's 'small-world' play is a useful example of the processes at work: people, objects, events, ideas, beliefs and feelings are playfully manipulated to create alternative scenarios, to those current in the here and now. The process can lead to fresh insights.[12]

In addition to its meaning-making function, narrative is also a powerful medium of communication. People can follow and relate to each other's stories.

Narratives may be personally or jointly constructed, as in children's social make-believe or fantasy play. Every culture also has its collectively held inheritance of myths and folktales, available for retelling to each generation. These merge with material from other sources in the creation of new stories. Narrative is a means through which adults and children can together reflect on life and help define what is real, important and worthwhile.

Paley's stories

This final section reviews and pays tribute to the work of Vivien Paley, referred to throughout this chapter. Paley's stories help to illuminate understandings of roles and relationships in early childhood education and the importance and power of the social context of learning.

Narrative and reflective practice often go hand in hand (Whitehead, 1994). Paley uses it not only to aid her own reflective processes, but also as a means of transcending time and space to connect people with the ideas, wishes, beliefs and feelings of others. The published narratives she creates, out of the raw material of the early years settings in which she practices, illustrate the meshing of individual narratives into new collective and individual wholes.

Paley's teaching career started in a southern state of the United States in 1969, where few schools were racially integrated. Ten years later, at a time of mounting racial tension, she moved to an integrated school in a white suburb of Chicago and began the process of coming to terms with the implications of diversity:

> As I watched and reacted to black children, I came to see a common need in every child. Anything a child feels is different about himself which cannot be referred to spontaneously, casually, naturally and uncritically by the teacher can become a cause for anxiety and an obstacle to learning.
>
> (p.xv)

From this point she adopts a critical, reflective stance in relation to her practice.

In turn, she examines many important social issues as these impinge on classroom life, like race and gender from her own and the children's perspectives. She resists the stereotyped labels of pathological discourse when struggling to understand children whose behaviour confounds the expectations of herself and the majority of the group. Such children cause her to re-examine her expectations. Through her eyes, it is possible to see how standardisation of either children or curriculum diminishes both.

Her case-study narratives span two decades. To read them consecutively, is to appreciate the slow and often painful process of teacher development. In sharing control of the curriculum, the teacher is as vulnerable as the children to the risk of contradiction and rejection. Teacher development, as that of the children, can be seen to involve both continuity and progression.

There is a dynamic relationship, as in all reflective practice, between Paley's teaching and her research methods. Each is continually modified in the light of experience and as the focus of attention shifts.

A tape recorder is central to the process and is placed near to where children interact freely. Her purpose in recording classroom interactions and proceedings is three-fold:

- to have her own contributions available for reflection;
- to gain insights into the children's concerns, which she can follow up with them;
- to gain a greater understanding of the symbolism and rules which give meaning to children's play.

A great deal of material is needed for this third enterprise, as other studies indicate (Garvey, 1983, 1991; Gura with the Froebel Blockplay Research Group, 1992). The fine grain of regular behaviour, is of greater importance than novel events. Geertz (1973) explains the need for 'thick' description, in the interpretation of meanings. Only by gaining exact descriptions of all the circumstances surrounding an event, can they be discussed with the actors and an accurate interpretation made.

This is very close to Paley's approach. She owns only one tape, which she says is used, transcribed and wiped daily, otherwise it is too easy to set aside. Each day she asks the children for guidance on aspects of the recordings she is not clear about. This enables the children to adopt an onlooker position in relation to their actions and to think about them in a way not possible when they are engaged in the actions. She shares with them any ideas she has gained from listening to the tape, relating to their concerns.

The insights afforded by the tape enable her to see possibilities for action and connection between emerging and changing themes and concerns. She acts, she suggests, much like a Greek chorus, commenting on events and providing continuity. She speaks of her ambition to connect everything which happens in the group, and uses knowledge gained from the tapes to refer children to each other, as well as to past events. She confesses to not having always been a good listener, and expresses shock at discovering she listened more to herself 'than to any of the children' (Paley, 1986, p.123). This was combined with a tendency, even when she did listen, not to let what she heard deflect her from her intentions.

Her earlier writing reflects a Piagetian perspective, and her role as a facilitator, responding to children as she found them. The more recent narratives suggest an increasingly participatory stance. There is a greater readiness to take the lead. Like many early childhood educators, Paley recognises that children cannot, any more than adults, consider and develop ideas they have not yet had. She takes a stand on behalf of children who are habitually excluded from group play by making a rule: *You can't say you can't play* (1992). The children are given several weeks in which to get used to the idea before it becomes the law. During these weeks they have the opportunity to air and exchange their views and through this to modify them and adjust to the idea of the new rule.

Paley scaffolds the process by shuttling between year groups across the whole early childhood age range in her school, putting the idea to each of them and reporting back her findings from one group to another. Thus the older children can ponder the thoughts of the younger and vice versa, with each gaining new insights on themselves and others through this distancing process. On each turn, as a result of what has been said, Paley refocuses the discussion. Acting as mediator, she helps a whole school engage in reciprocal dialogue.[13]

A unique aspect of her work is the development of strategies for enabling *children* to reflect on their behaviour. Each day she sits at the 'story table', which doubles as a general workshop. It is situated so as to be in the path of anyone crossing the room. She is there to take down the stories children dictate to her. When a child has finished dictating, she reads it back, so they can listen to it.

Children often stop by, to listen and comment on each other's stories. Participation is voluntary, although she sometimes suggests it, when it seems appropriate. Later in the day, children dramatise their stories, to a gathering of the whole group, choosing the cast for themselves.

The telling, writing down, reading back and subsequent shared enactment of a child's story, represents a series of shifts of personal narrative, from the private to the public domain, to be enjoyed, reflected upon, revised and taken on board at both collective and individual levels. By such means, personal, interpersonal and cultural perspectives continuously interact with, and transform each other.

Summary and conclusions

It is a matter of record that as early childhood educators, we are excellent caterers and facilitators in the *physical* world we share with children. Without seeking to diminish that aspect of our work, the main emphasis of this chapter has been to explore the means by which we can optimise the *social* context of learning.

A reflective stance has been urged throughout. Many of the practices we engage in create or maintain barriers to communication and learning. Reconsideration of these is vital to the creation of effective social environments. Children's need for 'space' to adjust to the social world of school has been discussed at length.

The importance of creating shared frameworks for learning was explored with reference to the peer group and narrative. Narrative has been acknowledged as a powerful and universally accessible form of meaning making and communication through which people can connect with each other, with ideas, the past, the present and future.

The work of one practitioner has been explored in some depth. The fine example of reflective practice afforded by Paley's stories, is not offered as a blueprint. She demonstrates clearly the idea that we teach who we are and of teaching as learning. Practice develops over time and is shaped by our lives and the lives of those we meet. Paley's work provides us with food for thought.

Her development of narrative frameworks could be extended by others into a wider exploration of symbolic forms. Despite its obvious power in meaning making, not everything can be expressed or explored through narrative. The work of Malaguzzi and his colleagues in Reggio Emilia highlights the fact that children have at their disposal *many* powerful symbolic languages. In the past, we simply have not bothered to explore them, preferring our own adult forms.

Just as we must be prepared to make 'small loans' to children from our experiential and cultural store, we should also be prepared to 'borrow' from them, as Paley does when she asks for their guidance in understanding their worlds.

Notes

1 A report from OFSTED (1993a) suggests teachers structured work too much and play too little.

2 Haste (1987), Vygotsky (1978). Wood (1988, pp.7–13) offers a brief introduction to the work of Bruner, Piaget and Vygotsky, indicating the commonalities and differences.
3 Bruce (1992) reflects on roles and relationships as they impinged on a study of children's blockplay; Jones and Reynolds (1992, pp.34–56) consider the pros and cons of the 'teacher as player' role.
4 Tutorial relationships: McAuley and Jackson (1992); the idea of children as apprentices or novices and the scaffolding process are discussed in: Bruner and Haste (1987a); Edwards and Rose (1994); Edwards *et al.* (1995); Froebel Blockplay Study Group (1992, pp.126–7); Waterland (1985); Wood (1988, pp.75–80); Wood *et al.* (1976).
5 Lee and Lee (1987) discuss antiracism in this context; Ministry of Education (New Zealand) (1993, p.13) lists six dimensions of 'appropriateness' to be considered in relation to the early childhood curriculum: human; national; cultural; developmental; individual; emotional.
6 Group glee, discussed in Garvey (1991, pp.21–3).
7 Thank you to M.M. for sharing this story with me.
8 La Fontaine (1991): analysis of references to bullying from the children's helpline Childline reveals categories of behaviour which adults tend not to recognise as bullying, like namecalling and exclusion, which apparently cause children deep hurt and anxiety; Mosely (1993); Rowe and Newton (1994), advise on creating caring climates in classrooms and schools.
9 Edwards *et al.* (1995) and Katz and Chard (1989), contain rationales for adopting a project approach which optimises the social context of learning.
10 The copyright to these stories belongs to St Peter's Eaton Square, CE Primary School Nursery Class, Westminster. I am grateful to Jean Ainsworth-Smith, the children and staff of St Peter's for sharing them with me and allowing me to borrow from them.
11 Any of the following will provide an introduction to the nature and role of narrative: Britton (1977); Bruner (1990); Meek (1985a); Rosen (1984); Whitehead (1990).
12 In the actual world our role is that of a 'participant' according to Britton (1972). In order to see ourselves in that role, we have to take up a position as a 'spectator', and in our imagination recreate the events of our lives.
13 See Note 8. La Fontaine's analysis of the Childline data indicates that children equate rejection with bullying. To be told 'you can't play' is obviously taken more seriously by children than we realise. Children find it hurtful and threatening.

Chapter 4

Working in a team

Lynne Bartholomew

Introduction

Working in a team can be enormously rewarding and satisfying, it can also be frustrating and disheartening. Reflecting upon and coming to understand the factors which underlie well-united teams helps to enable both leaders and team members to take part in the building and maintaining their own strong team. This in turn affects motivation and morale and ultimately the quality of provision offered.

One of the aspects of teaching in early years settings that brings challenge as well as reward is working with other adults. 'While some people still enter the field with the assumption that the focus of the job is with children, the reality ... is that the work of the early childhood practitioner requires effective interaction with other adults as members of a team' (Stonehouse and Woodrow, 1992, pp.207–23). This may be part of a whole-school team or within the classroom. However, this 'effective interaction' does not just happen – not only does the team need to be aware of the elements that go towards the functioning of a successful team, but also there are specific skills and qualities required of a team leader. To the student or newly qualified teacher this may seem daunting, so it is worthwhile unpicking the strands to understand the underlying principles, since 'the essence of a team is that all participants work together effectively to achieve a common goal' (Rodd, 1994, p.87).

Building a team: the Redford House experience

Our experience of building a team at Redford House, the workplace nursery which opened in 1989 at Froebel Institute College, has highlighted significant factors and offered many valuable insights. Among these have been:

- the need for the team to work together;
- a sound knowledge of child development and education theory;
- the importance of each person's contribution: everyone needs to have a voice;
- respect, valuing and support;
- sharing of team ideals, successes and also risks;
- confidence building;
- ensuring that one learns to value and use the personal strengths and resources within the team and focus on what can be done with these rather than feeling constrained by the fact that sometimes personal limitations or weaknesses may counterbalance such resources. (This may sometimes require a certain amount of 'creative thinking'.)

When Redford House was established, it was always intended that the nursery should offer a constructivist approach to children's learning and development, and that this approach would be based in particular on some of the very specific and exciting work carried out during the Froebel Research Project in the 1970s. There was commitment on the part of the coordinator to the principle that everyone in the team should have a voice, on the basis that everyone has something to offer and different knowledge and expertise to contribute. Additionally there was a clear expectation that the constructivist approach, i.e. focusing on what children *can* do as the starting point on which to build, rather than focusing on what they *cannot* do, meant that a minimum number of rules were formulated before the nursery was opened. These were: firstly, no use of the word 'naughty' (there are always reasons for children's behaviour); secondly, no shouting (on the relative basis that most adults would not like to be shouted at by a giant!); and thirdly, (as part of the belief that children's health is of paramount importance) no sweets for the children. The lavish use of the word 'good' was also discouraged, this initially being to avoid the gender differentiation of 'good girl'/'good boy', but also because, while it might appear to be positive praise, it does not acknowledge the *process* of achievement and the routes that a child has taken in gaining an objective. Responses such as 'You *have* worked hard', or 'Which bit did you do first?' or 'How did you make that?' or 'That reminds me of...' emphasise far more positively one's acknowledgement of the effort the child has made. Within the Redford House team, the sharing of thinking about the reasons for this has ensured a consistent approach by all members.

An essential part of the nursery ethos has always been that team members value each other and build on one another's strengths. Adults, no less than children, need to be positively valued and their efforts acknowledged – they need to be praised and given credit where it is due. Care and concern for colleagues and an interest in them as people, regardless of personal feelings, helps to make each person feel respected and appreciated. Similarly not forgetting to thank colleagues when they have made an extra effort is not only courteous, but also recognises their contribution. Ensuring that a constructivist stance is maintained among staff helps also to maintain a similar approach within the classroom.

It is important to stress how vital it is for adults working with children to act as a team. 'When adults come together and use their energy in an orchestrated way on behalf of the child, then quality and excellent progress are seen' (Bartholomew and Bruce, 1993, p.ix). The essence of this is encapsulated by Nias *et al.* (1989, p.60), part of whose research looks at collaboration within schools: 'Being a team did not necessarily mean doing the same job, nor working in the same teaching space, but it does mean working to the same ends.' This means 'sharing successes as well as concerns' and recognising and valuing 'the unique contribution of each member, teachers and non-teachers alike, to a joint enterprise' (Nias *et al.*, p.62 and p.60). Both team leaders and team members need to be aware that the responsibility for maintaining such a stance is shared. Yeomans (Southworth, 1987) refers to this aspect as 'valuing independence'. He suggests 'The characteristic of a team is that it is an *interdependent task unit*' (his stress).

In particular

1. Each member's function contributes to the team task
2. Thus each member feels responsible to the team and is valued by it
3. Each member responds flexibly to emergent team needs as s/he perceives them
4. Leading the team carries obligations as well as powers.

(1987, p.134)

At Redford House, regular staff/team meetings (as well as constant dialogue and discussion) have not only served as the forum for ascertaining particular responsibilities and appropriate delegation, and for tackling issues that have arisen, but have also been the means of developing staff thinking. The resultant strength of 'corporate thought' is very enabling and often individuals will come up with ideas or solutions that have not occurred to other team members.

The role of the team leader

The role of the team leader, either of a larger team or as a class teacher working with other adults, carries particular responsibilities. These are over and above those incumbent upon each member to contribute to the effective working of the team. It is essential to recognise that everybody – from school cleaner to team leader – needs to feel important and valued. 'While most people enjoy the companionship and support of teamwork, they also want recognition for their individual contribution. One of the most challenging tasks for any team leader is to create an environment where individuals can feel a sense of personal achievement and are offered a degree of responsibility consistent with their ability. In order to remain motivated, individuals need to feel that their achievements are recognised and that they are making a valuable contribution within the team' (Lally, 1991, p.12).

Many early years teachers will be working in small teams in nursery schools, classes or centres, or within early years units in first schools, particularly now that many four year olds are being admitted into reception classes. This often involves being a team leader or early years coordinator. Although the word 'leader' is used, in many cases this will simply mean the class teacher, who may not have perceived her/himself in this role. Others will be class teachers within a primary school team. There are many qualities demanded by such posts, but *confidence* must come high on the list. The confidence to be a team leader or a valuable team member stems from a sound grasp of education theory. Among others, Curtis and Hevey highlight professional attributes early years teachers should have as:

1. a sound knowledge of child development and education theory;
2. the ability to develop strategies to transmit knowledge to others;
3. a deep understanding of the subjects of the early years curriculum and the value of play.

(Curtis and Hevey, 1992, p.199)

Without a thorough knowledge of theory, it is difficult to fulfil these conditions – 'teachers need to be able to articulate, explain and even justify early years practice with confidence to other people, especially parents' (Cleave and Brown, 1989, p.65). When Redford House nursery was set up, because of a commitment to a specific approach and the fact that some team members were not familiar with this way of working, it was important in the early stages to add particular and related theory to their existing knowledge of child development.

Confidence also comes with experience and the willingness to listen, learn, reflect and adapt as circumstances demand. Confidence by itself is not a guarantee of success and may take time to build. If team members who are not leaders are helped to understand these points, they should be able to support each other and the efforts of the whole team. This of course applies also to student teachers, particularly in their final stages, when they begin to take over the role of class teacher and thus carry more responsibility. They certainly need to consider carefully the roles of all the adults involved and how best to liaise with them.

The dynamics of a team can be very subtle. 'Leader and member behaviour are often indistinguishable because an effective leader legitimises leadership from members ... when all are willing and able to talk and listen, all become leaders and members' for 'collective activity is a strong cement' (Southworth, 1987, p.134). Thus it is clear that corporate responsibility needs to be fostered and encouraged.

The importance of valuing and building upon one another's strengths within the team has already been stressed. This is very empowering and raises self-esteem. A helpful analysis of the foundations of self-esteem is given by Docking:

> One of the ways in which human beings vary in their self perceptions is the extent to which each considers himself to be capable, significant, successful, worthy (Coopersmith, 1967, p.5). Those who have positive self-concepts are said to be high in self-esteem and those with negative self-concepts are low in self-esteem. Self-esteem is thus about how we evaluate our own worth.
>
> (Docking, 1990a, p.78)

Clearly, maintaining a constructive stance and realistically fostering self-esteem either as a team member or as a team leader is of great importance. Everybody works better if they feel good about what they are doing.

Managing change

Part of the responsibility of the team leader or classroom teacher is establishing with the team the goals towards which they need to work. One of the things that can present challenges is that working out new goals may necessitate change – and this can be disturbing and sometimes appear threatening. This will clearly require careful handling. It is important to remember that changes need to be organic, that change takes time and that it needs to be owned by the whole team. Simply dictating what needs to happen may produce backlash. 'Working as a team is a process, not a technique' (Whalley, 1994, p.171). In *Learning to be Strong* Whalley describes the time it can take for a team to develop and how new goals constantly appear.

The team at Redford House took on effective record-keeping as a main goal – the process and change in practice took many months, with meetings to establish priorities, to iron out wrinkles, and to share ideas and concerns. It also took time for staff to feel confident in their ability to do the job properly. It was recognised that the process would take time and although all staff worked steadily towards the goal there was no pressure for new ways to be implemented without consensus.

Although it is unlikely that student teachers will be in a position to make changes, it is important that they reflect upon aspects of practice which offer examples which they may want to adopt in their future careers – or those which they most certainly may not want to! In looking at the process of change, Jillian Rodd says that 'change is one of the few certainties of life! Leadership for change requires vision and inspiration, careful planning, decision-making skills, confident conflict management and sensitive handling of people involved in or affected by the change' (Rodd, 1994, p.115). She makes useful points for practitioners to bear in mind when implementing change, which:

- is inevitable
- is necessary
- is a process
- occurs to individuals, organisations and societies
- can be anticipated and planned for
- is a highly emotional process
- can cause tension and stress
- is resisted by many people
- can be adjusted to by individuals and groups with the support of the leader.

(Rodd, 1994, p.115)

Rodd does not advocate change for its own sake; rather that it should only be considered if it is thought to be effective in furthering the organisation's mission and objective. Where team leaders have a voice, the sense of ownership of that change makes the change more effective. Fostering and promoting appropriate change requires sensitive and constructive encouragement. Indeed the leader's role 'may be compared to that of the conductor of an orchestra, drawing out from each group and player the highest quality of performance' (Everard and Morris, 1985, p.125).

What qualities do team leaders need?

It is not only an understanding of the process, but also the manager's personal skills and qualities in putting this into effect that go towards making a successful leader. 'It will be clear that although effective leadership depends on the teacher's understanding of what her task involves, there is also a personal dimension – in other words it is not just what she says but also the way that she does it' (Lally, 1991, p.15, quoting Stubbs, 1985). Although Lally's writing is particularly directed at nursery teachers, the attributes below would be applicable to other team situations. Drawn from INSET work with experienced teachers and nursery nurses, she lists as important qualities for team leaders:

- Commitment and enthusiasm
- Ability to deal with others
- Good communication skills
- Consistency and a sense of fairness
- Loyalty to the team
- Ability to earn respect by example.

(Lally, 1991, pp.15 and 16)

It is worth noting that Lally also considers in some detail the challenges that may face a team leader, as well as the positive aspects of leadership.

Not only does a team leader need to have the ability to earn respect by example, but also s/he needs to be aware that respect generates respect, for it is just as important for a team leader to respect team members as for them to respect the leader. All members of a team need to be aware of and value what is contributed by all their colleagues. Over-ridingly, in the words of Lally (1991, p.17) there is a need for 'clear principles, teamwork and respect for individuals'. Thus it clearly follows that a team leader needs to try and enable the team to work to the *best* of their ability: 'Leadership is lifting a person's vision to higher sights, the raising of a person's performance to a higher standard, the building of personality beyond its normal limitations' (Drucker in Riches and Morgan, 1989, p.161). Drucker describes this as the 'spirit of performance': 'The purpose of an organisation is to enable ordinary people to do extraordinary things' ... the test of an organisation is therefore the spirit of performance. It requires above all the realisation that integrity is the one absolute requirement of managers' (1989, p.161).

Confidence, respect, integrity and also courage go towards making an effective team leader. Courage to stand up for one's principles, to face resolving conflicts and also to earn respect by example, and to accept that mistakes are a valid part of the process. To be able to admit to a mistake or error of judgement takes courage and strength, but this is all a constructive part of learning and helps other people to do the same. Whalley illustrates this vividly when writing about working in a team and the development of the team at the Pen Green Centre in Northampton.[1]

> Above all I want to celebrate the many mistakes we made, mostly with good intentions, and to be clear that making mistakes has become a very important part of our learning process. Making mistakes implies that we have taken risks; taking risks assumes that staff have the self-confidence and the ability to take on personal responsibility.
>
> (Whalley, 1992, p.157)

There is a comfort in knowing, despite the best intentions, that 'getting it right' also involves 'getting it wrong' at times – this is part of the learning process. Drucker aptly says:

> The one to distrust, however, is the person who never makes a mistake, never commits a blunder, never fails in what he tries to do. Either he is a phony, or he stays with the safe, the tried and trivial ... The better a person is, the more mistakes he will make – for the more new things he will try.
>
> (Drucker in Riches and Morgan, 1989, p.156)

For beginning teachers at a time when there are so many new things for them to tackle, it must surely be a comfort to keep this in mind! It also needs courage for all members of the team to be articulate about the principles of early years education in the face of possible opposition. Again the necessity for a strong theoretical framework to support this cannot be over-emphasised, as well as constant reading, thinking and reflecting, so as to develop understanding and apply this in practice.

The teacher/nursery nurse team

Probably the most common 'team' is that of teacher and nursery nurse, particularly in nursery settings or in reception classes, so it is worth examining this in some detail. It is important to bear in mind a number of points in what can be a very sensitive relationship. It is highlighted by Moyles (1992, p.142) that if one is lucky enough to have a full-time nursery nurse or ancillary worker, it is important to be clear about the similarities and differences in the jobs undertaken. Cleave and Brown (1989, p.66) point out that 'the teacher and nursery nurse should work as a team, being "partners" in providing activities for children's learning'. They note that nursery nurses have two years training and that their:

> expertise should be used and valued. They should not be used merely to clear up activities but should be involved in extending activities, in following up ideas and in discussions with the children. They should also be given opportunities for in-service training.
>
> (Cleave and Brown, 1989, p.66)

Bruce (1987, p.25) gives examples of how the role of the teacher and nursery nurse can complement each other effectively. As she says, 'It is one of the most important professional partnerships that can exist.' Of nursery nurses she says:

> They are highly skilled in their knowledge of the whole of the child's life and in their training pay more attention to the under threes and health care aspects than does the

> teacher, as well as studying the child's educational development. The training of the teacher emphasises education, albeit of the whole child (not just the child's thinking) and concentrates on the three to eight years period.
>
> (Bruce, 1987, pp.125–6)

She goes on to say:

> Both partners need each other ... Both approaches to the child are valid and of use in different ways. They are separate, but overlap. They need to be integrated so that each participant is aware of and proud of her particular different and distinct contribution to the development of the child.
>
> (1987, p.127)

It means that both partners should share and participate in the more irksome aspects of the job as well as the pleasant ones. If a partnership is based on mutual respect, a strong team will result. Different early childhood workers 'need to be clear about their roles, what is expected of them, what their contribution should be. Because the early childhood educator and the nursery nurse literally work in the same room this becomes particularly important' (Bruce, 1987, citing Clift *et al.*, 1980). Heaslip (in Clark, 1987, p.29) points out that 'Too often the nursery nurse issue is swept under the carpet – yet it is probably the issue which causes the most concern to nursery teachers beginning their careers.' Whalley in describing the establishing of the team at the Pen Green Centre, writes of how they have created a 'side-archy' (Whittaker) as opposed to a hierarchy – a sharing of responsibilities rather than an imposition of responsibilities. Whalley also highlights an issue which, while in fact a major one, may not be sufficiently recognised or appreciated – that of the pay differential between teachers and nursery nurses.

> Clearly the pay structure ... implies some sort of hierarchy, with teachers' salaries being the most advantageous. Whilst it is obvious that differentials in salary do affect how people perceive their role, it is even more important that people feel valued for what they are doing.
>
> (Whalley, 1992, p.164)

The wider team

There are one or two additional points in the context of successful teamwork which, while not dealt with fully here, should not be overlooked.

Working with a wider range of adults, either within or outside the classroom, also means being part of a team, albeit an extended one. Working with parents is considered in Chapter 5 and so is not dealt with in any detail here. However, it is important to stress that parents need to be considered as part of this wider team, not just as helpers in the classroom but also as partners in observation – for the development of children does not just take place in the classroom; learning at home and at school is interdependent. The sharing of observations between teachers and parents plays an important part in supporting children's learning. Having parents or ancillary helpers in the classroom does, however, need careful consideration, planning and preparation. Moyles (1994, p.67) suggests working out objectives 'to ensure classroom helpers feel important and are clear about their responsibilities ... Knowing what learning is intended and what it is useful to look for empowers the helper to take on a high level of responsibility for the task'. Pollard and Tann (1987, pp.106–7) put forward two important pre-requisites:

> The first is to find time for adequate discussion with parents to find out what they have to offer and to help them relax in the school environment. The second is to think about how parents can be most educationally productive when they are in the classroom ... Parental partnership in the classroom needs careful organisation to use the time and talents of parents to the full. A related range of organisation issues could be applied to ancillary helpers. This kind of organisation means maximum continuity in and minimum disruption to the daily running of the classroom.

Involvement with other agencies also forms part of the jigsaw of the wider team, with different levels of involvement according to the situation. Establishing common ground with other professionals may take time, since different disciplines may have different priorities – e.g., social workers and health visitors – but all have important parts to play in serving the best interests of the children. The spectrum of other professionals may be broad and could include the speech therapist, health visitor, social worker, educational psychologist, special needs advisor, teacher of the hearing impaired and others, although naturally on a more intermittent basis, depending on the identified needs – and on availability! Working together and sharing knowledge adds strength – failure to do so may produce confusions which could be unhelpful or even damaging to the children.

Conclusion

This chapter has been about the elements which go towards the creation of dynamic and successful teams; about understanding the framework on which to build. It is important too to understand that this takes time and commitment – that those setting out on the journey, whether students, newly qualified teachers or established workers, need not be daunted or discouraged by the enormity of the task if they can comprehend and appreciate the framework and the processes.

Rodd (1994, p.86) stresses that 'Effective leadership and teamwork can have a major impact on the quality of the service offered.' Therefore if children are to be offered what they deserve, i.e. the best quality provision for their development and learning, which is what will influence their total future successful functioning, then we as educators, from all the disciplines and at all levels, must ensure we fulfil our responsibilities by working together in the most constructive way. What could be more exciting than working to achieve this?

Note

1 Pen Green is a multiprofessional, multidisciplinary centre for under-fives and their families, offering a range of community provisions based around a nursery centre.

Chapter 5

Home and school: a potentially powerful partnership

Sue Robson

Introduction

Go into most nurseries and first schools and you may see parents around. Look closer, though, at what they are doing there: are they in classrooms with the children, 'seeing' the head about their child, tidying up the PTA cupboard, digging a pond in the school grounds? Parents and schools cannot avoid some involvement with each other, even if they wished to, but what does this involvement look like? The ways in which homes and schools interact can be very different, varying from those schools which still have a line (real or imagined) in the playground, beyond which no parent may venture without invitation (or summons!) to places which act as a focus for their community, involving different family members, and providing a base for a wide range of services and facilities. Here, home and school act as partners, each respecting and valuing the other's knowledge, expertise and experience. In this chapter a range of reasons for the active involvement of parents in schools is offered, premised on a view of parents as partners, rather than as either problems or consumers. This is followed by suggestions for developing worthwhile relationships between homes and schools, related to the needs and wishes of both the schools and the parents concerned.

A brief look at history

Wolfendale (1984) suggests that over the past 20 years it is possible to identify a trend in parental involvement, along a continuum from no contact to partnership:

Figure 5.1: Parents and schools: continuum of contact and involvement

nil contact	**minimal contact**	**moderate contact**	**moderate involvement**	**considerable involvement**	**partnership**
	open evenings, concerts, plays, written reports	PTA	parent hears reading, helps with painting, cooking, Newsletters	home reading, maths, parents' room, home liaison, parent–teacher workshops, community base	

Source: Wolfendale (1984, p.5)

It should not automatically be assumed that one end of this continuum is always necessarily 'better' or more desirable than the other (although it is difficult to argue with the principle that a child's parents should be able to take an active role in their child's care and education, as represented by nurseries and schools). There are many ways in which schools and homes can and do work together, to the benefit of both, and what may be most worthwhile is an approach which gives parents opportunities to be involved at levels appropriate to both their wishes and the time available. 'The parents' are not a homogenous group, and do not all have similar needs or wishes to be involved. The policies we develop, like those in any other area of school life, will need to recognise and support this diversity and ensure that everyone feels valued and acknowledged for the part they play.

It may be useful to begin by thinking of the relationship as one between homes and schools, rather than between parents and teachers. Tina Bruce comments on the diversity of children's lives: 'it is no longer appropriate to write of "family" in the sense of two parents and their children, with father working and mother at home, or working part-time' (Bruce, 1987, p.107). In many schools and nurseries this 'traditional' family model may be a minority one. For many children, family life may involve a range of members – parents, step-parents, step-brothers and sisters, a parent they may see infrequently or not at all. Adults may or may not be in work, and the communities in which they live will be ethnically and culturally diverse. If we remain unaware of these realities, or even ignore them, we deny important opportunities for forging connections between home and school, and providing continuity for the children concerned. This continuity can provide the basis for shared understandings, through the knowledge each has of the other.

The alternative is, as Cousins (1990) points out, assumptions made on both sides, with young children in the middle, picking up messages from both. 'Is it', she asks, 'any wonder that some of them are confused?' (p.28). The central value, then, of nurturing good home and school relations must lie in the effects it can have on the children at the heart of it.

While parental involvement in schools has tended to be more a feature of early years settings than of later school phases, the rationale for it as a way of sharing understandings, and a recognition of the expertise of both schools and homes, is of relatively recent origin. Margaret McMillan was a rare figure, especially for her time, in her belief that 'The nursery itself should be attached to homes' (1930, p.12). The prevailing educational view remained that schools could assist and educate 'inadequate' parents, and compensate for shortcomings in the home. It is with this idea of remediation in mind that initiatives such as Head Start in the United States emphasised parental involvement. Even the Plowden Report (CACE, 1967), which advocated a partnership approach, saw that as being very much on the basis of parents raising money, and being kept in touch with classroom progress through regular meetings, open days and reports. Nevertheless, the Report did undoubtedly mark a turning point, in emphasising the importance of parental involvement, and the value of good communications between home and school. Around the same time the growth of the playgroup movement[1] demonstrated that a preschool service for children could be effectively run by parents, and that all concerned could benefit – the children, playgroup staff and parents.

Figure 5.2: Further reflection – welcoming parents

How do you welcome and respond to:

- mothers?
- fathers?
- single parents?
- other family members?
- working parents?
- parents who you see very rarely?
- parents who never seem to be on time?
- parents who seem to question the value of what you do (either explicitly or by implication)?

There is considerable evidence to suggest that many parents were not then, and are not now, content to have just a peripheral involvement with their children's schools. For example, Tizard *et al.* (1988) found that 97 per cent of the parents in their study were helping their children with reading when they were in the reception class, a figure which remained at 95 per cent by Year 2. Similar percentages are cited by them for mathematics. They point out that this was because parents were interested in their own children's education, and saw helping as part of their roles as parents, and not because they had any doubts about the schools. Such studies emphasise how mistaken it would be to assume that the vast majority of parents are anything other than deeply interested in what happens to their child at school, and, more than that, are keen to support them. Their reluctance, as Hannon and James (1990) discovered, may be more to do with fears about doing the 'wrong' thing, coupled with diffidence about asking teachers what they can do. Learning, then, can no longer be regarded as the sole province of the school, and to see parents as 'problems' in need of 'expert' help is a limited and limiting view for all concerned. Indeed, Tizard and Hughes (1984) and Wells (1986) have effectively demonstrated how most homes, right across the social spectrum, provide a rich learning environment for children.

Figure 5.3: Further reflection – talking to parents

Many studies (Barrett, 1986; Cousins, 1990; Hughes *et al.*, 1994) have concluded that parents want to know more about what their children are doing at school:

- How could you help them to know more?
- What do you think parents need to know and should know?
- Are there things you would not tell them about?

Central and local government, and legislation

So how is this viewed at 'official' levels? Under the 1944 Education Act parents have a duty to ensure that their child receives 'efficient full-time education, suitable to his age, ability and aptitude' (1944 Education Act, Section 36, as amended by the 1981 Act, Section 17). The Taylor Report (1977) also emphasised parental responsibility at the individual level of one's own child, but, in addition, suggested that parents should have a collective voice, and recommended that all schools should have individual governing bodies, on which parents were equally represented along with the local education authority, teachers and the local community. The 1980 Education Act which followed this report implemented these recommendations only partly, and it was left to the 1986 Education (No. 2) Act, to give parents equal representation with LEA members. This Act also obliges governors to distribute an annual report and to hold an annual meeting for parents.

From a home and school perspective, though, perhaps the most significant piece of legislation in the 1980s was the 1981 Education Act, which followed the Warnock Report (DES, 1978a) on special needs. This report, with its emphasis on 'the full involvement of [their] parents' (para.9.1) was one of the first official statements to recognise the importance of a partnership between parents and schools, for the benefit of children. In particular, the Act stressed the joint nature of the assessment of children's individual needs, with teachers, other professionals and parents supposedly acting in partnership. Although it seems clear that, in practice, such ideals have not always been realised (Docking, 1990b, p.42), nevertheless, their existence as part of the Act suggests government support for them as a principle, and a similar emphasis on partnership in the area of special educational needs is a feature of the 1993 Education Act.[2]

The 1988 Education Reform Act, the most far-reaching piece of educational legislation since 1944, among other measures, requires schools to communicate the results of assessments at the end of a Key Stage to parents, and to provide for parents to vote on the issue of their school applying for grant-maintained status. The emphasis here is on parental choice, a theme developed in much that has come from the DES/DfE/Department for Education and Employment since then. This emphasis on parents' rights as consumers underpins the Parent's Charter (DfE, 1994a).[3] The Charter itself suggests that parents can secure the best education for their child as an 'active partner with the school and its teachers' (p.25). It also points out that a parent's choice of school directly affects that school's budget, and that it is this purchasing power which gives parents 'the right to influence how your child's school is run' (p.18). It is interesting to note the comment of the National Commission on Education (1993) that 'treating parents mainly as consumers exercising legal rights is a limited approach' (p.168). Is it, though, what parents do want? Hughes *et al.* (1994), interviewing parents of infant school children over a three-year period, found that, while over that time there was some growth in the number of parents who saw themselves either very much or to some extent as consumers (68 per cent after three years as opposed to 46 per cent at the beginning of the study), it remained a troublesome idea for many. Irrespective of whether they saw themselves as consumers, many parents commented on their disquiet about the idea of applying 'market forces' to education, and seeing 'the school as [a] supermarket' (parent comment quoted by Hughes *et al.*, 1994, p.63).

Under OFSTED arrangements for the inspection of all schools (1993), including centres with children under statutory school age, inspectors should collect evidence of a school's documentation for parents, and information from pre-inspection parents' meetings. The report should include 'an evaluation of the school's links with parents and their contribution to school life' (section 7.8).

Over the course of the past 20 years, then, a range of legislation has not only supported the idea of a parent's right to be involved in what happens to their child at school on an individual level, but has also given legal status to parents' collective rights to govern maintained schools. Parent governors who sit on governing bodies have the same rights as all other governors, and the same responsibilities – deciding policy, paying staff, balancing the school budget. In practice, though, some schools have found it difficult to recruit enough parent governors, and parent governors may sometimes feel 'frozen out' on governing bodies (Docking, 1990b, p.72). Parental participation at a wider level in local authorities is similarly uneven. In some authorities they may sit on education committees and have access to the authority through consultative organisations (O'Connor, 1994).[4] In other areas the picture may be very different. The Labour Party policy paper on education (Diversity and Excellence: a new choice for schools, 1995), however, suggests that, under a Labour government, elected parent representatives would sit on local authority education committees throughout the country. The stated intention of such a move is to strengthen local accountability. Can, though, such accountability be legislated for? In practice, it will depend much more on the attitudes of those concerned, and their enthusiasm for real partnership.

Ways forward

There are, then, several ways of viewing home and school relationships. It seems clear that the 'parents as problems' deficit model is both inappropriate and unhelpful. What, though, of the other two – parents as partners, or parents as consumers? The evidence suggests that parents are not entirely happy with being cast in the role of consumer (nor, perhaps, for that matter are schools themselves), but also that ideas of 'partnership' are many and varied. What, then, is an appropriate way forward? If we build on the idea of a partnership as a sharing of knowledge and expertise, Marion Whitehead (1992), in the context of reading, talks of parents and teachers being 'equal but different partners in literacy'. Such a view, with its emphasis on complementary, but not interchangeable roles, may be appropriate to a wider field of home–school relationships than just literacy, and serve as a useful guiding principle. Looked at in this way, roles can be seen as mutually supportive, and not threatening to each other.

What, then, are these complementary roles, and in what ways are parents and professionals different? As Bruce (1987, p.108) points out, there are, in fact, many crucial ways in which parents and teachers have similar aims: for the children in their care to be happy, successful, well-behaved and popular, for example. For the teacher, these are aims he or she has for all of the children in their care, and their responsibility extends to each and every child. However, the range of roles that professionals perform in relation to children is limited. Parents, on the other hand, are interested in and care deeply about their own child, in every aspect, and are all things to their children. 'They need only find one arrangement, but their stake in the quality of that arrangement is immense' (Larner and Phillips, 1994). Parents and professionals may also differ in their beliefs about the means by which these aims may be accomplished (Tizard *et al.*, 1988). Home–school initiatives and programmes must acknowledge these central differences and can then build on them to their advantage. As Becher (1986) points out, home–school programmes are often least successful where staff suggest to parents that they repeat at home some similar activities to those carried out with their children at school. A more worthwhile strategy might be to take positive account of the different environments and relationships of home and school, and use them to work in different ways.

Why involve parents?

Thus far, we have seen that parental involvement in school is widely regarded as a 'good thing'. What, aside from an overarching principle of its possible beneficial effect on children, and the issue of parental choice suggested by the DfE, might be the reasons? Looking at these possible *whys* not only gives us insights into what the various people involved would like to get from this partnership, but may also help us to identify *how* it may be developed.

1 *Parents have rights, and schools will need to be accountable to them.* This accountability argument is represented, partly, by the emphasis on parents' rights in documents such as the Parent's Charter. Some of these rights are, indeed, enshrined in law, as we have seen. Others, no less important, are observed more as a moral principle. For example, that parents have a 'parental responsibility' (Children Act 1989) towards their own children, with regard to their care and upbringing, and therefore should have some rights over how this is effected in school. The United Nations Declaration of the Rights of the Child (1959) puts it thus: 'The best interests of the child shall be the guiding principle of those responsible for his education and guidance. That responsibility lies in the first place with his

parents.' This may have additional importance in the early years, when children have their first encounters with organised education and care settings, and when parents may be particularly anxious about how their child copes with these first transitions. Perhaps the most fundamental moral right, however, is a recognition of the parent as the child's first educator, and thus with a legitimate concern over how this is built upon once their child begins to step outside the home.

2 *Parents can have a positive influence on their children's attainment and progress in school, by the attitudes they themselves display, and the support they give.* As we saw (Tizard *et al.*, 1988), the vast majority of parents of young children take an active interest in their progress, helping them with activities such as reading. The school can take this interest seriously, and use it. The Junior School Project (Mortimore *et al.*, 1988) found, among other things, that children's achievement and motivation tended to be better in schools which both involved parents in school, and encouraged them to take an active part in their child's education at home.

3 *More direct involvement of parents in their children's school activities can produce a range of gains.* There is, as we have seen, evidence to suggest that parents have long taken an informal interest in their children's school work. Programmes like the Haringey Project (Tizard *et al.*, 1982) and the Belfield Project (Hannon and Jackson, 1987), have capitalised upon this interest in developing schemes which involved parents more directly. In both projects children took home books from school, accompanied by cards on which both parents and teachers made comments. The Haringey group at the end of the two-year project had made significantly greater reading test gains than the control group, a difference that seemed to remain a year later. The Belfield Project did not yield such impressive gains, but the authors of the project suggest several possible reasons for this (Hannon, 1987).[5] What both projects did find, however, was that working-class parents from inner city schools were most willing to become involved, and to maintain that involvement, in schemes to help their children with reading. Both projects also suggested other types of gain. In particular, they commented on the positive effects upon children's motivation in general, on classroom behaviour and on improved relationships between parent and teacher, and parent and child.

Similar schemes, often under the title 'PACT' (Parents, Children and Teachers) (Griffiths and Hamilton, 1984), now operate throughout the country, and the idea has been extended to other curriculum areas, such as science and writing. In mathematics one of the most widely used schemes is IMPACT (ILEA Maths for Parents and Children and Teachers) (Merttens and Vass, 1987), which uses materials for home activities that build on the mathematics of the classroom. These are intended not only to develop children's competence, but also to enhance parents' understanding and confidence in an area which many may have found problematic themselves.

4 *Parental involvement in school may help to avoid conflicting behaviour between home and school, and minimise confusion for the children.* The more each knows about the other, the less potential there may be for confusion and

misunderstanding, on all sides. Cousins (1990) found in her study of reception children starting school that parents wanted to find out more about what their children were doing, because they felt they needed to know, and because they were genuinely interested in the teachers' points of view. Liaison through schemes such as PACT and the running of workshops in curriculum areas can all help to give parents information about the school's approaches, but, just as importantly, they can provide a mechanism for parents to talk to teachers about what they are doing at home, and about what they themselves are unclear about in relation to school practices. Teachers, for their part, then have a much fuller picture of the children, and their lives both in and out of school. This can also be true for many other aspects of parental involvement, for example, the sharing of record keeping and observations on children. The growth of projects in which parents and teachers share their observations of children (for example, the PROCESS project discussed in Chapter 6) is an acknowledgement of the ways in which parents' informed observations of their children can give vital information to teachers and all professionals working with young children. This kind of continuity between home and school is important for social and emotional reasons, too, in helping children to feel accepted and competent in both settings.

5 *Parental involvement in school may enhance parental knowledge, skill and confidence.* Increased direct involvement in school life can give parents insights into how the nursery or school approaches activities – fantasy play, for example – and the values attached to it by professionals. Similarly, displays or workshop sessions tell parents more about how professionals work with young children, as well as explicitly acknowledging the parents' right to know. This sharing of insights can be done in ways which reassure and inform parents, but do not patronise them, and it can add to parents' knowledge about their children's lives at school, as well as contributing to their own knowledge and confidence. For example, we saw earlier that one of the intentions of the IMPACT project is to enhance adults' understanding and confidence in the area of mathematics. In addition, it may help parents to feel more confident generally about approaching the school. As a public institution, with some power over their children, it can often be a daunting place for parents, however welcoming we might hope we are.

6 *Parent–professional partnerships may enhance teachers' knowledge, skill and confidence.* Some of the comments recorded by Hannon and Welch (1993), after an initiative in which teacher-training students met and interviewed parents (among other things) included:

> I shall look at a child in a class as part of a family rather than a lone individual.
>
> It was very useful to be able to talk to parents, and see them from their point of view, breaking down my stereotyped ideas.
>
> (p.13)

The second comment is particularly compelling. Tizard *et al.* (1988) document how teachers' ideas about children's home lives tended to be at odds with the reality of what occurred at home, particularly in relation to parents' active support and encouragement for their children. It would seem that, for these students at least, it was personal experience and involvement which enhanced their knowledge, and helped them to view homes in less stereotyped ways.

7 *Parental involvement in school can be an effective way of building support for teachers and the school.* It is often those schools which seek to keep parents 'at arms length' which have the least support from them. By contrast, Hughes *et al.* (1994) found that, the more parents knew about their children's school, and the work of the teachers in it, the more positive they were in their support. The nurseries of Reggio Emilia, in northern Italy, display information for parents, in the form of records of their children's dialogue and activities, all around the walls, with the explicit intention of eliciting parental reactions and support for what they are doing (Edwards *et al.*, 1995). This support can have psychological benefits, in helping teachers to feel valued, but it may also come to have very practical ones too. In the United Kingdom in recent years difficulties in local authority funding have led, in some areas, to very real threats to the continued provision of nursery education. Parents and teachers have, in many of these areas, combined to form pressure groups, lobbying both local authorities and central government.

In all of these reasons for a parent–professional partnership we must not lose sight of what must remain the central justification, that is, the positive impact it can have for what it is that both sets of adults have in common, namely the child. Looked at diagrammatically we can see as shown in Figure 5.4.

Figure 5.4: Channels of influence and information

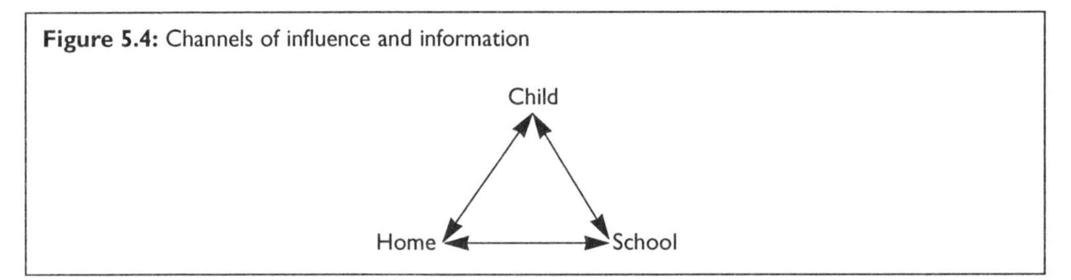

As the figure implies, the traffic of influence and information is two-way for all parties. All adults are working together for the good of the child, but there are opportunities for all, including the child in the middle, to have some impact upon the others. In recent years, much research has suggested a wide range of benefits, cognitive, social and emotional, resulting from collaborative working between children (see, for example, Bennett and Dunne (1992) and Galton and Williamson (1992)). If this is so for children, it may be that similar positive outcomes can result from adult collaboration, too. As professionals, it is our responsibility to ensure that what happens to children in nursery and school is as worthwhile and as positive as possible. Good relationships between the significant adults in a child's life may help this. By implication, the converse may also be true, that the potential exists for harm where relationships between home and school are poor or perfunctory in nature.

Before we go further, however, it is important to recognise and acknowledge possible reservations, of both parents and professionals. Docking (1990) suggests five categories of problem for teachers:

1 *ideological* – traditions about professional boundaries and who possesses the relevant expertise in educational matters;
2 *psychological* – feelings of being threatened through having one's work exposed to public scrutiny and one's perceptions and beliefs challenged by counter-perceptions and counter-beliefs;
3 *political* – the lack of adequate resources and teaching personnel;
4 *professional* – the lack of training in communicating with parents and working with them collaboratively;
5 *practical* – the lack of time to think about and implement constructive liaison strategies.

(Docking, 1990, p.8)

There may, too, be other dilemmas for professionals. In school, for example, anti-racist policies may present some children with different ideas to those they have encountered at home. Cultural differences may also lead some groups of parents to value different types of activity to those common in the nursery, for example, play.[6] It may be that discussion, both informally and in forums like parent–teacher groups, can be helpful, but there are no simple answers here, and change may be long and difficult to achieve.

Parents may have their own reasons for not wishing to become involved, either individually or as a general principle. As individuals they may not have the time or want to give it. They may also find the atmosphere of school offputting, either associating it with unhappy memories as a pupil themselves or because of what they may perceive an institution such as a school or nursery to represent. They may also believe that, as a general principle, 'education' is best left to the professionals. All of these reasons are within the school's control to potentially do something about. In the case of parents whose commitments preclude direct involvement, for example, because of work, it may be that they can contribute material from their work – old forms, telephones that no longer work, offcuts of wood. It may also be possible to arrange for groups of children to visit them in their work. It is the professional's responsibility to ensure that all parents have opportunities for involvement, and this necessitates taking a wide view of what involvement means. It also requires us to draw a distinction between the 'functional involvement' (Jowett *et al.*, 1991, p.137) of parental help in the classroom (although welcome) and true involvement, characterised by shared dialogue, expertise and experience. Whalley (1994) demonstrates well how this latter type of involvement can happen in practice, given commitment and will on both sides.

How can productive partnerships be promoted?

How, then, can we develop a constructive relationship between home and school? The onus must be on professionals here. In outlining what we can do, action falls into two broad categories: strategies designed to aid induction and transition, and initiatives and ideas for when the children are part of the school. All of them can be brought together into a policy for the nursery or school, jointly 'owned' by both professionals and parents, and always open to scrutiny and reappraisal.

Induction and transition

For some children the transition from home to nursery or school is a happy and successful one, for others the experience can be one of anxiety and confusion. Times of induction and transition are potentially stressful for both children and carers, and may be even more so when the children themselves are very young. Blatchford *et al.* (1982) found that, after their child had entered a nursery, over half of the mothers they interviewed admitted to experiencing various degrees of stress. This is clearly understandable in situations where a child has found this first transition difficult; what is interesting about Blatchford's finding is that even where a child had found the transition a happy experience, mothers often said that they had felt distressed or anxious. For the children themselves, the experience of starting in a nursery or school may be stressful in a range of ways. In particular, Ghaye and Pascal (1988) found that, for the four year olds in their study, the most stressful times were when three different kinds of activity were going on. The first kind was when children were separated, from home, parents, brothers and sisters, in the daily movement from home to school. The second occurred when children were involved in transitions in school, that is, from one activity to another, one part of school to another, and times such as dressing and undressing for PE. The third type of activity they identified involved incorporations of some kind, where children were expected to be a part of a group, in activities often closely associated with school: corporate activities such as assembly and eating together. Such knowledge can inform both the induction programmes we plan, and the ways in which we meet the needs of children and their families in their early weeks and months in school.

Transition and induction are, inevitably, times of change, and it can be argued that change is an important part of development. However, the quality of such change is central, and sensitive policy and practice and careful provision can all help to ensure that it is 'sufficient to be stimulating but not so drastic as to cause shock' (Cleave *et al.*, 1982, p.195). What, then, are some of the things we might do? An underpinning principle takes account of the triangle of influence and information looked at earlier, in particular the idea that induction into school or nursery is not a one-way process, in which the child, and his or her family, adjust to school. Rather, there should be opportunities for each to have some impact upon the others. In practice, this means that professionals will value and build on what experiences the child has already had, the knowledge and understanding they have gained before school, and the information that children and parents can provide. Wells suggests we look at it thus, 'entry into school should not be thought of as a beginning, but as a transition to a more broadly based community and to a wider range of opportunities for meaning-making and mastery' (Wells, 1986, p.68).

Preparing for induction or transition
The key need at these times is for all concerned to begin to get to know each other. Since the 1980 Education Act, all schools have been obliged to publish a prospectus or brochure 'which describes its achievements and what it has to offer' (DfE, 1994a), but this can be only a part of the documentation that schools provide for prospective children and their parents. Many schools and nurseries now have booklets which can be shared between child and parent, giving them valuable information about staff, about what sorts of activities will be available, and what to expect when they come in (see, for example, Bartholomew and Bruce (1993)). Schools with children who have a range of home languages will also need to make sure that this material is available in those languages, where possible. They may also provide photographs or videos for loan, showing the unit in action or activity packs for parent and child to do together.

Home visiting
While such information is vital, and the quality of it crucial, at some point parents, children and professionals must meet each other. How it is to be managed is a decision that must be taken by the school as a whole, for there may be practical and financial implications, as well as philosophical principles. The key question here will be whether to have a programme of home visiting. Projects such as High/Scope (see Hohmann *et al.*, 1979) have seen such visiting as central to their success, and an NFER study (Jowett *et al.*, 1991) showed that, of the parents in their study, nearly four-fifths were in favour of home visiting, particularly those who had received such a visit. In many instances, home visiting has served an interventionist purpose or has been part of a programme, such as Portage, concerned with special needs of some kind.[7] Its use, however, as an integral part of the school or nursery's programme may have a range of benefits. For the children, if the professionals that visit are those with whom they will come into contact upon entry, ideally 'their' teacher, nursery nurse or key worker, some faces will already be familiar. For parents a visit can provide the opportunity to talk both about their own child and about the school itself, allowing them to voice their concerns, to clear up any misunderstandings, and, hopefully, to lessen worries and fears. Most importantly, the location provides both parents and children with the opportunity to be on their own 'territory', in an environment where they may feel more confident and at ease. For professionals, home visiting is a chance to establish early, positive contact and to see the child in a familiar setting. Such visits may often also be a time for meeting other family members and people important to the child – aunts, grandparents, childminders, even the family dog. Once in school, this background knowledge can help professionals towards greater understanding of children, as well as providing shared contexts for conversations of the kind Wells (1986) has suggested are so important for young children, and which tend to be rare in school settings. Children will often refer to such visits even months after. Philip, at age four, five months after a very happy, calm start in the nursery said to me 'Do you remember when you came to visit me ... I was *awful*, wasn't I?' As he said this he looked at me knowingly and smiled. He had, indeed, been 'awful' – jumping off

furniture, rolling downstairs, and a host of other things, all to the embarrassment of his mother. As well as Philip feeling that we shared this experience, it was, for me, a powerful lesson in not making early assumptions.

However, as with parent–professional partnerships generally, there may be valid reasons why parents or teachers may be reluctant to become involved in home visiting schemes. Parents may not want teachers coming into their homes, and have the right to refuse such visits, which cannot, nor should they, be forced upon people. The most important feature of any home visiting scheme will need to be a shared understanding of its purpose and value. So, the information that goes to parents will be crucial in establishing these, both in order to reassure parents that it is not a time for snooping or prying, and so that they have some idea of what will happen during the visit. Children, too, need to know, as for many the idea of 'their' teacher coming to visit may be more important than adults often realise (Cousins, 1990, pp.32–3). Within the school, the decision to home visit can have budget implications, as it may be necessary to draft in extra professional support, from within or outside the school, while staff are out visiting, and all staff must see it as worthwhile. It may also be possible for professionals to visit children in other settings, too. Before entry to school, for example, a child may be attending a playgroup, combined centre, day nursery or nursery school, or be in a nursery unit within the school. Professionals can gain much from observing a child where he or she is settled and in control.

Visiting the nursery

None of this should be taken to suggest that opportunities for children to visit you are unnecessary. They may, indeed, be familiar with the school through coming to a pre-school club (Tizard *et al.*, 1981, p.136) or accompanying an older sibling, but visits to their new school or nursery remain just as vital, and are often very special to children, particularly if they have had a card or invitation, giving them a time to come, and a welcome from the adults they will see there. When they do visit, what they find should be welcoming, too. Notice boards can carry messages in a range of languages, and nursery workers will need to be ready and prepared to greet children and parents. The nursery or class itself can also be prepared, with already named pegs, for example. Such visits may also be a time when parents and children make judgements about the school, and form opinions about their child's 'readiness' (Ghaye and Pascal, 1988, p.201). As a consequence, it is better to invite only a few families at any one time, in order that staff can make time to talk to these 'new' children and parents. In general, these visits will also occur during the unit's working hours, when current children are in attendance: it is important to remember that too many unfamiliar faces and crowds in 'their' nursery may also be disturbing for them.

What happens at the point of induction?

Children may actually be received into school or nursery in a variety of ways. Again, decisions about how this is managed are fundamental to the school, and need to be carefully considered. Many units have found that a system of staggered entry over time, where appropriate, allows each child to feel more at ease, as well as giving professionals more opportunity to spend time with individual children, and to comfort and reassure any who may be unhappy.

Whether or not parents or carers stay with their children at the beginning is also a question which the school must consider. For many parents and children this may be important, certainly in the early days. The child has the support of a parent or carer in this new situation, and they, for their part, have the chance to see their child there. When parents do not stay, their children should know that they are going (with a clear 'goodbye' and reassurance of their return) and, upon return, will need to know how their child has been. Although, as Goldschmied and Jackson (1994, p.185) point out, this can be a sensitive area, with a need to avoid giving the impression either that the child has not missed them at all, or that they have been inconsolable. Cleave *et al.* (1982) give a poignant reminder of the need for careful thought here, in their description of Wayne's mother who 'plucked up courage to ask' after three weeks:

> The teacher, who was impressed by Wayne's outstanding ability, responded to the inquiry with a surprised 'Why on earth do you ask?' The mother interpreted this to mean that she had no right to ask and vowed never to go there again.
>
> (Cleave *et al.*, 1982, p.103)

This need to know applies not just at induction, but also when changing from class to class within school. What will be most useful to parents are specific comments, often about activities undertaken, episodes with other children, incidents of conversation etc. Again, the commentaries on the walls of nurseries in Reggio Emilia are there to give parents just this information. Schools in the United Kingdom also use display space for this purpose, as well as other ideas, such as a 'link' book, which goes back and forth, between home and school. In this, professionals write brief notes of how the child has spent the day, with occasional incidents described in greater detail, and the family contribute accounts of events at home, aspects of the child's behaviour and conversation (Goldschmied and Jackson, 1994, p.184). In other nurseries, professionals, parents and children all contribute to a 'parent held development diary', which is begun before entry, and may contain messages, accounts of important events, and even collections of leaves and bus tickets (Ollis, 1990). While such devices are important throughout the child's time in the nursery, they can be particularly helpful during induction or transition.

Schools and nurseries are in a position to smooth induction and transition, as far as possible, by the ways in which these times are prepared for and organised. Clear procedures, useful information and a welcoming atmosphere (including public recognition of its importance by the presence of a person such as the headteacher or head of the centre upon the child's entry) can all go some way towards this.

Working in school or nursery

In the normal course of nursery and school life there are as many ways of developing home and school links as there are parents, and what follows here is really no more than a checklist of possible beginnings and initiatives. What will be most important is that whatever is provided is there because it suits your situation, and meets the real, expressed needs of the families concerned.

If we return to the continuum of contact and involvement on page 57, 'minimal contact' is seen as open evenings, parental attendance at concerts and plays, and the completion of written reports. The emphasis here is on the provision of information, from school to home. Even within this minimal contact, however, there is scope for productive home–school liaison. 'Open Evenings' can be seen in a much wider way than the traditional brief interview between parent and teacher. At the very least, such parent interviews can be held at a variety of times, during and after the school day, which can allow shift workers, for example, to come in more easily. In cases where a child's parents have separated or divorced, it may be necessary to ensure that both have the opportunity to come in at separate times. The purpose and format of the meeting itself also need careful consideration and a shared understanding. Is it to be an opportunity to discuss individual children's progress, or is it a chance to look around the class and see the type of activities available? In both cases, it could be combined with other displays and events, and in the latter case it might also occur during working hours, giving the children themselves the opportunity to be experts, taking their own parents round and sharing things with them. When discussions about individual children are the prime purpose, the material gathered during the year – diaries, observations, samples of work, photographs, etc. – provides a common focus for shared understandings.

Sharing records

This documentation may begin, as we have seen, before entry with link books and home–school diaries. These books can continue throughout the child's time in school, often developing into treasured family possessions. Because they are a continuous diary, they can encompass a child's activity and interest in all areas – social, emotional, physical and intellectual, both at home and at school. A nursery headteacher involved in such a scheme had this to say:

> The excitement is infectious ... We are discussing what is happening; enabling parents to take an active role, to have knowledge and insight into the school ... Another advantage is that you are jointly responsible for the record. No longer is there the view that this is 'my department'.
>
> (Ollis, 1990, p.24)

Similar principles underpin observational records, now used increasingly across all early years settings, as a mechanism for sharing insights and facilitating appropriate provision. At Redford House, described in Chapter 4, Parent Observation Sheets and staff observations come together to help assess children's current progress, and to identify possible future needs (Bartholomew and Bruce, 1993).

Schools are obliged to provide an annual written report on a child to his or her parents, but this can be seen as the coming together of all of the observations made and insights gathered throughout the year, by both parents and professionals. The Primary Learning Record, developed by the Inner London Education Authority initially as a Primary Language Record, gives just such an opportunity (Barrs *et al.*, 1990), and includes provision for parent–teacher discussion and child conferences. The Elton Report on Discipline in Schools (DES, 1989) suggested that schools send letters home when a child's behaviour has been good and not just, as is so often the case, when it is a cause for concern. In nurseries and first schools, where parents may be seen more frequently, both face to face and written or telephone messages can be used in this way. All of these mechanisms take events such as open evenings and written reports much further along the continuum of involvement than 'minimal contact'.

Parental involvement in school

Moving on to the category of 'moderate involvement', parents' roles are more extensive, although still essentially passive. Parental help in the classroom may centre around cooking or painting, or 'hearing' children read, but it may also be about much more, and in ways which draw upon parents' (and other family members') own interests, skills and knowledge. The way in which professionals seek this help and the status they accord it, will, in some measure, condition what help they get. Soliciting general help and using parents just as another pair of hands, may not be as effective as talking to parents about what they would like to do, what they would feel happiest doing, and then providing opportunities for that to happen, as well as giving specific tasks to others. This, as well as being most useful, helps to convey the message that the parent's time and involvement is valued and respected.

We looked earlier at the need to provide clear, welcoming material at induction, and the principle remains the same for all communications from the school. Regular newsletters are a way of keeping everyone informed and may be particularly useful to working parents and others who cannot often get to the school. Within the nursery, noticeboards and displays can tell parents about the activities of the nursery, both current and planned, as well as giving information about other services in the area. Such displays and school booklets, can be made available in a range of languages, to suit the needs of the school. Help in translation may come from the local authority or from within the staff of the school, but it can also be another way of involving parents and families. Providing videos for loan (itself a possible collaborative parent–professional project) during the year is a good way of showing parents both the work of the unit in general and their own child in particular.

All of these are, however, ways for the school to talk to parents and do not take account of parents' needs to talk to the school. In a crowded day it can be difficult, if not impossible, for a parent or carer to have the opportunity to discuss something with nursery staff, or even to pass on useful or important information. It may be possible to arrange staffing so that at least one member of staff is free at the beginning or end of the day, or to have an arranged time before or after the session, when parents know you are available to talk and are not either getting ready or clearing up.

Teachers and parents: shared responsibilities

The final two categories on the continuum of involvement mark a shift in parent–professional relationships. Characterised by their reciprocal nature, they embody a sharing of responsibilities, with both sets of voices being heard. Thus, parents and professionals may work together to tackle specific difficulties, for example, in relation to a child's special need. They may also work alongside one another, in parent–teacher workshops exploring curriculum ideas and innovations. A variety of home–school curriculum partnership projects, such as the PACT programmes looked at earlier, are in operation at all levels of school and nursery, and are well documented (see Docking (1990)). Less widespread, but growing, is the practice of involving parents in other kinds of programmes, for example, the construction of codes of conduct, anti-bullying and equal opportunities policies, and reviews of the school's development plan.

If such schemes are to be most effective, however, they will need to be about truly joint development of policies, across the whole spectrum of school and nursery life. Ultimately, the governing body, on which parent governors sit, bears responsibility for the school's policy statements and development. In practice, construction of these policies can draw on a much wider field of parental involvement. Indeed, this is one of the two key ways in which homes and schools can truly be said to be acting in partnership, the other being joint management.

Such joint operation cannot, of course, happen overnight, and brings with it problems which are not always easily resolved. For example, how can parents jointly manage a service that is, ultimately, the responsibility of the local authority? How will staff feel about their 'professionalism'? How much more difficult might it be in combined centres, which may involve education, health and social services departments? Some staff decisions will always remain 'non-negotiable' (Whalley, 1994, p.16), but, as the same author points out, 'We learnt that if we wanted real participation then we needed to share decision-making from the word go' (p.148). Decision-making and consultation can also be through a variety of mechanisms, from the governing body or management committee, through the PTA, to the provision of school forums and other meetings and suggestion boxes. Participation and trust by parents will grow over time, as they see that what they have to say does have an impact upon the school.

Many of the features which we might identify as marking 'considerable involvement' (it may be more useful to think of it as 'collaboration'), go some way towards creating the conditions in which true partnerships can flourish. Central to them all is a view of the nursery as a part of the community, an idea which we can trace right back to Margaret McMillan, in the early years of this century. So, facilities such as a parents' room and a drop-in centre, equipped with refreshments and adult-sized chairs, acknowledge the parents' right to be in school, and provide a meeting place and a setting for a whole host of activities. Parent–toddler groups, toy libraries, resources for parents, caring for and developing the environment of the school, playschemes and after-school clubs are examples of joint activities, which can be run by either parents and professionals or by parents alone. As we saw earlier, joint action by parents and professionals can also take the form of campaigning on issues of shared concern.

Alongside this, the school can be a centre for services for the parents themselves, acting as a base for adult and community education, as well as a link with other services for families (Whalley, 1994). Parent workshops and Parenting Groups (Braun, 1992, p.182) can provide support for all parents and enable staff to learn about their concerns.

If we return to our continuum, it may now be as illustrated in Figure 5.5.

Figure 5.5: Home and school: continuum of relationships

◄——— *uni-directional* ———►			◄——— *reciprocal* ———►	
information	**contact**	**involvement**	**collaboration**	**partnership**
open evenings	open afternoons	before school day access	home liaison home visiting	
written reports			diaries, observations, home reading, working together to tackle specific difficulties	joint construction of policies
	children's assemblies	displays – plans, information, book weeks, newsletters,	parent–teacher workshops, joint videos	
		parent hears reading, helps with cooking	parent as skilful expert, author, etc.	
concerts and plays	PTA	social events	joint activities parents' room, drop-in centre, toy library, parent–toddler groups, after school clubs, community ed., liaison with other services, clinics	joint management

Summary and conclusion

This chapter has advocated a partnership between homes and schools, where shared understandings and expertise contribute to the insights of parents and professionals in dealing with the children in their care. A move from a passive 'recipient' model of parental contact, towards active involvement characterised by reciprocity has been outlined and suggested as a way forward. At the same time, an acknowledgement that all schools may be at different points along a possible continuum is important in helping us to assess what the next steps might be in each case.

In conclusion, then, developing home and school relationships is an inescapable professional responsibility for those working with young children. The Start Right report (Ball, 1994) places the active involvement of parents firmly as one of its five defining features of high-quality early education. It is, however, more than just a responsibility. For professionals the rewards, intellectually, in the knowledge it can give us of children and their families, socially in the relationships it can enhance, and emotionally in the extra job satisfaction it can yield, are considerable. Tizard and Hughes suggested that it was 'time to shift the emphasis away from what parents should learn from professionals, and towards what professionals can learn from studying children in the home' (1984, p.267). As professionals we should do well to remember that parents are, in effect, sharing their childrearing role with us, and doing it with the things most precious to them. This partnership can be a most productive, positive experience for everyone. Athey (1990, p.66) concludes that 'Nothing gets under a parent's skin more quickly and more permanently than the illumination of his or her own child's behaviour. The effect of participation can be profound.' Perhaps it is time, as Whalley (1994, p.149) suggests, to stop feeling we must continue to justify this work and instead begin to count the cost of *not* doing it.

Notes

1 Later to become the Pre-School Playgroups Association and now renamed the Pre-School Learning Alliance.
2 The importance of the role of parents at an early stage is a key feature of the Special Needs Code of Practice, established as a result of the 1993 Act.
3 Sally Beveridge (1992) provides a good critique of the Parent's Charter, part of the 'Citizen's Charter' initiative, in '"This is your charter...": parents as consumers or partners in the educational process?', *Early Years*, vol.13, no.1.
4 She cites the director of education services in Haringey: 'Parents are key partners at all levels in the education service, from direct involvement in schools to membership of the main education committees.'
5 He suggests that Haringey might have offered greater scope for improvement than Belfield. The latter had both a stronger tradition of parental involvement and fewer children for whom the language of the home was not English.
6 Goldschmied and Jackson (1994) cite a survey by Newson and Newson (1989), which found that at home nearly all four year olds were smacked, often several times a day, and that almost two out of three mothers admitted smacking babies under a year. In maintained schools in this country all forms of physical punishment are against the law.
7 This home teaching model originated in the 1970s in Wisconsin, USA and is now found throughout Britain.

Chapter 6

What we see depends on what we look for: observation as a part of teaching and learning in the early years

Jane Devereux

> Once we have trained ourselves to become keen observers, we can turn our attention to becoming shrewd interpreters of what we observe. What we see, will naturally raise questions as to what actions we might take, identifying, recording, hypothesising, questioning, theorising, changing, these are all part of the cycle of discovery for every observer.
>
> (Irwin and Bushnell, 1980, p.3)

Introduction

The above extract highlights the fundamental importance of observation as part of the teaching and learning process, showing clearly what it is we stand to gain from the process. It summarises the major issues to be addressed in this chapter and provides a starting point for discussion and action.

Observations can help teachers and other adults working with children to develop their knowledge of the child and of their developing competences, schemas and personal interests. Key questions that I have asked myself throughout my teaching career, are: why am I doing this activity or action with these children in this way? Is it the best way to enable the most learning to take place for all of the group? Why do I want them to learn this now? Is it informed by my knowledge of the learners' interests, needs and wishes? How do I know this?

The learner must always be at the centre of the process. The rights of learners, as Drummond (1993) says, 'create responsibilities that all teachers are obliged to accept'. A key duty of teachers is to monitor the effects of their work in order to provide evidence of the learning that has taken place and therefore of the effectiveness of the provision made: 'The responsibility to assess, to watch and to understand learning is an awesome one; but the exercise of this responsibility is the only real fulfilment that teachers can know' (Drummond, 1993, p.10).

This chapter will explore how watching children provides the core and basis for all future actions. It will provide a clear rationale for planned observations of children's learning and for the need to keep objective records of that achievement in order to best serve the needs and interests of the learner. This knowledge provides an informed basis from which to work to support, challenge and extend children's learning.

Why observe?

According to Stierer *et al.* (1993) there are four key purposes for observation. These are:

1 gaining knowledge of children's strengths and areas for development;

2 reviewing provision;

3 forward planning;

4 for summative reporting.

The DES Report *Starting with Quality* (1990) supports these with its emphasis that observation-based assessment should be a fundamental part of the process of understanding children's learning and of reflecting on the effectiveness of the provision, as well as having both a formative and summative role. OFSTED Criteria for the Inspection of Education for Under Fives (1993) also stress the importance of observation as crucial to 'ensuring breadth, balance and continuity of learning'.

We can look at some of these possible reasons in more detail.

Observations can provide formative evidence of children's competence. This is defined by the PROCESS team (Stierer *et al.*, 1993)[1] as 'the gradual building up of a picture of young children's learning and development, through everyday observation of them engaged in classroom activity and through discussions with parents' (p.1). Observations provide the information on which to base future action and develop our knowledge of how children think and learn, as well as providing evidence of their developing competences, persistent interests, dispositions (Katz and Chard, 1989) and schemas (Athey, 1991; Bartholomew and Bruce, 1993). These aspects of competence related to children as learners are explored in more detail in Chapter 1 and taken together provide a theoretical basis for observation. For teachers of young children, therefore, it is important that observation is seen as a fundamental part of the process of teaching and learning if the goals described above are to be achieved. It is not an end in itself, because some kind of action should normally be a consequence of those observations, even if it is a decision to do nothing, yet, or to gather further observations before planning changes in provision.

Watching children at play and work I am constantly surprised by their creativeness, inventiveness, persistence and talent. While watching a student teacher on placement in a nursery I heard the following discourse between two girls at work in the writing corner, set up by the student. Having noted an interest in teddy bears by a group of children, she had provided some teddy note books which these two girls were using and discussing as follows:

> Victoria (3 yrs 8 mths): What's that you've put in your writing? [Points] There!
> Louise (3 yrs 11 mths): Oh! That's a full stop. [She makes it bigger and darker]
> V: What's it do?
> L: It stops my writing going on.
> V: Oh I think I need one of those! Let me put one here. [Puts in large full stop at end of her writing.] That's stopped that writing. Good.
>
> (personal observation)

For me, this was a magic moment – being in the right place at the right time. It is only a short observation but provides a whole wealth of evidence about young children as learners and also of possible lines of development to take with those two girls. It does not imply that one must prepare a formal lesson on the use of full stops, but it does suggest that it would be valuable to gather more evidence of the children's understanding of their use e.g. to collect samples of their writing over the next few days and weeks to see if there was any consistency or pattern in the use of full stops. I may have done some shared writing with groups, including the two girls, and talked about full stops there. I may also have read some familiar big books at story time, encouraging children to help me with the reading. This would have created opportunities to talk about features of written language, such as full stops.

Observation raises our awareness of our own beliefs and values, and encourages us to be more conscious of how these affect the interpretation of what we see. Differences in children's experiences, for example, in relation to gender and culture, will be highlighted by observing what they do. Our expectations of the children will also be influenced. It is therefore vitally important in early years' settings that all adults are involved in the process of gathering observations so that a range of voices can inform the team's approach to provision and interaction with the children. Included in this notion of 'all adults' must be the parents and carers of the children. They have been the foremost influence in the child's life and have provided the crucial basis of their early learning. How we can develop this aspect of partnership will be discussed later in this chapter, and partnership in a wider context is the focus of Chapter 5. But important to note at this time is the way that our observations and those of the parent and/or carers can help provide continuity in the learning of the child between home and school. Each can inform the other of concerns and developments that can enable all to enhance the learning experiences of the child.

Gathering observations of competence will provide teachers with evidence to report to parents, receiving teachers, heads, LEA inspectors, OFSTED and other outside agencies concerned with the child's progress. This summative use of evidence allows for 'a stock-take' (Stierer *et al.*, 1993) at significant points in the child's educational life, such as the transfer from nursery to reception or from one school to another. It can inform the discussions that take place between some or all of the above groups.

Vital within this justification for observation is the need for evidence if there are concerns about a child's progress or lack of development. For example, children who have difficulty settling into a new setting, find it hard to relate to others, have difficulty communicating with others or have speech difficulties. Teachers may need to seek expert advice and support for the team and/or the child. Gathering information about children will help to refine our understanding of any problem, or alleviate our anxieties by refuting our initial concerns. Having information and detailed observations enables us to approach the appropriate agency(ies) from an informed basis and so initiate action as quickly as possible.

At all times in our work with children we should be able to justify the actions we take, on the basis of our detailed knowledge of their needs and experiences. Observation is, therefore, a vital skill that teachers need to develop from the very beginning of their careers. However, many experienced teachers will admit that it is not as easy as it sounds. How, then, do we get started and what do we do with the observations as they are gathered?

Factors to consider when observing

Getting started

Who, how, what, when and where to observe are important questions to address in getting started. This can seem a rather daunting list and inhibit some from even attempting to observe. It will be different for each teacher as it depends on individual experiences of observation and on the skills already developed. The most important thing is to make a start, and to reflect on that experience and learn from it. Sharing experiences with other team members or colleagues in different situations will help clarify the process of observation and may highlight needs.

Figure 6.1: Activity

Getting started

- Plan to observe during a session when you can be less involved with the children.
- Have a notebook with you and write down what you can see happening and/or what the children are saying. If you can tell any other adults in the room that you are planning to observe they can help by redirecting children away from you at that time.
- Reflect afterwards on the observations you have made, sharing your findings and experiences with another adult, and thinking about any difficulties you had.
- Plan another observation for the next session, building on this experience.

Who should do the observations?

The whole team should be encouraged to be involved, but some members may need support and encouragement to begin. First, it is important to just have a go. Watch an individual who interests you or causes you concern. Record what you see on some form of note pad or proforma. The more people who are involved in the observing the more varied will be the evidence about each child. If that produces a consensus of evidence then the assessment of that child's competence is stronger, and decisions about ways to extend and challenge that child will be better informed. Parents, as has already been mentioned, should be part of this process too, but it is important to be sensitive to the different ways that parents both want to be and can be involved in their child's school time education. The start of children's time in the nursery or reception is a crucial one to be in contact with parents, to welcome them but also to share their knowledge of their child's learning up to that point. Parents are the first educators of the child and do not stop being such when children start school, but their role is, as Robson suggests in Chapter 5, different and complementary to that of the school.

Both Bartholomew and Bruce (1993) and Stierer *et al.* (1993) offer ways of involving parents that allow them to contribute their observations in order to help build up a comprehensive picture of the child as a learner. The Parent Discussion Book explained in *Profiling, Recording and Observing* (Stierer *et al.*, 1993) is an example of one of many different versions of parent consultation that have been developed by teachers in different localities and educational settings and which provide opportunities for parents to share their understanding and knowledge of their children as learners, through informal discussion with the teacher. It does not replace the initial home visit which may sometimes be carried out prior to starting school, as the purpose of this is quite different. Bartholomew and Bruce (1993) develop this idea and shows how parents can feed observations into the early years setting to help inform the school's assessments. This is, of course, a two-way process and school-based observations may help and inform parents/carers, facilitate learning beyond the classroom and provide continuity for the child.

This discussion may also help assess whether or not observations are providing the information needed about the child as a learner. If the information from parents does not concur with the teaching team's developing picture of the child it may indicate possible areas for further observation, or changes or additions to the provision already on offer. It may be that the quality of provision does not allow children to operate at an appropriate level, important questions may need to be asked about how the environment is organised, about how children are able or unable to access resources, and about the support and interaction that takes place between children and adult. Tightly prescribed tasks with control in the hands of the teacher may limit children's opportunities to display their creativity, imagination and expertise, and discussion between children and adults where children's efforts are directed towards guessing what answer is inside the teacher's head may affect the development of their own thinking strategies and skill in solving problems.

Play is a vitally important part of a child's activity. The provision of opportunities for play can allow children to practise and develop new skills and competences, to explore emotional situations, to experiment with ideas, to take risks and to solve problems. Involving all those who work in the early years team in observing children at play and work is therefore vital to gain a clearer picture of each child's competence.

When is the best time to observe?

In reality, as soon as we enter an educational setting, we begin to watch and look. At first this is to gain an overall view of what is happening within the room, and the provision that is on offer. This will include noting the areas of provision, the adults involved and their location and the forms of interaction that are taking place. However, it is very important that our observations go beyond this, since 'understanding the process of assessing children's learning – by looking closely at it and striving to understand it – is the only certain safeguard against children's failure, the only certain guarantee of children's progress and development' (Drummond, 1993, p.10).

For the very reason that observation is part of the process of teaching and learning and is happening all the time as we listen to and interact with children, it is important to take care that its vital role is not lost. If observation is not planned for specifically, then it often does not happen. How will we know what children are achieving, if we do not spend time watching and listening to what they do and say? At times we will want to observe as we interact with the children, and many of our questions and actions will be in direct response to the children's actions. The more we know about individuals and about child development in general the better will be our observations and, ultimately, our judgements. Planning for observation is, therefore, important and should be part of the general routine. Questions about how many observations can be made during a session, and by whom, need to be considered. In particular, the goals set for the number and type of planned observations must be both realistic and achievable, if they are to stand any chance of happening.

Many nursery teams meet briefly each day or regularly during the week, to share significant information, including observations about children, provision and resources and to plan the next day's provision in the light of the day's events and the children's experiences. The allocation of people, and time, to observe as well as who or what is to be observed, may be some of the decisions taken at such meetings. Observations can be made:

- at regular intervals during a day;
- at incidental or opportune moments;
- at the start and end of sessions/activities;
- during activities while participating with children;
- during activities but not participating.

The timing of the observations and the form they take will be determined, to some extent, by the kind of information it is hoped to collect, and we shall consider *what* to observe later in this chapter.

How can observations be made?

In observing the current interests and schemas that dominate the child's interactions and actions in school or nursery we need to look at the whole child, and the interplay of intellectual, social, emotional and physical aspects that are vitally important and feed and support each other. We need to be aware that we can and do bring our own experiences and expectations to bear when we observe any action. The old saying that 'what we look for is what we see' carries an important warning for all those working with children that we try to see what the children are *actually* doing and not what we *think* they are doing, or even what we *want* to see. As DES (1990) suggests, it is important to remember that the context within which our values and beliefs operate may be different to that of the child and we must respect this difference and individuality.

Observations should be as objective as possible given all the influences that can come in to play as we watch. The use of language is, therefore, very important. There is a world of difference between recording that a child 'wrote his name from right to left in the top right hand corner of the paper starting with the first letter in the extreme corner and moving along from the right to left' and saying that 'he wrote his name in the top right corner of the paper but it was written wrongly as it was back to front'. The first is both more factual and less judgemental than the second entry. Judgemental language may work to lower teacher's expectations for individual children, and close down options for them. In this example, use of the word 'wrong' does little actually to describe what the child has done and to provide information about how his understanding and competence can be developed. It may also be that this child's first or home language is one in which reading and writing *are* carried out from right to left. Ignorance or insensitivity to such factors are ways in which our observations can be affected.

Statements such as 'has difficulty in concentrating', 'is a slow reader', 'has poor gross motor skills' sometimes appear in children's profiles. What evidence, though, can be given to justify such comments? To reach such conclusions the observers would need to have seen things which led them to believe them to be 'true'. To write such statements, however, sometimes even based upon a single observation, suggests that general conclusions are being drawn too easily. For example if we take the comment 'is a slow reader'. The child in question may have had difficulty with a particular text or been called away while in the middle of another activity in which s/he was deeply involved.

At this stage it is useful to consider two types of observation – participatory and non-participatory. The use of either will be dependent on such issues as staffing levels, resources and the information that is being gathered.

Participatory observation

All teachers, as part of their everyday work with children, are involved in participatory observation, but this does not always lead to written entries in the child's record. Participant observation may initially seem more difficult to manage, in that notes must be made either at points during work with the children, or immediately afterwards if the knowledge and evidence is not to be lost. We think that we will remember something and will be able to note it down later. Given the pace at which events can develop in the nursery, however, these observations can easily be lost or inaccurately remembered. Having 'post-it' notes, clipboards with paper or note pads, placed strategically around the room will help provide both the incentive and the means with which to record the incident, briefly, as it happens. Another practice is to ensure that you always carry a notepad with you, from place to place. Such pads often become the focus for children's attention, too, with them leaving messages and writing their own 'notes' down.

Observations made in this way may often be incidental and unplanned, e.g. the writing corner described earlier. Like the planned observations, these can be incorporated into the general system of observations which add to the developing picture of a child.

The habit of recording observations almost automatically comes with practice and notes often become shorter, but more telling in their content, with increasing experience. One teacher in the PROCESS Research Project (1993) said that as she became more experienced at observing she wrote less but it told her more!

Non-participatory observation

Non-participatory observation means that the observer stays outside the activity in order to concentrate on the child or aspect being watched. If a single child is the focus it allows the observer to watch that child both as an individual and in the setting of an activity. Similarly, a focus on an aspect of provision or on a particular activity, allows the observer to concentrate on that aspect of the nursery alone, without having to keep an eye on anything else.

If the observation is to be non-participatory, children need to know which adults are available for help while that person is busy observing. One teacher in the PROCESS project (Stierer *et al.*, 1993) used to wear a hat when observing, and the children knew that they had to go to the other adults while this hat was being worn!

Where to sit while observing in this way is also important, but becomes less of an issue as children become used to seeing adults watch them. Sitting too near or far from an activity may affect the quality of what is seen or heard, and even the observer's ability to do so. What is most important is that where an adult sits does not have a limiting effect on the children's activity.

A range of formats or ways of observing are also possible, which may be appropriate for particular purposes and at specific times.

Time sampling

Time sampling involves making observations at pre-specified intervals, for example, every ten minutes during a session or morning, of a targeted child, group or area of provision. Possible questions one might have in mind when observing a particular child, for example, might be:

- Where is he?
- Who is he with?
- What is he doing?
- What is he saying?

Similarly, in observing an area of provision, or piece of equipment, the observer might be considering the following:

- Who is using the equipment?
- What are they doing?
- What are they saying?
- Are adults involved?

Time sampling is particularly useful for tracking children's activities and interactions over a period of time, for building up a picture of particular children, and for appraising the value and use of equipment.

Frequency sampling
Frequency sampling is a way of tracking incidences of particular aspects of behaviour in a child or group of children. In this, the observer identifies a feature of behaviour and notes whenever this occurs. For example, a child may appear always to play alone in the nursery. Observations would focus on whether or not this was indeed the case, and would include looking at whether s/he approached another child, children or adults, whether s/he initiated any interaction, how any interaction was initiated, and where in the nursery this occurred. As its name suggests, frequency sampling can be useful in giving an accurate picture of the frequency of aspects of behaviour, and can be used to monitor both progress and concerns.

Duration observation
Duration observation is a way of accurately tracking how long children spend at particular activities or using certain equipment. It may seem sometimes as if a child or group of children spend *all* of their time in the construction area or riding the bikes: duration observation is a good way of establishing just how much time they *do* spend in these areas, and can help to ensure that the observations we record are accurate. 'Kuldip spends all of his time on the bikes' may, in reality, be 'Kuldip chooses the bikes first, generally spend half an hour on them and then moves on to other activities.'

Focused observation
In this method, the observer selects an activity, child or children and records everything that happens for a pre-specified period of, for example, five minutes. Focused observations can be helpful in giving a complete picture of children's activities and achievements.

Who and what should we observe?

Decisions about who or what to observe will be driven by the individual's or team's responsibility for the children in their care, and their interests. The following list shows something of the wide range of possibilities:

- new children;
- individual children or groups – gathering general information;
- children giving cause for concern;

- areas of provision;
- use of particular areas;
- resourcing of areas;
- movement around areas.

How these are to be observed will vary, according to the reasons for the observations, and in relation to the information needed. A look back at the previous section, on how observations can be made, will help in reaching decisions about the most appropriate forms of observation for particular situations. Whether observations are to be of one child, several children, or an area of the nursery or classroom that is being monitored to assess the effectiveness of provision, as was stressed earlier, it is important to write what is actually seen and heard.

Providing a rich and varied environment plays an important part in the observation process. Quality observations arise out of quality provision. What constitutes quality provision will be briefly discussed here, but is considered in greater detail in other chapters. Young children's learning is deeply embedded in the context in which they are operating. Hughes (1986) describes the higher levels that children can operate at when that learning is in a context meaningful to them. A responsibility for professionals working with young children, therefore, is to provide contexts that will facilitate such learning.

DES (1985) describe nine areas of experience – linguistic, mathematical, scientific, aesthetic and creative, human and social, technological, physical, moral and spiritual. Children need experience within all of these areas if they are to develop as well-balanced individuals. Again, it is part of the role of teachers to ensure sufficient knowledge of the children, in order to support, challenge and extend their learning in the above areas of experience, in ways appropriate to each individual child. Observation in each of these areas of experience is a vital way of getting to know the child's needs and competences. Stierer *et al.* (1993) suggest the following aspects on which to focus, all of which may occur in those nine areas: children's' interactions, attitudes, investigating and problem solving, communicating, representing and interpreting, and any particular individual needs.

Keeping a record of the areas in which a child has been observed should raise questions for the professionals involved. A question such as why a child does not go to some areas is worth asking. It will be useful then to look closely at that provision: is it not interesting to others as well? Is it that the child has not had access to that kind of experience and thus may need the support of an adult to initially explore its potential? What *are* the particular interests of that child? From these records it will be possible to see the balance of observations one has of all of the children and build into planning the times necessary to observe children for whom there is less evidence.

Which children are confident with books? Does Simone ever go into the block area or outside to play? Does Jane settle at a task for more than a few seconds? Does Kuldip use provision other than the bikes? Who does Marcus play with? How good at solving problems is Hassam? Does he persist? Does he ask for help? If so whom? These are all questions that can arise about individuals, for which planned observations may help to find answers.

What happens to the observations?

Management and storage

As the notes and 'post-its' and pieces of paper accumulate it is important to have some way of managing the volume, both in the short and long term. These pieces of paper initially provide support and information for the planning of future work with the children: they have a *formative* purpose. They are also needed for the *summative*, report-writing stage, when statements are made about the child's progress, often for communication to others, in particular to parents or carers, and other teachers. In the long term, developing a manageable form of filing system for the observations is important if all of these observations are to be most useful, and are not to be lost. A pocket file for each child, ring binders and a section in a filing cabinet are all possibilities, but solutions will be individual, dependent upon available space and storage facilities and the time to support them. Keeping these samples of evidence is, however, very important both in order to inform planning, and for when it comes to the summative stage(s) in a child's time in the nursery or class. They give insights into the child that can inform the understanding of parents, headteachers, inspectors, educational psychologists and other agencies, and provide evidence that can support statements made of the child's competence, in a wide range of contexts and areas of experience.

The short-term management of observations includes the sharing of these with other staff at the end of day or at team meetings so that everyone is aware of the successes, efforts and concerns about individuals, areas and resources. Gaps in professionals' knowledge about particular children can be identified, and plans can be made to fill these gaps.

Sharing observations

How these observations and records are shared with parents/carers is an important aspect to consider, and ways of doing so need to be developed. Not all parents are able to collect their children at the end of a day or session. This does not, of course, mean they are not interested in their child or do not care about supporting them. In order for all parents to have the opportunity to share such observations on a regular basis the school may have to examine ways of making time available for teachers to do so, time which may involve extra resourcing and have staffing implications. Having another adult come in to take a story session at the end of the morning or afternoon for half an hour a week, or putting groups of children together for a period at the end of the day, may give some time, but a range of options need to be considered if as many parents as possible are to have the opportunity to participate. Bartholomew and Bruce (1993) describe how parents who cannot come in actually contribute observations to the records via a parent observation sheet, which feeds in to the nursery's records.

At summative stages, at the end of the school year, not all of the observations themselves will go forward to the following teacher or setting. They do, however, form the basis for formal records and report-writing, with evidence for the statements being drawn from the observational records. The summative statement or report then goes forward, the observations that fed it are stored or discarded, and the process begins again with the next intake.

Summary

Watching children explore and make sense of their world provides valuable insights into their developing competences. In exploring observation as part of the role of the adult working with young children it is hoped that its vital role in relation to many aspects of early years work has been articulated. Collecting evidence of competence, creativity, persistence, imagination and socialisation gives us insights into the child's growing intellect and personality, and enables professionals to provide the best supportive learning environment for each individual. As Drummond (1993, p.10) says about the early years professional's roles and responsibilities: 'Paramount among them is the responsibility to monitor the effects of their work so as to ensure that their good intentions for children are realised.'

Note

1 'PROCESS' is an acronym for the project 'Profiling, Recording and Observing Competences and Experiences at the Start of School', carried out jointly by the London Borough of Merton Education Department and the Faculty of Education at Roehampton Institute London.

Chapter 7

Meaningful interaction

Shirley Maxwell

Introduction

A young child in a nursery setting is playing shops. Dressed in a white overall and a white baker's hat, she stands behind a counter on which are displayed trays of things to sell. There are other 'shopkeepers' to whom she talks and with whom she interacts, but much of what she is concerned with is her own preoccupation. She calls out, 'closing time, closing time, you can't buy any more, I am closed now', as she sets about putting all the trays under the counter. She turns an OPEN sign on the wall behind her to CLOSED as she does this. Presently she turns it again, 'I am open', she says, 'shop's open!', but no sooner has a customer arrived than she is again calling 'closing time, closing time!' An adult approaches saying, 'this is a nice shop, are the customers paying you lots of money?' The small shopkeeper looks at the adult blankly, making no response at all, for that was not her game. Her prime concern and interest had been opening and closing the shop. The adult in question was bringing her own agenda of shopping behaviour to the situation and was not observing and building on what was the child's concern. This was not a fruitful adult–child interaction (*Play for Tomorrow*, BBC).

As viewers of this documentary we are not privy to background knowledge about the origin of this role play. What we can clearly see is that this child is deeply engaged in what she is doing, and that she is participating wholeheartedly in playing out something that has attracted her attention. Her interest is in playing out her ideas about closing and opening times in shops, for her at that time, and for whatever reason, an important feature of the business of shopping. This is the significant aspect of her play that is useful knowledge for the practitioner.

Substantial evidence suggests that the school experience is not particularly valuable for considerable numbers of people. Examples of parents who did not themselves feel they learned anything, media reports of pupil failure, and literature depicting disaffection from school all point to the fact that learning opportunity could be improved. I am reminded of Donaldson (1985) who said that, as schooling is a relatively new concept in the development of mankind, we need not be surprised that we have as yet not become very effective. However, she admonishes, it behoves those responsible to set about forthwith to create improvement.

> each day will be important to a child's development.
> each child can only live this day once.
>
> (Honig, 1990, p.61)

This chapter is about the significance of interactive experiences in the learning and lives of young children. If adults, at home and at school, are to help children make the most of their earliest experiences they must carefully consider their view of children, children's learning and children's development. They must also reflect on themselves, their formative experiences and the influence of these on their expectations of children. For children spend the major part of their early years under the guidance or control of adults, at least for the most part in the western world. It may be this nurturing role that can lead adults to overlook the young child as a thinking, feeling and competent, if inexperienced young person, and act instead as if children were somehow 'owned'.

Promoting a culture of shared meaning

Adults who do unwittingly consider they 'own' children tend to speak for them, make their decisions and generally overlay their communication with much of their own adult agenda. Children respond to this in many ways, but often learn very quickly that their voice or their thoughts are not of much consequence. In school it is not unusual to see children bewildered by what an adult says or, alternatively, believe that what is said does not apply to them. A worse scenario is when children learn to switch off when in adult company and either keep their thoughts to themselves, or believe they really do not have any thoughts.

Young children do have rights, the right to enjoy genuine and meaningful conversations with other children and with adults at home and at school, to learn to take responsibility for their own ideas and to feel that they are people who have ideas. This is not only important for self-esteem but also for the development of their attitude to themselves as learners.

What young children do *not* have is wide experience of the world around them, so it is important that they have opportunities to interact with recognised and loved people and things, while also enjoying new and novel activities. Things that interest *them* are important as is an acceptance by the people they meet of their inherited and very idiosyncratic personal disposition. The earliest experiences in the home offer the first opportunities for becoming skilled in interaction. Later, children must come to understand and make the most of the school experience.

Professionals in early years settings then have much to take account of. Do they, for instance, really take notice when they listen to children, do they really look them in the eye, and is there warmth in their body language? Cousins' (1990) description of Sonny Boy serves to show that the institutional demands of school can be bewildering for children and can even seem foolish. However, to promote a culture of shared meaning making in the classroom is a complex and challenging matter.

A community of learners

The term community of learners presents a picture of togetherness and sharing. In the classroom or at home, it can be children and adults who become involved in a shared agenda, an agenda that allows children to use their own ideas and to gain confidence in themselves as thinking and questioning people. Such an agenda must begin with the parent or professional showing a willingness towards an informed perspective of children's interests and understandings. The adult must be able to see the world through the eyes of a child and accept, as a starting point, the perceptions a child might hold.

Giving children real attention

Attending and listening to children is as much an attitude as a feature of interaction. It shows respect and love for children and a willingness to enjoy their thinking. It is usually based on a recognition of growth and development in the child. Clay (1979) helped New Zealand teachers to learn to observe and recognise children's growth and development as readers. She taught them that it was not important to know everything about observation before they began, but rather to start somewhere and to notice a few things. Before long they would become aware of more things because of what they had already noticed in the process. Child watching, then, was an essential pre-requisite for first understanding the process of development and second, interacting in effective ways.

A knowledge of oneself

A third feature essential for adults who wish to develop appropriate and sensitive interaction with children is an in-depth knowledge of themselves. Only by becoming aware of *why* we react and interact the way we do, as professionals and as people, will we better enhance and develop our skill in the doing. Danish students, studying at Roehampton Institute in recent years, have highlighted the importance given to this phase of development in Danish teacher training. During the entire third year of training these students, accustomed as they were to working to the motto – 'to dare is all' – really questioned their *own* ability, their awareness of creativity and their management of children's learning.

It would appear that promoting effective classroom situations demands practice, the willingness to research and explore, and personal space and support. There *are* competences and practices which a professional can employ to create effective interaction in the classroom. In my own experience of training, now a considerable time ago, the study of this was termed PPT, the Principles and Practice of Teaching and it held a significant place in the business of teacher training. Such learning must still take place, for current attention to curriculum content will have little success unless the manner in which this content is offered and shared with children makes a difference in some way to children's lives.

The practices and underpinning theories, that I intend to highlight in the remainder of this chapter will, I hope, offer possibilities for ways of working with young children, which might provide for effective teaching and learning. These practices are not in fact new, but could be described as tried and tested, and offered here with a new flavour.

Early interactive experience

> like throwing a ball – first ensure the child is ready with arms cupped to catch the ball, throw gently and accurately so that it lands squarely in the child's arms. When it is the child's turn to throw, the adult must be prepared to run wherever the ball goes.
>
> (Wells, 1986, p.50)

This example of the behaviours involved in reciprocal ball play might be paralleled across much effective adult–child interaction. One thing that cannot be overlooked is that the onus for creating a successful interchange inescapably lies with the more experienced person, the adult. Therefore, 'if the adult and child are to succeed in elaborating a shared meaning over a number of turns the adult has to make the effort to understand the child's intended meaning and to extend it in terms that the child can understand' (Wells, 1986, p.17).

Field studies concerning mother and child interaction have played a significant role in the development of understandings of interactive behaviours, and research into language acquisition and development has frequently highlighted the fact that it is the *nature* of the early verbal dialogues between parent and toddler which is significant to later language development and understanding.

Protoconversations, as described in Wells' work, those earliest interactions when communication between parent and child involves the infant gestures being replicated and expanded upon in a sort of conversation without words, provide a good place to start thinking about interactive communication, at least in western society. As they communicate with their babies, parents treat them as if they have intentions, so the babies in time come to have them. The babies in these interactions receive *culturally appropriate* feedback. This is within a *regular structure* where they can gradually understand and *predict* more and more the kind of response they will receive. The baby's early environment is often *highly repetitive*, and involves the satisfaction that comes from the recognition of predictions fulfilled. The infant becomes well advanced towards communicative behaviour, for they have discovered how to take part in interactive turn taking.

Notions of intersubjectivity are crucial to effective communication. When something is the focus of joint attention, the adult and the child are not only communicating with each other but they begin to communicate *about* something else, a feature from the world outside is drawn into their interaction and made the subject of joint attention. This may not appear to be a complex matter, yet, if anyone interested invests time and energy in listening to interactions taking place between young children and adults in the world at large, for instance on public transport, in shopping precincts, at leisure centres, this triangulation of interaction can frequently run awry. Often the child begins with a statement concerning something they have noticed and they make a comment or an observation. But the adult in response does not check that they have attended to the same thing and their response does not relate to a shared third feature, it is actually concerned with a fourth, and different feature altogether. What of the responsibility already suggested that the onus for understanding is in fact on the more experienced person the adult. 'It is very important that we listen to children and that we also listen very hard to ourselves when we talk with children' (Paley, 1995).

Adults, particularly those who believe they must think and talk for children, sometimes have difficulty in remembering that children generally have a great propensity to notice and to be interested in all that surrounds them. Through their first single words, through two-word utterances, and on to more complex sentences, children quickly grow in their worldly understandings, particularly if they have others to talk with them. They talk about the things they have noticed, the things they are doing, what they have read, experienced in the outside world or seen on television. Anyone who takes children seriously knows that it is not the simple basics to which children are attracted, the names of things, their colour or how many there are. These nearly always arise from an adult's agenda. It is the feature which interests that the children notice – 'why does that duckling drink water like that – why doesn't he drink like a cat?' (example in Tovey, 1994). To suggest adults should discuss simple words and phrases describing simple things, shows a complete lack of understanding about child growth and development and does grave injustice to the intellectual competence of young children.

Following the more experienced lead, or acting out the words and manners of older people, is a further feature of interactive development. Holdaway (1979, p.54) states, the child 'works assiduously at understanding complex cognitive structures' becoming not only very good at making sense out of situations but also at using other people's language. This willingness to reconstruct the sayings that they hear and which attract their attention, even though they may be ignorant of the full meaning is very characteristic of young children. John, aged four, when asked the name of another child in his class, replied, 'I don't know what his name is but he's got lots of vitality!'

Wells' (1986) findings from the Language in Interaction project suggested that there were in fact no non-verbal children at the start of school. There were differences, however, from one child to another, resulting, it was believed, from the manner of interaction children had previously experienced. Those children whose questions and comments had been valued and treated as serious attempts to make sense of the goings on around them, were the most advanced in their language abilities. Features such as the length of their utterances, their ability to comprehend what was said to them, and the breadth of their vocabulary were all indicators of this growth.

What persuades children to interact in the first instance? Wells would hold that the most important factor of all, urging children into speech is their desire to communicate their intentions more precisely. My experience would also suggest that children frequently interact because they wish to come close and feel near to adults, the desire for warmth and acceptance being also a strong motivator. Either way, the value placed by the adult on what children want to say is crucial to their later confidence in having relevant things to say and interesting ideas to express.

The following example of Amy, aged 29 months, confirms much that has been suggested. Amy and her mother are standing in the kitchen for much of this dialogue, except when Amy moves outside the door. Beyond the kitchen door is a small porch with a fire extinguisher on the wall, possibly the connector for Amy with her play around petrol stations. It seemed possible that she played out the game of petrol stations because the fire extinguisher in the porch reminded her of them. A further feature concerns the shared knowledge between Amy and her mother that when you drive into petrol stations children must not get out of the car, they must stay in their seats.

A: I got some, I got some, I got some spiders
M: What have you got?
A: I got some spiders
M: Some spiders?
A: Yeah
M: Where?
A: In my hand
M: In your hand? What are you going to do with them?
A: I gonna throw them in the petrol station.
M: Your going to put them in the petrol station?
A: Yeah I going to get petrol
M: You're going to get petrol?
A: Cos, you stay there
M: I'll stay here? OK
A: You see, don't worry 'bout me
M: Mm
A: Don't worry 'bout me. Don't come in
M: Don't come in?
A: Don't come in the petrol
M: Where's the petrol station then?
A: I don't know. Now don't come in with me
M: I'm not allowed to come in with you?
A: No, not cear [come in here?] in the petrol, not go in the petrol with me.
M: I see, [pause], and the petrol station's out there is it?
A: It's out in the garden
M: It's in the garden?
A: Petrol station in the garden. I see you later on. Never come ear [in here] me. Never come ear me
M: I'm not allowed to follow you?
A: No not collow. You stay there. I'll get the petrol – Bye [from outside the door] don't come in with me ... [then back inside] I've come back in. I've got some spiders, come and geat [get/eat] them, [self correcting] come and EAT them
M: I don't want to eat your spiders
A: I go and get some spiders/I go get some spiders

M: Are you sure there are spiders out there?
A: Yes I go get some in your hand
M: You're going to put them in my hand are you?
A: Bye Bye
M: Bye
A: Bye Bye [waving] don't come in with me
M: I won't come in with you. I will sit right here
A: Sit on right there. Sit right still. Sit right still.
M: OK what are you going to do?
A: I go get some spiders ... ssssss
M: Are you?
A: I go get a snake
M: A snake
A: Yeah
M: How big is it?
A: It's bigger, bigger
M: It's very big is it?
A: Yeah – I go get some. You stay right there You be right there
M: I'm not moving anywhere. I'm here
A: Bye. don't come cere [come in here] in with me Don't, you can't get in with me Don't come in with me. Don't FOLLOW me
M: I won't follow you.

There is much here to show that what has been jointly constructed with adult assistance is far more complex than the child could have managed alone. This is largely due to the role played by the mother. The mother in the first instance is treating the child as if she has intentions, that what she (Amy), is saying is a serious matter, deserving of her full attention. She uses the strategy of checking – 'What have you got?', as if she is not quite sure, then affirming, 'Some spiders?' Her rising tone at the end of these questions might be a real indicator to the child of interest, I am listening, now go on to what you are going to say, an extremely important feature in effective interactive strategies on the part of the adult. Mother then asks a leading question – 'where?' which Amy can easily answer, 'in my hand' and to which mother reaffirms her understanding by repeating her response – 'in your hand'. This is followed by 'what are you going to do with them?' another leading question. Amy probably was not ready for that, and settled immediately for something that was in her mind at the time, she was going to throw them in the area beyond the door that reminded her of the petrol station. The evidence of chaining complexes (Vygotsky, 1962), with one idea leading to another, is clearly in play here, as it is again later when the ssss sound seems to make her think of snakes, a new element introduced.

Opportunities for independence in play, for being in control, for enjoying the power that such feelings of control offer, are in much evidence in all the commands to mother. 'You stay right there', something Amy herself usually experiences, is reiterated over and over again. Once again her mother constantly checks that she has understood through her own repetition, raising the tone of voice for her questions, then responding with agreement.

The instances of self-correction are interesting. Amy says 'come and geat them', which she then corrects to 'come and EAT them'; 'not cear' (come in here) which went wrong in the saying is changed to 'not go in the petrol with me'. Holdaway (1979, p.45), would suggest that Amy is at this time 'processing primitive grammatical operations, and mastering different aspects of the language'. 'Cear' sounds as if it might be short for 'come in here', but she knew there was a mismatch and repeated 'not GO in the petrol'. 'Never come ear me', at first thought might be never come near, but adults who know her believe it to be more likely that she is saying 'Never come in here'. The later example 'come and geat them', a mixture of get and eat, is self-corrected to come and eat them.

Instances of Amy's developing competence as a result of the mother's interaction are also very significant. When her mother first says, 'where is it?' (the petrol station), Amy's response is 'I don't know'. When mother says 'the petrol station's out there is it?' Amy now manages to think of a place for it – 'it's in the garden'. When her mother introduces the word 'follow', a word Amy probably does not know, Amy actually repeats a word – 'collow' at that stage in the conversation. Much later she returns to this with her 'Don't, you can't get in with me. Don't come in with me. Don't *follow* me.'

Just look at the amount of *repetition* throughout by Amy, to make her point and by mother to ascertain that they have *shared understandings*. Consider the *culturally appropriate feedback* within the shared context which both understand. Amy has reached an advanced stage in knowing how to take part in interactive turn taking, but she can only maintain this position because the topic being discussed is totally within her command. When mother first leads off elsewhere, e.g. 'where is it?' Amy has no idea about this.

There are probably two reasons why conversations like this are valuable, says Wells. Adults may recognise the active and autonomous nature of the child's construction of his or her linguistic repertoire, instead of trying to impose fully developed adult systems on the child. Secondly, the conversations are rewarding, a meeting of minds, where the child realises that communicating with adults is interesting and that it is worth continuing to take opportunities to do so.

Although there is so much confirmation of the competent child in theoretical literature, why is it so difficult to take account of it in the school setting?

> Adventurous growth, and the educated guess flourish when children risk approximations to adult language, when their [language] attempts are accepted by those who matter, and when adult responses are made initially to the meaning of what is said, rather than to inaccuracies of form or detail. Risk taking is a way of learning but children do not take risks unless they feel self-confident.
>
> (Department of Education (New Zealand), 1985b, p.13)

Of course this applies to all emerging forms of representation and not just to talk.

Developing such reciprocity as was shown between Amy and her mother in the wider base of an early years setting requires serious attention and this is to be explored in the next section of this chapter.

A shared book experience: creating a shared classroom agenda

The scene is a new entrants classroom in a New Zealand primary school some time in the early 1970s. Twenty-six five year olds cross-legged on the mat are listening to their teacher, who is seated on a low stool, his body inclined toward them and his eyes almost level with theirs as he reads with lively intonation about the adventures of Corduroy.

> Corduroy is a bear who sits on a shelf in a large department store and waits with all the other animals and dolls for someone to come along and buy him and take him home. One day a little girl stands before him with bright eyes, saying 'oh look there's the bear I have always wanted'. But her mother says ...

'What do you think her mother says?' the reader asks of the children, and there is a chorus of replies, 'lets her have it', 'says she hasn't got any money', 'says you've got a bear already'. The reader continues:

> 'Not today dear, I have spent too much money already. Besides, he doesn't look new, he has lost the button to one of his shoulder straps.' Corduroy watches sadly as they walk away – 'I didn't know I'd lost a button' he cried. 'Tonight I will go and see if I can find it'. So that night when all the shoppers had gone and the store was closed Corduroy climbs carefully down from the shelf to search for his lost button.

The reader stops at this point, looks at the children and asks 'Do you think Corduroy's button might be in our classroom?', 'Might he have lost it here?', 'It just might be.' 'Shall we have a look and see?'

On hands and knees he and the children together crawl between tables and chairs looking for Corduroy's button. 'Is it here? Don't think so ... Over here? I don't think so. Oh, perhaps he didn't lose it in here after all.' Presently the reader reseats himself on his low chair, holds the book so the children can see and begins to read again – 'Suddenly, quite by accident'... and by the time the first page is finished all the children are again sitting with rapt attention in front of him.

As he continues – 'someone else was awake in the store that night', he withholds the picture so as not to give away clues, then asks – 'Who do you think might have been in the store' and the children answer spontaneously – 'robbers, a policeman, skooby doo, superman'. The reader replies, 'perhaps, might be, could be, you never know'. The session continues in this manner for a further 15 to 20 minutes until the story is all shared. Later, and over the ensuing weeks, much writing, drawing, play and language experience evolve. Parents ask questions about the bear story as they leave or pick up their children. One parent makes green corduroy overalls for her child's bear and brings it in for the class to see.

The teacher sharing this story is Don Holdaway, lecturer in teacher education and author (Holdaway, 1979). The children listening are in the very early stages of their schooling, and are enjoying their very first experiences of shared school situations. The setting is an inner city Auckland school, with its mixture of Polynesian, indigenous Maori and Pakeha children.

The most remarkable feature of this story session is that it illustrates many opportunities for making meaning by the children, while allowing flexibility in their response. Each child can use their own idea to shape their own meaning. As in the earliest interactions children can talk about what they know but the story provides a *shared structure* to which all can relate. There is, in Holdaway's own terminology, the experience of ego-sharing and not ego-uppance, and *real involvement* and exploration on the part of the children. There is practice in the skill of *prediction*, who might be awake in the store, and where might the lost button be? Children can see that there may be not one correct answer but there could in fact be many possibilities. They are offered the opportunity to become actively engaged in the story during the telling, and they are enjoying the experience together with others. The sensitivity to young children's understanding and levels of development dictate the pace of the session without the need to intervene with negative calls for attention or to gain control. Holdaway has chosen a subject, teddy bears, which he knows is of universal appeal to young children. One consequence is that the children themselves can be equally as powerful as their teacher in having a voice in the story. They are able to offer *culturally appropriate responses*. The teacher uses all the skills at his disposal, involving energy, facial and bodily expression, close eye contact and an interesting and interested presence. He capitalises on the 'teachable moment' (Honig, 1990) drawing out memorable language to describe, for instance, how sad, mournful, unhappy Corduroy feels. Administrative practicalities such as the time of the day have been well planned, and provision has been made for plenty of space to move and comfortable places to sit.

Holdaway believed in the creation of positive situations where learning might be successful and joyful. The example shown here suggests that he enjoyed stories and the company of children alike, and that he was in fact very experienced and skilled in his interaction with both. He described his work as 'a career of child-watching and child-admiration', wherein he was all the while determined to apply genuine developmental principles to classroom challenges. He favoured respect and honesty where children were concerned, knew how to see through the eyes of a young child, and liked to adopt a teaching style which promoted shared interaction and participation within a community of learners, a community where everyone might explore their ideas together, without being slaves to pressures from outside the classroom.

Holdaway is certainly treating the children as though they have intentions and is giving them some control in the story telling. There is engagement and two-way communication, together with the creation of an agenda for exploring background knowledge and a classroom context which helps the children to express themselves. It seems there is evidence of joy and personal security in the situation for these children. There is much which might form a sound basis for later shared learning.

Watching this story session was a turning point in my teaching career. It taught me to study more carefully and reflect more critically on the way I viewed children. My interactions with them changed as a consequence. For the interaction taking place before me bore no resemblance to former ideas I had held, of children sitting still and passive as they listened to a story, of being allowed to ask their questions, or worse still, answer mine, only when it was finished. Instead of demanding relevance which suited the adult ear, Holdaway was being accepting of all answers. He was also confident enough to allow, in fact even encourage, children to move around the room in the midst of the telling. The ensuing enjoyment which such practice brought out suggested to me that enjoying stories in this way could be generalised to attitudes to all interaction in the classroom.

For Holdaway's concern was 'to support' a tradition of sanity and deep concern for the children who need not fail (Holdaway, 1979, pp.11 and 12). His beliefs mesh well with what was considered in the previous section on early interactions:

> We want children to be able to make effective use of their faculties. Mothers make use of the close proximity they enjoy with their infants by talking to them as if they understood, and in a fundamental sense they do in fact understand. Parents reward children with adult attention, approval and affection, the most powerful reinforcers for learning.
>
> (Holdaway, 1979, p.21)

However, in reality in school classrooms we constantly 'intervene in corrective ways, thus tending to inhibit the development of those vital feedback systems which sustain healthy functioning' (p.14). How often do we allow children to share what they have noticed and how often do we put down their idea with too quick a denial. The following shows just such an example. Children in a nursery class are standing together around a table. The adult is making jelly, all are helping to stir and she asks – 'Where shall we put this jelly for it to set?', 'In the cooker', was one child's instant response, 'No, no no, where will I put it?', 'In the frig' says a second child, 'Yes that's right', is the adult's answer.

Would the jelly have set in the cooker? Very probably if it was not turned on. Did that family perhaps keep jelly in the cooker through lack of space anyway? What could have been explored about that answer. Yet the feeling of being cut off – the urge to please – the knowledge that your ideas are not good ones is not conducive to further risk taking unless you have a very strong self-image.

Possibly even worse for processes of development, might be the child who is complacent, who feels as a result of her experience that learning is a matter of 'covering' rather than 'uncovering' the knowledge one seeks (Duckworth, 1987, p.7). A recent example seen in the Science Museum involved a young girl who is brought by her parents to the museum every Sunday. She moves around the launch pad exhibits, rather in a manner of 'ticking off' each as it has been attended to. One wonders whether there is enough curiosity, or wonder in the interaction, and what learning is in fact taking place. Is this an unquestioning stance? Will it result in an ability to transfer what she has learned to new situations? Without curiosity, one must wonder.

Interaction: the teacher

> the teachers in this project were aware of and endorsed constructivist views of learning and the teaching approaches generally associated with them. They were industrious and child oriented in the sense that they recognised and valued children's

> perspectives on problems. Despite their constructivist attitudes however the teachers were dominant in classroom interactions and their ideal teaching practices were rarely enacted.
>
> (Desforges, 1989, p.164)

Teachers have been described as facilitators, chairpersons, enablers and people who can give evidence, guidance and encouragement (Wells, 1986). What we, as teacher trainers, try to inculcate in students is the ability to adopt a teaching style which encourages the children to take a proactive part in their learning, for at the heart of such practices, classroom interaction gives to children more autonomy for choosing issues, exploring problems and questions and offers responsibility for sharing and thinking on ideas (Desforges, 1989, p.158). Yet, on the evidence of research carried out (outlined in Desforges and Cockburn, 1987), Desforges suggests, there is a tension here for the teacher between the needs of a group and those of the particular child. He suggests three possible reasons for this conflict. The first is the possibility that teachers believe children to be easily confused or distracted in the getting of a proper grasp of a concept, that they are 'intellectually vulnerable'. The second is that the teacher perhaps believes that there is a 'correct' version of the particular concept that the child should be able to go to immediately (the antithesis of what they *say* they believe). The third is that they are driven by 'minute by minute dynamics of their interactions with children' and become anxious when the children seem confused or unhappy.

Despite a rationale which demands that the teacher be responsive to the needs of the children by providing what might be termed 'active learning' on the part of those children, most research shows that teachers lead and direct discussions, doing most of the talking, initiating and sustaining while terminating most of the activities, and demonstrating the procedures to be used on task (Desforges, 1989, p.158). Although teachers showed considerable powers of 'perception, interpretation and management', they experienced a persistent demand for decisions which they found to be exhausting (p.161). Added to this it was obvious that teachers were always aware of risk to children's confidence and therefore avoided the exploration of children's errors. The needs of the group, issues of pace and attention, were seemingly always in conflict with the needs of the individual child who needed more discussion. Teachers lacked overall time to consider their responses to children, they believed they lacked proper resources, and they felt anxious about longer or more individual interactions which might threaten classroom order.

Desforges states, if there is to be change it is obvious that rhetoric and exhortation based on developmental psychology will not suffice. Instead the teachers' thinking will have to be based on their perceptions of their working conditions and the ways they might make adaptations to these changes (p.159).

Robinson writes that we cannot force anyone to learn or even to interact but it is possible for a teacher to promote a classroom situation that promotes learning. As did Holdaway, she would suggest what she calls 'humanising' interaction, that is to give caring, sharing and supporting, pride of place in the classroom and to allow each member of the community to have their voice (Robinson, 1994, p.123).

She further states that teachers who are experimenting with more open-ended dialogical practices are themselves already responding to an openness to change in their children and the children in their turn respond to the teacher's openness.

She makes two important points, insights which are well supported in other literature. The first is, 'the problem of focusing on the intellect ... is that the brain lives in the body and can't function without the body's co-operation' (p.62). The second is, 'the important thing that children need to be able to see is that learning has to do with life' (p.75). Both these points are well taken care of in the earliest interactions set out already in this chapter, that which children enjoy in the home setting and the first classroom experiences in the Holdaway mode. Yet difficulties arise once the demand is made for what is seen as more important or more formal learning, as if that is somehow acquired in a different way. In Holdaway's words, is it the sanctity of conventional schooling or the matter of academic analysis which causes the anxiety to creep into the early years classroom. Why does the professional no longer see the child as a knowledgeable person, feel obliged to set the entire agenda, and feel concerned if children, sometimes aged only four, are not conforming to the patterns of school? I am much heartened by the words of Lord Judd speaking in 1993 about what he termed educational recovery. 'Schools', he said, 'should play a leading role in building a community, a sense of belonging, and social cohesion.' I was also pleased to hear a recent voice from the parliamentary quarter saying 'what we want is more idiosyncratic behaviour and not less, if we are to tap the creative energy of our young people'.

No one could exemplify these points better than the work of Sylvia Ashton Warner (or Mrs Henderson as she was known in school), who taught in various outback Maori schools in New Zealand from the mid 1940s to the 1970s, and who produced much writing concerning her work. The community surrounding a typical school would comprise a Maori pa, a church, a store and a hotel. Ashton Warner was a flamboyant, yet tortured personality, prone to enormous creativity yet unable to sustain real consistency in her life (Hood, 1988). However, her effect on the children she taught was unforgettable.

In her biography of Ashton Warner, Hood says, 'In many ways her [Ashton Warner's] approach to teaching was consistent with the times.' The difference was that while other teachers were committed to education, Sylvia was committed to creativity. Her emotional survival depended on it. So while most teachers felt that keeping the lid on their pupils' more explosive emotions was essential to effective teaching, Sylvia was determined to rip the lid right off: 'I see the mind of a five-year-old as a volcano with two vents; destructiveness and creativeness. And I see that to the extent that we widen the creative channel, we atrophy the destructive one' (p.134).

A well-known feature of her work was her 'key vocabulary', the 'organic' words which she encouraged her pupils to collect.

> Back to these first words, To these first books. They must be made out of the stuff of the child *inself*. I reach into the mind of the child and bring out a handful of the stuff I find here, and use it as our first working material. Whether it is good or bad stuff, violent or acid stuff, coloured or dun. To effect an unbroken beginning. And in this

> dynamic material within the familiarity and security of it, the Maori finds that words have intense meaning to him.

Her pupils learned to read from their personal key vocabularies. Nearly every day from their experiences at home or at school Sylvia helped each child select a new key word. She wrote the word with heavy crayon on a stout piece of cardboard and gave it to the child. The words became as precious to the children as the imagery they represented. Children who had laboured for months over 'See Spot Run' in the new Janet and John readers took one look at 'corpse', 'beer' or 'hiding' and suddenly they could read. Sylvia said, 'Pleasant words won't do. Respectable words won't do. They must be words organically tied up, organically born from the dynamic life itself. They must be words that are already part of the child's being' (p.136). If on looking them over for the day, a word could not be remembered it was discarded, thrown in the bin. The stories from which the key words were born were told in colourful Maori-English. Sylvia recorded them faithfully on to big sheets of paper and pinned them around the walls:

> 'I caught Uncle Monty pissing behind the tree. He got wild when I laughed at him.'
>
> 'My Dad gave my Mum a black eye.'

Hood writes that this wasn't exactly what the Education Department had in mind when it advocated the use of children's experiences, but it was successful, and the excitement and sense of relief created by the use of children's own language brought unprecedented enthusiasm from the children for their learning in this classroom.

Intellectual and affective engagement, two-way communication, sharing background knowledge and a classroom context which helped children to express themselves are all in evidence here. There is a chance that the brain might have the body's cooperation in these classroom situations because of the interactions which are allowed, and there are certainly links with life outside school. A simple matter to incorporate these features into learning for our classrooms? I like to believe it is possible but of course it is not simple.

For the way that interactive discourse develops in a classroom is a complex business, connected with classroom management. The way teachers were brought up to believe things should be, influences the way they think their teaching role should take shape and values and beliefs are crucial to the development of a classroom community. Most teachers can equate with Robinson when she notes 'the ingrained need for silence' which is as she describes, so hard to uproot. Before it *can* be uprooted it first needs to be noticed. We can empathise with the situation of a student teacher who in the space of 20 minutes, shushed her children into silence 23 times, yet there were no disruptions which took place. 'I didn't hear myself do it', she said. Controlling is in the vocabulary of most teachers, some need it there, others want to be rid of it (Robinson, 1994, p.128).

A recent article by Solity (1995) suggests that while professionals call for more child development in teacher education they ignore the fact that most of the psychology to which teachers are usually introduced focuses on children and their development. He outlines alternative psychological theories which might help teachers to become learners themselves, their family background and its impact on their classroom behaviour. He suggests early years teachers should address the nature of their own needs, and reasons that, being more sensitive to their own social and emotional development, they will better be able to foster children's emotional and social needs through constructive 'straight' interactions.

Inherent in Solity's ideas is the notion that psychologists who, in the past, have only been involved with children experiencing problems, might instead be asked to help teachers evaluate their overall interactional style with children or each other with a view to establishing more constructive relationships. In this way teachers might become more aware of their own behaviour.

'The developmental models emerging from the Piagetian child-centred perspective rarely acknowledged the learning process as an interactive one', asserts Solity (1995, p.10). He suggests that although Piagetian theory, in terms of seeing children as individuals enjoying their own unique development has seen much acceptance in the professional early years field, Vygotsky's views, emphasising how children are taught and the ways in which cultural experiences influence learning, are 'more challenging and less comforting for teachers' (p.8).

Interaction: the classroom

The complexity of providing real involvement in school settings for children of differing cultural experience and competences is seriously important and a challenging matter at any time. Barth, a Swedish citizen living in France, explored issues of interaction that she saw in her children's school experience. She began by referring to Piaget's premise, that it is not the subject matter children do not understand, but the lessons they are given, when she asked 'why is it so difficult to teach for understanding?' She describes her emotional concern for the large number of children she believed were not learning very well when her own three Swedish children joined the traditional French schooling system. Children who appeared to be poor learners, she states, 'did not seem to be able to use what they had learned. They were said not to understand or not to have sufficient capacities of abstraction. This situation made them develop poor attitudes and learning dispositions and affected their self image in a negative way.' She realised that this was not only a French problem and that many international studies have documented such concerns (Barth, 1995, p.76).

A summary of the fundamental concerns Barth held about the ways children and adults worked in these classrooms are features which have already emerged throughout this chapter:

- a lack of engagement, both intellectual and affective, on the part of the children;
- classroom interaction which seemed to offer only one way communication, with hardly any common activities, or reflection between teacher/children or children themselves;
- no real agenda for exploring shared background knowledge;

- nothing in the classroom context which helped the children to express themselves.

Considerable success for effective work with children can be gained when real attention is given to children's genuine concerns. For instance, early childhood practitioners have become aware of initiatives in the Emilia Romagna region of Italy, where 'the cornerstone of [the region's] experience, based on practice, theory, and research is the image of children as rich, strong, and powerful. Educators, politicians, and parents in this region uphold the children's need and right to communicate and interact with others, as emerging at birth and an essential element for survival and identification with the species' (Edwards *et al.*, 1995, p.103). Evidence gathered from the 29 schools of this region shows that prolonged and sustained periods of interaction between adults and children, based around children's interests, results in mature and well-developed cognitive, emotional and social growth, and shows the development in children of extraordinary representational skill. Extensive and wide-ranging documentary evidence is offered to parents, who in their turn observe and better develop their knowledge and understanding of what their children are doing. The ensuing interaction between home and school is significantly positive in terms of confidence, optimism and shared responsibility for the development of, as the people of the region see it, their citizens of tomorrow.

Other institutions held in world-wide regard for an emphasis on child involvement and social interaction are Danish nurseries, where practitioners are said to 'pay little heed to formal instruction, competition and achievement, and instead emphasise self-expressive games, the role of the imagination, creative activities, and the attainment of social maturity through group activities' (Vedel-Peterson, 1992).

Our own rich nursery traditions also offer evidence of most effective interactional experiences. Isaac's four year olds in the Malting House school are clearly supported and encouraged to develop their own thinking and problem-solving powers (Isaacs, 1930), while McMillan's attention to social life and healthy development affected not only the children and their families who attended her East London school, but many others throughout this century (1930). There is much valuable evidence available, in, for instance, such projects as Tizard and Hughes (1984), which concerns four-year-old girls, and their interaction at home and at school. This study is especially enlightening for the picture it portrays of children's strong propensity to enquire into and question the elements of their surroundings. Children, they say, are concerned with their social world, with people and their motivations and activities. This, of course, is a guiding principle in the Italian and Danish perspective. Tizard and Hughes comment that, 'the puzzling mind of the four year old has no outlet in a setting where the child's basic role is to answer and not to ask questions'. Other very significant contributions, well used by practitioners in this country come from the research of Heath (1983), Athey (1990) and Wells (1986).

What of the substance of the interaction in an early years setting? Can it be about anything at all? These questions hold major significance if interactive experience is to build upon shared background knowledge or offer the opportunity for children to feel able to express themselves? The people of Emilia Romagna, for instance, do not hold hierarchical theories about what is and what is not an admissible topic for school learning. In fact they are critical of what they see as western practices where teachers purport to be child centred and willing to start with the interest of the child, but where such favourites as barbie dolls and turtles are banned because they are considered to be unsuitable topics for school activity.

Katz offers a further point in her discussion of the notion that individuals cannot just relate to each other, but they have to relate to each other about something. She cites Bruner's suggestions that the content of teacher–child dialogue as exposed by his research in 1980 showed interactions to be predominantly concerned with managerial issues, and dominated by a concern on the part of the teacher for the child's performance, with comments such as, 'well done', 'very good', 'you got that right'. She suggests practitioners should instead be concerned with discussion of the task or the idea itself, especially if they are to shed the mother or surrogate parent image. They must know how to value development and learning, and that is what the interactions should be about (Katz in Edwards *et al.*, 1995). Duckworth (1987), Astington (1994), Swann and White (1994), and Paley (1981, 1990) have offered much that is also valuable to this debate.

For we will interact with children in ways which reflect our beliefs about people and the kind of person we hope a young child should become. Tobin *et al.* (1989), in their survey into the ways in which practitioners worked with young children across three cultures, showed that when workers and administrators from the three separate countries were asked to make comments on the challenging behaviour of one particular child, these comments varied considerably. While some believed the child's behaviour should be ignored, others thought him to be spoiled and in need of punishment. Some considered him to be bored, some believed he had emotional problems, yet others thought it quite natural for boys to behave as he did. It is consistent that the ways in which these professionals would think about and interact with this child would depend on the ways they perceived his behaviour.

For those who are prepared to reflect deeply on this matter, there would be rewards in reading the work of Paley, well renowned for her observational and interpretative studies of young children and their thinking, and whose work is referred to elsewhere in this book. This master teacher talks of her experience with a student researcher, who joins her in her classroom, and observes her interaction with the children. He showed her that, where she perceived a particular child, Charles, to be a troublemaker and leader of aggressive play, when systematically observed and evaluated, this proved not to be the case. However, it *was* the case that 75 per cent of her own interactions with Charles were negative. She began to listen properly to Charles and as a result realised that he actually provided his classmates with 'an unending supply of characters and plots'.

'Hey, Tom, y'wanna play castle? This is a drawbridge.'
'I got the key for it.'
'You can't. There wasn't keys invented yet. This is the only place keys can go. Okay, put it there. It's a fighting spaceship. It can kill someone by it's power. Hurry up, pull up the drawbridge. The invisible bees is here. Quick, get your magic key. Pretend this is magic. Touch it and we turn into dragons!'

(Paley, 1990, p.16)

Paley, by means of her sensitive and perceptive professional approach, came to better understand what the children in her classes were thinking and feeling. By means of long hours spent translating tapes of children interacting with each other and with herself she learned how to follow their ideas and so help their development toward more mature and logical understandings. It is through the provision of such a shared community as exemplified by Holdaway, Ashton Warner, Robinson, Paley, Athey and the people of Emilia Romagna, that I would see ways forward.

Conclusions

If teachers can take a lead from the studies of parent–child interaction in the home setting, the wealth of shared meaning and shared attention, and replicate this in some way into their work in early years settings, this would provide a much stronger stage upon which to build meaningful and interactive dialogue in school. If children's ideas are to be extended it is essential that adults take more responsibility for developing the sharing process, by listening more sensitively, in the first instance to the children and in the second to their own response.

Practitioners who develop a deeper understanding of their own attitudes and beliefs, as suggested in this chapter, will be better fitted towards promoting true engagement with children through real two-way interaction in the classroom. This will, in turn, help to promote a real agenda for the exploration of shared background knowledge, thus providing a context where children feel able to express themselves.

Paley (1986b) writes that if a teacher is well read in theories of development and instruction and well supplied with human empathy, the result can be a rare blend of science and humanism. However, he or she must start with the child's thinking rather than the teacher's rule.

Figure 7.1: Further reflection – some ways to think about interaction

When we are thinking about working with children it may be helpful to have some very specific strategies which help the kind of interaction we wish to develop:

- Are we attending to what the children are in fact noticing?
- Do we take account of children's joy when they recognise something familiar to them?
- Are we introducing enough that is new?
- How do we react when children talk to us and what does our body language suggest?
- Are we willing to accept the non-standard answer and follow along with a child's thinking?
- What are we prepared to accept as useful information to share in the classroom?

Chapter 8

Working for equality and equity

Sue Smedley

Introduction

Early years teachers have a privileged and responsible position. Theirs is an important moral and intellectual task; and it is one which draws heavily on teachers' personal values and experiences, particularly in working for equality and equity with young children. But it is also a wider issue, as every classroom is part of broader social and cultural contexts, which include inequality, discrimination and prejudice at structural and institutional levels. To counter inequality involves several different, but related strands: it involves critical reflection on personal values and experiences in relation to race, gender, disability[1] and class; it involves working with children, parents and other professionals to create an ethos of equality in the classroom; and it involves understanding and sometimes challenging and working to change the wider context within which we live and work.

The terms we choose to use in educational discourse are significant, and not static. The terms equality and equity define the area of study in question here, in order to emphasise justice and fairness, rather than sameness. 'Equality of opportunity' might be a more familiar term, but sometimes this familiarity can be a disadvantage; the term can tend to trip off the tongue all too easily. Equality of opportunity may also seem like rather a tired term – and familiarity can breed contempt, at best indifference, or feed into a backlash that claims that equality of opportunity is no longer an issue. Responses could be too personal and not recognise the structural inequalities that are also part of the picture. Equality issues may be treated superficially as a request for everyone to 'be nice' to each other. Tight budgets of schools and local education authorities might mean that equal opportunities initiatives are squeezed out, especially with the current, dominant emphasis on the subject content of the curriculum.

Equality of opportunity can seem to imply a passive stance, if it is taken to relate only to access. The implication is that if individuals don't take up the opportunities, it is their own fault. But it is counter-productive to blame the individual and not recognise that the individual is entangled in complex social and cultural contexts. Equality and inequality are issues that need to be considered at personal and institutional levels. Equality needs a 'social justice' perspective and to address outcomes, the realisation of potential – hence the terms equality *and* equity.

Words are shaped by and shape our thinking. As Roaf and Bines (1994) argue in relation to special educational need, there are problems and debates relating to current concepts; to talk only of needs, or rights or opportunities, for example, may not provide a sufficient way forward, 'where the desire to meet needs has developed into debates about opportunity, it has tended to be weak unless buttressed by the language of rights and social justice' (1994, p.61). To focus attention on access and opportunity could simply result in the provision of better access to an unjust system. Therefore we need to look more widely and think about equality, justice and tolerance and think about these as the basis for community; a sense of community where rights and responsibilities are recognised and where differences and similarities are actively recognised and accommodated.

In recollections of schooling, everyone can remember good experiences and bad, and, quite probably, the bad ones relate to experiences of not being fairly treated or of being misunderstood, bullied, disregarded, excluded. They may be experiences that pivoted on the way individuals were defined in terms of race, gender and class. Such experiences can be intensely felt by children, may be continuous and may have long-lasting impact. Paley (1992) writes of the way children build, 'domains of exclusivity in classrooms and playgrounds' (p.22) and describes her practical response to this '*habit* of exclusion' (p.117) by establishing a rule: 'You Can't Say You Can't Play'. Paley also makes a telling point when she observes that teachers may work for equal participation in the classroom, but not in the world of children's free play. But this should be fundamental, 'free acceptance in play, partnerships, and teams is what matters most to any child' (p. 21). This must not be underestimated by adults working with young children.

Equality and equity is not just about the discriminatory practices of individuals one to another, important though that is, but is an integral part of a wider social picture of inequality. There are very specifically personal, and broader political angles to considerations of equality and equity, which mean teachers must act both on an individual basis, and on a more collective basis, which acknowledges and addresses the wider hegemonic structures of inequality; it would be naive and a failing to children, to work only on an inward-looking basis that did not recognise these wider contexts of inequality.

The nursery or classroom, as a community, is a microcosm of the wider society. With the children and parents, the early years teacher has a responsibility and to some extent still, the freedom, to create and shape that community. Although it is not an isolated community, an 'ivory tower', neither is it one which is passively moulded by outside influences. Within, and sometimes even in spite of, more formal legal frameworks, early years units and schools, and individual teachers must decide and determine the nature of the community of their classrooms.

It is from this starting point of the nursery or classroom as a community that I want to consider issues of equality, justice and tolerance. There is much emphasis in the history of early years education in this country on the needs and importance of the individual, and in many ways, rightly so, but that is not the whole story. Child-centredness can ironically undermine the very equality it seeks to promote and may need to be redescribed and redefined (see Pound, 1988). It is, however, perhaps important to put alongside this individualism, and to re-emphasise, the strength of a sense of community and responsibility to others. There is a real need (not just a sentimental one) to feel a sense of belonging and confidence in that community, that is necessary for learning. The culture of the classroom must be relevant and understood by all who create it. Paley (1995) describes exactly this when she writes of a 'community-in-the-making' (pp.113–14).

Commonsense arguments?

Promoting equality, justice and tolerance is not straightforward and uncontested. Indeed it is a complex and debated area, which elicits strong feelings, although it can be treated simplistically and superficially. There are, for example, commonsense arguments which make a case for less rather than more attention and energy to be put into these fundamental issues. Take these imaginary, but representative, comments about equality issues, for example:

'Young children are not aware of differences of race, class and gender'
Young children are learning all the time; they learn from their experiences and from the attitudes expressed by others. This includes learning about race, class and gender. It would be naive to assume children are not learning about such things, and indeed it would contradict what we know about children's learning generally, that children are active meaning-makers (Wells, 1986). More specifically, much has been researched and written indicating that children are aware of differences of race, gender and class, for example, Siraj-Blatchford (1994b), Browne and Ross (1991), Milner (1983), Walkerdine (1989), Weis and Worobey (1991), and Wright (1992). The Children Act (1989) states, 'Children from a very young age learn about different races and cultures including religion and languages and will be capable of assigning different values to them. The same applies to gender and making distinctions between male and females roles' (6.10).

'We should just treat all children the same'
There is a problem with 'sameness': it presupposes that sameness is desirable and implies one cultural norm should be established. This would mean one set of beliefs and attitudes be imposed on everyone; in practice, that single, dominant, cultural norm tends to be that of white, middle-class men.

Sameness has also been considered by Browne and France:

> it seems that the philosophy of treating children all the same, no matter how well intentioned, serves to blur several issues:
> [for example]
>
> - differences do exist between children in the nursery
> - how can equal treatment help children to cope in an unequal society?
> - is equal treatment a cover-up or reluctance to be anti-sexist, as it is too political?
>
> (Browne and France, 1986, pp.123–4)

'We want our children to add, subtract and not to learn anti-racist maths – whatever that may be.' (Margaret Thatcher, quoted in Davies *et al.* (1990, p.3)) This is just one example of the lack of understanding and the ridiculing of aspects of classroom practice relating to equality of opportunity. Similarly, Lawlor (1990) writing of BEd courses commented that, 'Questionable emphasis is given to "special needs", "multicultural education", "gender" and so on' (p.29). Issues become belittled and undermined, especially as the implication is that they are the focus of teaching to the detriment of children learning more basic and important skills. Issues of equality are not seen as an important part of the curriculum.

The seriousness of striving for equality of opportunity in general has been further undermined by the movement for Political Correctness, which has prioritised an apparently pedantic care over the use of words and phrases, without recourse to the serious debates which originally questioned language and its usage, e.g. the use of the generic 'he' or 'man'.[2] Being politically correct or 'PC', means being 'culturally sensitive' (Beard and Cerf, 1992, p.87), although as they point out, it is in itself a term which has been 'co-opted by the white elite as a tool for attacking multiculturalism' (p.87). It has become a means to scorn debates about the excluding aspects of language and the social and cultural structures and inequalities they reflect and reinforce. And it is done humorously; this can make those who argue about the serious nature of the use of language and the offence caused, seem over-zealous, extreme or cranky.

As with all aspects of teaching, teachers' values are centrally important to the reality of what happens in the classroom. Early years teachers' values, experiences, feelings and priorities will influence the way they interpret equality issues in practice. No one is exempt from this influence, though that does not mean teachers are passively subject to influences. As Anning (1991) comments, most teachers' family backgrounds are middle class or skilled working class, and 'there is evidence that teachers present a set of values and aspirations to pupils which reflect white, British, middle-class assumptions' (p.63). The consequence of this can be the subtle, if not overt excluding of children from the community and the discourse of the classroom – it would be like not being part of an 'in-joke', except that it has much more serious consequences and is also part of a wider picture of discrimination and disadvantage, which results in children and adults being unable to take up opportunities that exist or realise their potential.[3] Not only might children not learn effectively, but they may also be learning that inequality must be the way of things. Early years teachers' ideals should relate to the sort of society they aspire to, not lapse into a defeatist acceptance of the way things are – taking a stand in this way is something those involved in early years education and care have always done. In her chapter, 'An entitlement curriculum for early childhood', Gura writes of those 'who have taken on the established order of the day, defying received wisdom', people who have challenged others, questioned long-accepted ideas (or argued to retain them) and worked to provide the best experiences for every young child with whom they worked.

There are different kinds of reasons for working for equality and equity, some personally and professionally based, or moral and humane in nature, and some grounded in legal requirements, 'The concept of equality of opportunity was first given official recognition in the 1944 Education Act though since then our interpretation of its meaning has undergone substantial alteration' (Weiner, 1985, p.6), for example in relation to the recognition of wider issues of power and subjugation of certain groups or debates about positive discrimination. The Education Reform Act, 1988 requires a 'broad and balanced curriculum' be provided for children between the ages five and sixteen years, one which 'promotes the spiritual, moral, cultural, mental and physical development of pupils at the school and of society'. The Children Act (1989) states that, 'Children have a right to an environment which facilitates their development' (6.28) and goes on to consider rights in terms of children's sense of identity, including the right to individuality, respect, dignity and freedom from discrimination such as racism and sexism. Siraj-Blatchford (1992, p.110) describes the Act as 'an exciting move towards equality' and the 'first piece of legislation on the care of children which refers specifically to catering for children's racial, religious, cultural and linguistic backgrounds' (p.110).[4] Legislation, however, crucial as it is, needs to be brought to life by people.[5]

Social class, gender and race can all provide the basis for discrimination and inequality. Each will now be considered as a separate focus, but it is clear that there are themes which are common between them, and that class, gender and race intersect with each other and overlap, in the way they are experienced by children and responded to by adults.

Social class

One of the ways children can be discriminated against and prevented from realising their potential in school, is through the assumptions that are made about them in relation to their social class. Membership of a social class is usually defined for research purposes by the occupation of the parent(s). In the classroom teachers may be defining children's social class through observations of appearance or speech, and perhaps going on to make assumptions about academic ability. The importance of knowing children well is generally accepted, but it is interesting to stop and think sometimes where that knowledge has come from and to what extent it is based on relevant evidence – is it just assumptions and crude categorising?

Anning (1991) provides an overview of some of the research carried out in the 1970s and 1980s into teachers' attitudes towards class and the ways it affects teachers' behaviour towards children. Anning refers to the 'myths about "working-class" homes being without books, culture or indeed "language"' (p.65). To say 'working-class' homes are without 'culture' invariably implies a narrow definition of culture as white and middle class. This establishes a covert norm against which other cultures are to be measured and found lacking. Such myths and assumptions are curiously persistent and are based on a lack of understanding and reflection; they rest on an uncritical acceptance of discredited views of verbal deprivation. Wells' research on language development, for example, led him to conclude, 'all the dimensions of social difference that we investigated led to the same conclusion: stereotypes are not appropriate' (Wells, 1986, p.134).[6]

Inequality and discrimination can arise from one dominant and defining group treating another as second class, ridiculing or ignoring the choices and preferences of others and, in fact, their lives. And importantly this operates on a wider, institutional basis as well. The cultural norm, specifically defined, becomes institutionally established as a dominant ideology. To change this situation requires not just a change of outlook, or pleasantness and good intentions (valued as those should be, as long as they are not patronising), but a more fundamental change to existing structural inequalities.

Children's social class, as perceived by teachers, may have significance in terms of educational achievement and therefore equality and equity. Wright (1992) refers to the 'classic study' carried out by Rosenthal and Jacobson in 1968 (p.12). Wright outlines the findings and outcomes of this study and explains that, 'a "self-fulfilling prophecy" was at work in many classrooms and ... the under-achievement of working-class children could be accounted for partly by low teacher expectations' (p.12). The key issue, as Tizard *et al.* explain, is whether 'teachers judge children's academic potential accurately, or whether in some cases they *cause* under or over achievement, by basing their expectations on considerations other than children's academic potential. In this way, the expectations become a self-fulfilling prophecy' (Tizard *et al.*, 1988, p.15). And in this way children can experience inequality and injustice.

MacGilchrist provides a comprehensive summary of aspects of access and entitlement and emphasises the link between disadvantage and achievement, 'socio-economic inequality is a powerful determinant of differences in cognitive and educational attainment in children' (MacGilchrist, 1992, p.13).[7] But the research of Athey (1990) shows that teachers can improve the educational achievement of disadvantaged groups, through informed provision of curriculum experiences for children and through involving parents.

The deficit view of the working class applies also to parents, as they may be assumed to be 'less effective in the preparation of children for academic success' (Edwards and Knight, 1994, p.112). The implications of this deficit view for working-class parents and carers is also a serious consideration for the children and for the parents and carers themselves.[8] Whalley (1994) describes the ways staff and parents have worked together successfully at Pen Green, a neighbourhood service for under-fives and their families. The philosophy underpinning this community service is one which genuinely values the contributions and needs of all parents, and shares decision-making. In this way the power base is also shared.

Walkerdine and the Girls and Mathematics Unit (1989) have investigated girls' and women's attainment in maths from preschool through to secondary school. In so doing they provide a complex and wide-ranging debate about gender, which also has much to say about social class. Walkerdine looks at the subtly embedded expectations teachers may have of children. Teachers 'tend to expect intellectuality from middle-class girls and teacherly helpfulness from working-class girls' (p.52).

Walkerdine *et al.* (1989) take the argument further and show how the working-class mother is assumed to be inadequate and 'lacking' (p.54). She does not know the ways of school and according to Walkerdine is already defined as 'wrong and reactionary' (p.54). This can lead to difficulties of transition from home to nursery, for working-class girls; middle-class girls also have difficulties. (Boys are not the focus of the study.) Walkerdine sees the working-class girls of her study as *failing*, compared to middle-class girls, although they are, in fact, not doing badly at six (p.91). 'But they are not deprived, their mothers are not inadequate, pathological' (Walkerdine, 1989, p.58). The defining norm is middle class; by seeing working-class girls and their mothers as pathological (i.e. a deviation from the normal) the status quo is maintained, the problem becomes focused on the working classes, the response being, for example, compensatory programmes of the 1960s.[9]

In their research Walkerdine *et al.* (1989) studied children at four and then at ten years of age. Two children in particular are described and discussed in detail. Walkerdine *et al.* present a complex and detailed analysis of the two girls, Julie (middle class) and Patsy (working class). The point most pertinent to the concerns here is the classteacher's way of talking about the two ten year olds. Julie has a block in maths but is basically bright, while Patsy is described as not bright and also babyish (p.110). Julie *could* achieve with help; Patsy could not. The children had achieved equal scores in a standardised maths test. 'So here were two girls, with similar attainment, judged by the teacher in class-specific ways.' Walkerdine is not arguing that Julie has no problems, indeed the thrust of her argument is about the anxiety experienced by both children as girls. However, in terms of thinking about social class and the impact of class differences, here is a specific example that shows that teachers' interpretations seem to hinge on social class. Similar ways of describing achievements or otherwise hinge on gender and race and intersect with them.

Evidence collected from teachers at a South East London Infants School by Lee reveals 'the "classless" view of society' which she sees as working against recognition of any wider social conflict (Lee, 1987). The teachers denied the existence of notions of social class and rigidly defined class analysis. However, Lee found their comments still revealed assumptions about social class differences, which they felt some particular individuals were able to transcend. Hence, the interpretation was based on an individualistic concept, which according to Lee can only result in people having to adjust to the systems, rather than achieving any adjustment to the systems themselves. Lee is very critical of any thinking or practice which does not recognise the structural dimensions of inequality and argues for the need for a wider more political view that recognises the role that power plays in discriminatory practices and inequality.

Gender

The sex of a person can work as a defining feature, influencing expectations and responses. Young children are aware of this; young children learn through active meaning making, through making sense of their social and cultural environment. This process of learning about gender begins early, 'Before they are three, children begin to develop scripts for their gender' (Weis and Worobey, 1991, p.114).

Delamont provides a review of the research in the 1970s and 1980s into gender differences in the early years (1994), giving numerous examples of the ways boys and girls are responded to, specific to their sex. She considers aspects of classroom management, making reference to King's research (1978), which gives examples of sex and gender being used as a management strategy – instructions are given to boys or girls, or a boy is asked to complete a particular task. These examples may now appear dated, as such overtly sexist strategies, but are still important in drawing our attention to the potential genderedness of teachers' responses to children. Hartley's more recent observations of teachers' comments to children suggest that such differentiated responses do still occur. Considering the ways boys and girls were perceived in the nurseries studied, Hartley presents the following examples of staff's comments:

> 'Boys! Leave the girls to play in the Wendy House.'
> 'That's it, Lorna. Show the boys how to do it!'
>
> (Hartley, 1993, p.124)

There is evidence and research to indicate that boys and girls focus their play differently, and that boys and girls gravitate to single sex groupings in play. Browne and Ross (1991) talked with and observed young children and discovered they have clear ideas about play preferences and about which toys are for boys, which for girls. Jones and Glenn (1991) found that girls showed more pretend play than boys, and that most play occurred in single-sex groupings.

Paley's observations of young children's play in the kindergarten leads her to reflect on the genderedness of play and the stereotypes that seem to abound. She observed few successful intersections of boys' play and girls' play (1984). Paley writes, 'I must be careful: So eager are the boys and girls to have separate play worlds that I am almost fooled into believing they don't need each other' (p.37). This single-sex play was also observed in the blockplay area. The Froebel Blockplay Research Group's observations of children in blockplay areas suggested that it was boys rather than girls who were playing there; this is described as, 'a self-perpetuating cycle that becomes inextricably bound up with territory and dominance' (Gura and The Froebel Blockplay Research Group, 1992, p.166).

The Equal Opportunities Commission (EOC) defines sex stereotyping as,

'Making assumptions about people – their roles, behaviour, ability, etc. – on the basis of what is thought to be appropriate or to be expected of their sex, so failing to recognise and encourage their individual aptitudes and talents' (EOC, 1992, p.7). The notion of stereotyping is one with broad relevance in thinking about equality of opportunity issues, but is of particular interest here because of the arguments around socialisation related to sex stereotyping. It highlights questions about how gender issues are researched, debated and discussed. Gender issues have been widely studied and there are many examples which confirm that particular images, characteristics and behaviours are reinforced differently or distinctly in girls and in boys. Browne and France (in Weiner, 1985) for example discuss sexist talk in the nursery and draw attention to sex-specific terms used by adults, which 'clearly define the type of behaviour and characteristics deemed acceptable in girls yet unacceptable in boys, or vice versa' (p.152). For example, a child observed to be organising others, would be described as 'bossy', if a girl, and as a 'born leader' if a boy.

France (1985) identifies the family network, professionals (e.g. in health, education and social services), community and peer group, and the media, as four groups who will provide advice to parents, which in many ways simply serves to reinforce the status quo in terms of expectations made of men and women, boys and girls. They also argue that differentiated sex roles and very clear distinctions between the attributes and expectations of men and women, serves to retain things as they are, and work very much against change on a wider scale. So, sex-role theories can reinforce sexism, 'one can fall into the trap of attempting either to prove exactly what girls lack so that it can be put right, or to demonstrate that there is no lack at all ... such approaches trap us ... like flies in a web, into playing the game by patriarchal rules' (Walkerdine, 1989, pp.1–2).

To accept the idea of children being socialised into very specific sex roles, for example by influential parents, causes several contradictions with other ideas, which might be part of an early years teacher's thinking. For example, this notion of a child being socialised so effectively, does not take account of the child being an *active* learner. It is a view which pays too much regard to the individual and not enough to the wider structures which can also influence the way children and adults can be. Davies (1989) develops this line of argument and discounts the sex-role socialisation model of thinking about gender for several reasons, one of which is the way it focuses on individual identity, rather than looking at the power relations that exist between male and female. Davies also puts forward a different way of thinking about the whole idea of what an 'individual' is. This is an important strand in thinking about gender issues, as some theoretical positions can perpetuate gender differences that are disadvantageous to women and also to men. Thinking about gender from the basis of a rigid acceptance of fixed and clear differences between men and women, will perpetuate the differences, leaving no way to work for change on the necessary wider and more fundamental scale. Walkerdine *et al.* (1989) and Davies (1989) conceptualise individuals as complex, and multiple, involved in creating and recreating themselves, through different discourses. This results in individuals experiencing particular situations differently, according to the way they are positioned in the discourse. According to Walkerdine *et al.* (1989), it is not always the case that girls are weak and dependent in play situations, but they appear to be engaged in a 'struggle' with the boys to create and read situations, e.g. in the home corner, where they can be powerful (see Walkerdine *et al.*, 1989, ch.5).

Walkerdine argues that girls' and women's power in the nursery must be understood in 'a different way from the rigid stereotypes and poor, weak and defenceless little girls scenario' (p.63). This is not saying gender differences do not exist or that they are not important, but it is arguing very forcefully for a different way of looking at the situation in relation to boys and girls. Otherwise the way of looking simply perpetuates the inequity it perceives. Existing arguments, states Walkerdine, claim there is something wrong with girls. The fieldwork carried out by Walkerdine and Walden (1982 cited in Walkerdine *et al.*, 1989) fails to support the idea that there are huge differences in play between boys and girls.

What we can be sure about is that any argument that says girls and boys are simply taught how to behave, and to achieve equality and equity means providing dolls for the girls in the blockplay area and Power-Rangers for the boys in the home corner, is painfully inadequate. Teachers must take account of the struggle that goes on through discourse and play, through which children construct their identities, establish themselves, learn who they are and who they can be.

Race

As in other areas of education the meaning of terms is often debated and 'race' is no exception. Siraj-Blatchford (1993) keeps 'race' in inverted commas, in order to 'emphasize the problematic nature of the term' (p.6). Massey (1991) tackles the wider issue of the clarity, or lack of, in the terminology used in anti-racist and multicultural education and in so doing explains the background of the term 'race'. It has a historical background in the concept of genetic superiority of one race of people over another, which was grounded in theories that claimed intellectual and physical characteristics to be entirely hereditary. This 'eugenics creed' was popular during the Edwardian period, and accepted by many in the years after the First World War (Brown, 1988, p.295).

The need to look at our past in order to understand racial inequality is clearly argued by Siraj-Blatchford (1994b). As Britain and other European countries took control of newly discovered lands, 'they stigmatised certain "race" groups as inferior and sub-human, so as to justify their exploitation' (p.14). This dates back several hundred years and although this 'scientific racism' (Massey, 1991, p.31) or 'pseudo-scientific doctrine' (Wright, 1992, p.2) is now no longer accepted, it is important to remember that this belief is part of the history of racism. Wright explains how the concept of 'race' and the hierarchical classification of people was used to define the superiority of white races. Wright provides a useful redefining of the term 'race' by explaining that it operates now as a metaphor, 'the meaning of which reflects socio-cultural characteristics such as language, religion, custom, mores and life-styles, thus emphasising social characteristics rather than genetic endowment' (p.2).

There have been changes in attitude and approach to issues of race, during this century, which can be summarised as a shift from essentially celebratory white liberal multicultural education to active anti-racist education. This shift is significant as it represents a move to a politically more proactive stance. Massey shows how this shift in response to the cultural diversity of Britain, took place at school and local education authority level. Massey identifies six phases:

1 Laissez-faire
2 Assimilation via language and numbers
3 Integration through compensation
4 Multiculturalism: from compensation to cultural pluralism
5 Anti-racism – from saris and samosas to struggle
6 Anti-racist multiculturalism – a practical synthesis?

(Massey, 1991)

Roaf and Bines summarise this same move, as they draw parallels between the shifts in perspective and policy related to children with special educational needs and children of ethnic minorities:

> a needs-based perspective emphasising assimilation and integration characterised the 1950s and 1960s within which the needs of the immigrant communities were those defined by the host community. In turn this was succeeded by a perspective emphasising diversity. This was an improvement, conferring a greater sense of community and equality of opportunity but in a notably weak form. It has had to be strengthened by policies emphasising the active reduction of prejudice and unfair discrimination, through the courts both national and European if necessary.
>
> (Roaf and Bines, 1994, pp.61–2)

'The colour of a person's skin is significant, and for carers to pretend otherwise is both harmful and false. Children, however young, are not "all the same"' (Durant, 1988). Young children are aware of racial and cultural similarities and differences and in making sense of the community of the classroom will be learning about perceptions of race. This will also have an impact on their sense of identity. Bruce (1987, p.158) argues that children should select their own identity, rather than have to be defined by others; sense of identity and self-esteem are fundamentally important and formed from birth onwards. It never actually reaches a point when it is 'finished', but is a life-long process. However, we are inevitably partly defined by the way others perceive us and respond to us. This is also where awareness of identity can be experienced differently. Being part of a white majority does not necessitate awareness of identity; being part of a black minority does. As Paley says, white teachers and children don't need to know they are white, 'They simply *are*' (Paley, 1995, p.16).

The examples given in Wright's study show black children experiencing a fundamental conflict between perceived expectations of their background and the requirements of their school. Wright gives an example of Asian girls in a nursery school whose behaviour was regarded by the teacher as 'over-sensitive and modest' as they sought some privacy to undress for PE, rather than acknowledging their behaviour as part of the cultural and religious expectations of their background (1992, p.18).

Wright is not talking here about blaming teachers (individually), although individuals clearly have a significant role to play, but is arguing for the recognition that some teachers feel insecurity about working with ethnically and linguistically mixed classes (p.106). Teachers may feel unsure about how to respond to young children's comments or behaviour or feel it is easier to pretend not to see or hear. There may also be a sense that these are issues that are too difficult to discuss with young children. Paley (1995) shows that this is not the case and that in fact children are 'devoted to philosophical enquiry' (p.9). Young children should be thinking about concepts of fairness and justice and indeed these may well be among their main concerns, were we to ask children themselves. Paley's examples certainly show that children's fears relate to fundamentals like exclusion, inadequacy and oppression. Paley argues that through story children can address and explore these issues in ways that move their thinking forward and is not superficial, tokenistic or threatening.

Wright also gives examples of the interactions between a teacher and Afro-Caribbean children which highlight the children's genuine concerns for fair treatment. The examples seem to indicate differential treatment particularly of Afro-Caribbean boys, the 'frequent control and criticism' experienced, for example by a four-year-old Afro-Caribbean boy in the nursery (1992, pp.20–1).

Siraj-Blatchford (1992) gives examples of the 'propagating notions' (p.105) that continue to reinforce the idea that black people are second class, less important and inferior. She lists the press, television, books, graffiti, jokes, language and traditional British tolerance (pp.105–6). We are all influenced by the representations or omissions of black people. White therefore becomes established and reinforced as the norm and black children can feel excluded and inferior, with poor self-image and self-esteem. These processes influence our thinking and actions and perpetuate stereotyping and racism (see Siraj-Blatchford, 1994b).

There are critics of anti-racist multicultural education, and one of the most well known has been Honeyford. Massey (1991, p.55) provides a concise summary of the Halstead's account of Honeyford's arguments. Honeyford's opinions centre around claims that multicultural education is a bandwagon, is socially divisive as it gives concessions and privileges to certain groups, and is part of a progressive, political agenda to radicalise pupils and change society (Halstead, 1988, cited in Massey, 1991).

Strategies for equality and equity

As has been argued throughout this chapter, equality issues have an individual as well as a much wider social and political dimension, and the strategies and practice necessary need to reflect this. All adults working with all young children have a responsibility, legally, morally and professionally, to address equality issues, to think about and to discuss them, and to act positively. Kidner (1988, p.52) considers the children's perspective, in terms of what children deserve:

- They deserve adults who are prepared to look objectively at their own practice to see how it affects different groups of children.
- They deserve a curriculum that values a range of cultures, languages and lifestyles and is supportive of their own.
- They need to be exploring concepts and ideas which will eventually be consolidated into an understanding of racism and other forms of oppression.[10]

Working for equality and equity could be treated as a passive role where not preventing children from participating in certain activities is adequate practical response; perhaps coupled with a little attention paid to resources, for example the books available to children, artefacts on display or resources in role play and home corner areas. Again such responses are not to be sneered at or derided, but they are inadequate if issues of equality of opportunity are viewed rigorously in terms of the creation of social justice. What happens then is that a much more far-reaching task presents itself; more demanding on the teachers, parents and children and more long term. Central to any consideration of equality and equity needs to be a recognition that there are issues of power and control, which operate at a level beyond that of the individual. Weiner (1985) writes of the 'constant competition for power and control; between men and women, black people and white, and between class interest' (p.10). This is not to suggest a sinister 'plot', in any simplistic terms, but emphasises the wider and profound struggles and tensions that exist in society and in the ways cultures are constructed and function. As Weiner (1985) explains, 'expanding educational opportunity is not just a question of juggling resources ... It is far more fundamental than that' (p.10).

In thinking about the principles and practice involved in issues of equality and equity and working with young children, both the more immediate and individual responses need to be considered, and the more global, more political and perhaps less tangible. Both are relevant and important to early years teachers. Working to create a socially just community in the classroom is not straightforward or formulaic – classrooms are part of the wider social and cultural world and as such are influenced by it; but that should not render teachers, children or parents passive in the wake of inequality or injustice. Indeed it makes everyone's efforts, and specifically the early years teachers', all the more necessary and urgent. The role teachers can play is considerable, and to prioritise social justice, tolerance and a sense of community must surely be a responsibility teachers take very seriously indeed.

Keeping this wider dimension clearly in focus, will help to prevent strategies and practice that is superficial. 'Ignoring or being unaware of such a structural and therefore political context will render most well-intentioned practice as ineffective and tokenistic as is the majority of "multi-cultural" practice that occurs in classrooms' (Lee, 1987, p.113).

Classroom practice and the underlying understanding of that practice must not be separated. It is teachers' professional understanding of the issues and the educational aims that helps to make equality and equity practice meaningful and genuinely worthwhile. Simply to provide resources that superficially reflect cultural diversity is probably better than not doing so, but alongside it must be a clear rationale for their presence and use.

The work of Davies (1989) provides an interesting perspective here. In reading anti-sexist picture books to nursery children, Davies discovered a wide range of responses from the children, which did not all accord with the children learning anti-sexist ideas from the stories. Learning is, as we know, a complex process that cannot be explicitly controlled, but with this awareness, it may be possible to improve the quality of practice by ensuring an appropriate level and depth of interaction with children, to move towards more real exploration of the intended issues. And this is good early years practice generally too. It involves listening to children; it involves acceptance and openness, informed by rigorous principles, rather than unchallenged freedom, which shies away from intervention, and challenging children's thinking. Teachers need strong thought-through principles and the courage and integrity to act upon them.[11]

Paley (1984) focuses on the crucial importance of fantasy and pretend in extending children's understanding of the possibilities that are open to them. This is encapsulated in an example where Paley invites Franklin, a kindergarten boy, to *pretend* to be boy who knows how to let others use their own ideas in the block play area. A more collaborative scenario develops which implies that the use of make-believe is enabling (pp.86–7). Paley is not claiming that such role play results in long-term changes in behaviour, but it may well prove to be a good strategy for breaking patterns of behaviour which are embedded in discrimination or exclusion. It gives a less confrontational basis for talk, easier to move forward. '"Pretend" disarms and enchants; it suggests heroic possibilities for making changes, just as in fairy tales' (p.87).

Teachers' interactions with children are centrally important in order to promote equality actively. This does mean taking sides if children or adults are jeopardising the equality and equity teachers are working towards, but this stand must be taken with sensitivity as well as strength – it is about taking a positive stand for equality and justice for all. It is not about taking a stand 'for girls against boys', for example, although it may well involve challenging boys' habits and behaviour to gain access to certain play areas for girls. To work for equality is challenging and requires determination and thought. The need for dialogue, open discussion and sharing of perspectives, is important with children, parents and professional colleagues.

It highlights the fact that it is necessary to ensure young children have the time and space to express their own ideas and understanding – through talk, play, drawing and story (see Graham, 1993), to provide the basis for productive dialogue. Pound (1988) acknowledges that children's free play might have allowed children to practise racism, but that 'it could have had, with adult support and guidance, another important function' which is to explore other possibilities, in terms of their thinking and their actions. Paley (1995) uses children's own storytelling and stories she has created herself as the forum for children to explore their prejudices. Hers are interactions broadly based and exploratory.

Anning (1991) describes a helpful framework for thinking about teachers' responses to 'classroom incidents that reflect children's awareness of complex social problems' (p.68).

She identifies three categories:

1 involvement or extension – teachers listened to children and talked with them, but did not express their own views;

2 direction or manipulation – teachers made their own views clear, sometimes giving reasons;

3 delay or diversion – teachers ignored the children or attempted to distract them.

This provides one model for thinking about short-term responses to children's play, where equality and equity are issues. Longer term responses would need to look at the planned provision for play and children's access to it; also the way ideas of equality might be specifically addressed. Butterworth (1991) describes a range of intervention strategies used to tackle gender inequality in the nursery and concludes that praising children of both sexes for playing cooperatively, and providing 'girls only' block-building days were effective strategies (p.6). The Froebel Blockplay Research Group did not pursue the idea of girls only sessions however, arguing that this could be seen to support ideas of gender difference. In its place they adopt a collaborative policy, which demands the 'personal involvement of adults *long term*' (p.166) to achieve equality of access.

So, working for equality and equity is not just about responding to problematic incidents, but also involves a much more proactive provision of resources and discussion; it means enabling children to take up and make the most of, opportunities in the classroom. Teachers need ways to open up possibilities for children and to show they value each child's contribution. Who decides what counts in the classroom and what is valued? It is important to remember that the classroom culture is not fixed but dynamic and should be shaped by all who have a stake in it – teachers, children, parents at least.

Stereotypes form subconscious frames of reference that need to be made explicit and questioned. Teachers cannot step outside contexts, but need to stand back and inspect them. The generalisations that are made about people or groups of people can be very limiting and excluding; they involve power and control. The prejudices they represent are exposed as serious and invidious, in particular, when these stereotypes become institutionalised. And some stereotypes can unwittingly be reinforced through attempts to counteract them. Siraj-Blatchford argues that focusing on a specific aspect of an ethnic group's culture can be seen as tokenistic and can result in children seeing 'them' as different, exotic and odd. Far more productive to focus on a theme or provide resources that reflect a diverse cultural background and society (Siraj-Blatchford, 1992, p.114).

Children's experiences and understanding, just as the teachers', need to be viewed in the wider social and cultural context. Neither is in isolation from this. This is why as well as thinking about personal perspectives and how teachers' own social and cultural gendered backgrounds might shape their teaching and values, teachers need to look at the school context and think about equality issues. To what extent are the adults in the school valued for their work – are some people's opinions more important than others? What assumptions have become institutionalised into the structures of the school?

Concluding thoughts

Teachers' sense of identity and their understanding of their cultural backgrounds (shaped by gender, class and race) are important if teachers are going to be able to work with children constructively and sympathetically. This is not idle reflection or indulgent self-observation, but involves working at critical appraisal of one's own cultural positioning, recognising that beliefs, ways of life, priorities, perspectives are socially and culturally constructed and reconstructed continually through our lives – it is part of the life-long learning process about ourselves. That recognition must include reflection on gender, class and race. And being in a majority group – which in the case of early years teachers is white, middle-class female – may militate against reflecting on that.

Actively recognising this should encourage teachers to reassess the importance of trying to 'see things from the child's point of view', because that point of view is also socially and culturally determined. The fundamental need for dialogue is clear from Paley's account of her reflections on what it really means to belong to the school culture (Paley, 1995).

A part of that reflection must be thinking about the cultural identity of the teacher within the context of the culture of primary teachers generally and primary school. Michael Annan (1993), a black male teacher in a primary school, recognises that he brings his personal experiences to his teaching and argues that different perspectives and practice should be accommodated in primary schools. There are stereotypes of primary teachers and of primary practice which should not be passively accepted, but which should be continually discussed, debated and reshaped where necessary. That is a slow process. 'Human growth is not like rhubarb. It can be nurtured and encouraged but it cannot be forced' (Fullan and Hargreaves, 1994, pp.67–8).

Inaction or denial – being caught up in what Paley describes as 'webs of indifference' – will be to the disadvantage of all children (1995, p.114). A classroom community underpinned by prejudice, exclusion and fear would be one no teacher would want to create, but inaction could lead to just that. Discrimination might be subtly embedded. Young children learn from their experiences, they learn about who they are and what school is going to mean, or not mean, to them. This is a particular responsibility of the early years teacher – children who feel excluded in their early experiences of schooling are at a real disadvantage.

But it is important to remember that, 'Race, class and gender inequalities are *structural* inequalities as well as having personal manifestations. The "individualistic" ethos ... must be replaced by collectivism, collaboration, communality and political action' (Lee, 1978, p.113). It is not a question of simply reflecting on personal likes and dislikes, or of hoping all early years teachers will be 'nice' to all the children – there is a more political dimension, which has moral and social as well as intellectual aspects.

Children need to be able to make sense of experiences in the early years classroom but also to develop and extend those experiences – the classroom culture must encourage children to take risks, ask questions, suggest alternatives, make meaning. Children need to have their say. Teachers should encourage this, and also be prepared to take risks. They should recognise they are inducting children into a school culture, but also be prepared to think actively about how that classroom culture should be shaped. Faust talks of 'defining the world of the classroom' (Faust, 1987) and this should be a collaborative, on-going task.

There should be a sense of collective responsibility – continually asking, how can we make this better? There is a need to work with parents and the wider community of and beyond school. The dialogue must be kept open. If some children do not seem to fit into the classroom culture or do not seem to be participating fully, then we are wise to look at the culture and deeper structures of that classroom culture, and ask questions of it, as well as observing the child.

Teachers, children, parents and professionals need to talk about important issues. Given the opportunity, children often ask searching questions that relate to the global perspective of equality and equity – e.g. about there being children in the world without food. These are serious questions that deserve time and attention. Early years teachers, above all, must not lose sight of important, fundamental concerns, get buried in minutiae or bureaucratic pressures, and leave equality to chance; the foundations for equality and equity are too important and early years teachers have a vital role to play.

Notes

1 For consideration of issues relating to disability, not a specific focus in this chapter, see Rieser and Mason (1990). For a focus on special needs, see Peter Long's chapter in this volume; also Wolfendale and Wooster (1992).
2 See Cameron (1992) for a clear discussion of the phenomenon of common gender.
3 Language diversity is an important consideration in relation to children's ability to participate fully in the life of the classroom. See Barratt-Pugh (1994) on multilingualism; see Bain *et al.* (1992) for a wider consideration of the significance of children's language histories.
4 See Burgess-Macey (1993/4) for a consideration of equality issues, the Children Act and the Education Reform Act, 1988.
5 For an outline of the legislative framework relating to equality issues, and extracts from the relevant documents, see The Runnymede Trust (1993).
6 For arguments and evidence to challenge views that working-class children underachieve because their language is deficient, see, Tizard and Hughes (1984).
7 MacGilchrist cites: ILEA (1983) *Race, Sex and Class 1. Achievement in schools.* London: LEA. Mortimore, P. and Mortimore, J. (1986) 'Education and Social Class', in R. Rogers (Ed) *Education and Social Class.* Lewes: Falmer.

8 For a consideration of parental involvement and equality of opportunity in general, see Edwards and Knight (1994, pp.112–14).
9 For example the 'Headstart' projects set up in the USA, see Whalley (1994, ch.5).
10 Kidner is writing about race, but his points are also more widely applicable to gender and class issues.
11 See Siraj-Blatchford (1994b, in particular pp.64–7) on child-centredness. See Walkerdine *et al.* (1989, ch.5, especially pp.65–8), where Walkerdine analyses the transcript of an interaction between nursery children and their teacher.

Figure 8.1: Further reflection

The following quotations highlight two distinct strands in attempting equality and equity:

> Where, in our society, teachers have been able to bridge the gulfs of race, class, gender, and to meet children who are very different from themselves, it has been through a very personal entering into those children's worlds. Only through lived personal experiences is it possible to learn something of the situation of strangers.
>
> (Salmon, 1988, p.45)

> Educators are not generally powerful in economic or policy terms ... However educators *are* powerful in terms of the power they have over the children in their care. If educators are to exert any influence over economic decisions they need to apply their understandings of government policy and legislative effects at both national and local level.
>
> (Siraj-Blatchford, 1992, p.109)

- Can you identify ways to work for equality and equity, at both personal and policy levels?
- How can you develop your understanding of the children with whom you work?
- How can you work more collectively with colleagues within and beyond your own workplace?

This final quotation encapsulates one dimension of Paley's aims in working with young children:

> '"Maybe our classrooms can be nicer than the outside world" I suggest.'
>
> (Paley, 1992, p.22)

- Do you share this aim?
- Is it realistic?
- What could be the advantages and disadvantages of thinking about the classroom in this way?

Chapter 9

Special educational needs

Peter Long

Introduction

In addressing special educational needs within the context of early years education, this chapter sets out firstly to give the reader an introductory historical and legislative background to this aspect of practitioners' work. The second part of the chapter raises a number of issues, points and arguments pertinent to students involved in teacher education and explores matters in relation to SEN in the early years setting. Student competences and the dangers inherent in labelling children; baseline profiling and screening in the early years; working with colleagues in aligned professions and the importance of parental involvement and whole-school policy, are areas addressed which it is hoped will encourage those intending to pursue a career working with young children, to be reflective and evaluative about their own practice.

Historical and legislative background

'There are lots of special needs children at that school.' 'I have eight special needs children in my class.' Have you ever heard these sorts of comments made by colleagues, whether they be experienced class teachers or students describing their school experience? The problem with these types of statements is that they tend to be sweeping generalisations about a wide range of specific learning difficulties or physical disabilities, or a combination of both, which pupils may experience in varying degrees. Such remarks also tend to label children in a negative sense rather than address any need which may have been identified. What may be perceived as special educational needs in one setting or by an individual or group, may not be seen in the same light in a different context or from another viewpoint. In considering special educational needs in early years education, it is difficult to establish some sort of 'catch-all' working definition of what we mean by SEN as children have very different needs which have to be addressed through a range of flexible programmes and approaches.

Robson (1989, pp.14, 15) traces the impact the Warnock Report (DES, 1978a) had for the first time on special educational needs in relation to the 'preschool' child and some of the innovatory ideas within the field of special education contained in the resulting 1981 Education Act. The Act brought about a new concept of special educational need, stressing the importance of early intervention and empowering local education authorities to assess and provide educational services for children with special needs below the age of two years, if parents wished this course of action to be taken. For children over the age of two years and under the age of five, the Act stipulated that if parents made what was referred to as a 'reasonable' request, the local education authority must carry out a formal assessment of a child's special educational needs likely to be followed by a statement regarding what was considered to be appropriate provision and/or placement to meet those needs. Despite the empowering of local education authorities to become more actively involved in the assessment of and provision for children with special educational needs prior to statutory schooling, it is interesting to note that this piece of legislation still left the onus very much on parents to seek educational assistance for their children.

In an attempt to gain greater consistency between schools and local education authorities dealing with children's special educational needs, to establish what is meant by the term SEN with a greater degree of clarity and make more explicit the responsibilities of schools, governors, LEAS, health and social services, the 1993 Education Act introduced a SEN Code of Practice to be followed by all schools including those offering educational provision for the under-fives. Webster (1994) points out that when the new Code was announced in the House of Commons in the autumn of 1994, government ministers described it as 'setting a whole new framework for special education in the future'. Although it must be acknowledged that against this political rhetoric, a number of local education authorities had been working for some time on a staged framework to address SEN. The Code clarifies the role of the school in five stages leading up to the formal assessment and statementing of children identified as having special educational needs. The precise way in which the Code is interpreted is left to individual schools to determine, but this has to be set out in a published policy which all schools were to have in place by 1 August 1995. In consultation with parents, schools decide which stage is suitable for a child, which means action may be taken at Stage 2 or 3 of the Code regarding a child's special educational needs, even though previous action may not have been taken at Stage 1. In this way it is intended that the Code can be used flexibly to meet individual needs and a child does not have to progress through Stage 1 if it is felt that his or her needs can be best met by action initiated at Stage 2 or 3. Schools are required to have a designated teacher responsible for monitoring SEN policy and practice, to keep a register of all children with SEN and record the steps taken to meet pupils' needs. Inspectors from OFSTED are responsible for monitoring how effectively the Code is being implemented in the planned four-yearly cycle inspection of schools.

At the time of writing it has yet to transpire how well the Code will work in schools and what benefit it will be to children and parents. However, from my experience as an OFSTED inspector involved in six inspections of primary schools during the academic year 1994–95, there was a marked variation among schools in the amount of preparation undertaken for implementing the new Code, with one school inspected in July 1995 having no SEN policy in place, in spite of a 'deadline' of 1 August – the following month. Moreover, it is a moot point whether or not OFSTED will be able to carry out the intended four yearly inspections of schools, including assessing the impact of the SEN Code of Practice, with the current number of inspectors available, an issue featured in a range of letters and articles in the national and educational press during 1994–95 and underpinned by OFSTED's advertisements in *The Times Educational Supplement* during February 1995 for additional inspectors.

Nevertheless, for students entering the teaching profession, a working knowledge of the SEN Code is a requirement which must be seriously addressed. Whatever shortcomings or problems may develop from implementation of the Code in the future, those intending to teach need to be mindful of their responsibilities in this area and critically evaluate the Code as one of the tools of their chosen profession as they gain experience and expertise. The Code is applicable to all children in state schools, including nursery schools, nursery classes and units, and therefore, is particularly relevant to student teachers and other practitioners intending to work in such institutions. The identification of the special needs of younger children during the pre-nursery years, which may in turn lead to the registering of special educational needs at a later stage, continues to be part of the work of other professionals such as health visitors and GPs, whose role it is to detect such problems at an early stage.

The SEN Code of Practice – a skeletal outline of the five stages involved

Stage 1

This involves the gathering of information, initial identification and registration of a child's SEN, with increased differentiation by task and learning outcome in the curriculum offered. Here the responsibility for the child's educational programme remains with those involved with the child on a daily basis, such as the class teacher(s) and nursery nurse(s) in the early years context; this should also entail the close involvement of parents. Stage 1 is initiated when a teacher, parent or other professional (such as a health visitor) has evidence that a child is showing signs of SEN. A record must be kept of the nature of the concern and SEN, what action has been taken, targets set and when progress is to be reviewed, which should be within a term to six months. If after two reviews at Stage 1 satisfactory progress has not been achieved, Stage 2 may be reached.

Stage 2
Here those working closely with the child may seek further advice from individuals such as the school doctor or professional agencies such as specialist teachers of children with visual or hearing impairment. In addition, an Individual Education Plan (IEP) should be created. This will include:

- the nature of the child's learning difficulties;
- special provision; staff involved; frequency of support; specific programmes/activities/materials/equipment;
- assistance from parents at home;
- targets to be achieved by a given time;
- pastoral care or medical arrangements;
- monitoring and assessment arrangements;
- arrangements for review.

Again, parents need to be kept fully informed of progress and development and their views sought and taken into account, especially if it is thought necessary to move on to Stage 3 of the Code.

Stage 3
At Stage 3 the school is able to call on outside assistance such as the local schools psychological service. Responsibility for pupils with SEN at this stage is shared between the class teacher, the school SEN coordinator and the relevant outside support services whose expertise has been requested. A new IEP will be drawn up with input from the support services and, as in previous stages, a review will be arranged by the SEN coordinator including the child's parents. If at the outcome of the review it is considered that the child must be referred to the local education authority for a statutory assessment, the school has to provide a range of written information to support the referral detailing the action taken during Stages 1–3.

Stage 4
Statutory assessment by the LEA may come as the result of a school or parental request, or a request from another agency, where it is felt that a child's SEN is not satisfactorily being addressed in the classroom context despite the efforts of the school and support services to meet these needs, with parental assistance and involvement. The new Code states that the statutory assessment should be carried out within a period of 26 weeks and lays down procedures which have to be followed during the assessment. A wide range of cognitive, social, emotional and physical factors have to be considered during the assessment.

Stage 5
A formal statement of special educational need will be drawn up by the local education authority once it is established that a child's learning difficulties are:

- significant and/or complex;

- have not been met by measures taken by the school and support services; or
- may call for resources which cannot be reasonably provided within the budget of a mainstream school in the area.

To this end the statement should provide the means of access to extra resources and establish a formula in an effort to meet individual children's needs based on accurate, detailed and comprehensive assessment taking into account the views of parents and the children themselves, as well as professional opinion.

So we have a legal framework within which we are required to address SEN in the early years. However, for student teachers and practitioners working with young children, there is much more to providing quality educational provision, which effectively meets the needs of those pupils with specific learning difficulties and/or physical disabilities, than just adhering to the requirements of an obligatory Code of Practice. We also have to evaluate our attitudes, assumptions, beliefs and expectations about children with SEN, what preconceptions we may have regarding such children's cognitive, social, emotional and physical development, and how this influences what we think they are capable of achieving as individuals within their own right.

Issues we have to address in dealing with SEN in the early years

Student competences and the dangers of labelling

All student teachers in order to gain Qualified Teacher Status have to be assessed against a range of criteria which are competence based, and universities and institutions of higher education involved in teacher education have developed a range of such criteria. For example, in Year 1 of a four-year BA QTS Programme at the Roehampton Institute, London, students are required to:

> 'Assess the learning of individual children in your teaching group in relation to your (teaching) plan.' Focal Competence 3
>
> 'Set up activities which helps you identify the learning needs of children in your teaching group(s).' Focal Competence 4
>
> (Roehampton Institute, 1995, p.B6)

Second-year students are obliged to:

> 'Create opportunities within your teaching for diagnostic assessment.' Focal Competence 1
>
> 'Incorporate prior assessments into planning.' Focal Competence 3
>
> (Roehampton Institute, 1995, p.B14)

Similar Focal Competences have to be tackled in Years 3 and 4 of the Programme as part of a developmental progression in students' knowledge and understanding of how children learn. In effectively addressing such competence-based criteria, students have the opportunity to raise their awareness, sharpen their perceptions and ultimately feel a greater sense of empowerment when supporting children in the early years who have been identified as having some form of SEN. This is of crucial importance if we are to avoid what can be referred to as the labelling syndrome which employs an implicit deficit model of the child – the vessel to be filled. This concept of the child incorporates a possible range of achievement correlating with chronological age in terms of which an individual may be considered to be 'average' an 'overachiever' or an 'underachiever'. An example would be a child achieving a National Curriculum Standard Assessment Task (SAT) Level 1 or Level 3 at the end of the infant phase of schooling, when the 'average' seven year old, according to the National Curriculum Council 1991, would achieve a SAT Level 2. Such notions beg many fundamental questions, not least, what or who can be defined as the 'average' seven year old?

Similar criticisms can be levelled at a consultative paper published by OFSTED (September 1994) which gives guidance for the inspection of institutions accommodating children under the statutory age of schooling. Under the heading 'Standards of achievement' the paper states, 'Most children between the ages of 3–4 years of age should be able to ... relate to more than one adult ... use equipment and resources including IT constructively and imaginatively ... be aware of and able to use their own bodies in different ways.' The paper goes on to assert that 'Most children between the ages of 4–5 years of age should be able to...' and another list appears incorporating statements such as 'demonstrate increasing independence and the ability to take the initiative ... show more confidence in making choices and in giving reasons for their decisions and actions', more than what is not explained, 'be able to co-operate with other children leading to instances of collaborative play as well as working independently', how play and working independently differ, is not made clear. The main failing of this paper is that it lacks any theoretical framework regarding child development or how young children learn, resulting in lists of unsupported generalisations and assertions. It is acknowledged by numerous sources, e.g. Lindon (1993), that there are broad areas of physical and cognitive development, e.g. sitting up independently, crawling and beginning to walk, using sound and body language to call for attention or imitate others, that most children reach by certain ages. It is a somewhat sweeping statement, however, to claim that most children of three to four or four to five '*should* be able to'. Moreover, what if they cannot fulfil the criteria set out? Are they to be deemed as having some form of SEN at this early stage of their schooling with the educational provision they are offered designated as lacking in some important aspects?

Learning at any age is individualistic; our ability to assimilate knowledge, concepts, skills and attitudes, and effectively utilise these in a wide range of situations to benefit ourselves and others, depends upon many factors. This is particularly the case with young children working at their own pace and coming to terms with the world in which they find themselves through explorative, practical, investigative endeavour. Each child is unique and needs to be seen as so, thus, it is inappropriate and misleading to label children in the early years in terms of being 'underachievers', 'overachievers' or 'average'. The lumping together of children into age groups with categorical statements about what a particular group 'should' be able to do, as if the individuals within that group constituted some sort of homogeneous entity, is equally untenable and, more importantly, is totally at odds with the main thrust of this book that education in the early years is essentially individualistic and holistic in nature, embracing the development of the whole child.

Baseline profiling and screening in the early years – the impact on SEN

The 1988 Education Reform Act brought many changes to the work of primary schools particularly in the areas of curriculum, funding and assessment. In a climate of much greater teacher and school accountability generated by the Act, one development which has had a marked impact on the work of early years practitioners has been the development of baseline profiling or screening as children enter infant school. A number of justifications serving very different purposes have been proposed for this initiative, among which are those made by the National Association of Headteachers (NAHT) (1989a,b). Establishing such a baseline, it is argued, is an indication of a child's readiness for National Curriculum Key Stage 1. It also serves as a reminder as to what stage of development a child has reached on entering school, so that his or her progress can be assessed when oral and written reports are made to parents indicating what has been achieved between the ages of five and seven as the child leaves infant school.

It is also maintained that profiling or screening children as they begin school serves as an aid to indicating school effectiveness. This is aptly illustrated in a Report commissioned by the then DES (1988b) and compiled by management consultants Coopers and Lybrand. In listing the factors relevant to performance indicators for schools, under the heading 'Input Considerations', we have among other criteria:

> (a) Pupil Intake:
>
> | | |
> |---|---|
> | Socio-economic background | Cultural background |
> | Innate ability * | Handicaps * |
> | Levels of expectation | Academic attainment on entry to each phase * |
>
> (p.51)

The factors I have marked * would no doubt be particularly relevant to the idea of establishing a baseline at five and in addition to identifying children who may be perceived as potentially having SEN in the early years. They also give, within the context of school performance, an indication of the 'raw material' the school is receiving as part of the 'input considerations'.

As the effects of the Education Reform Act began to have an impact in state schools during the late 1980s, the NAHT (Bulletin, 15 September 1989) made clear their view about the importance of performance indicators for schools and the contribution which screening or establishing a baseline for children at five years of age could have: 'Monitoring and evaluating schools are going to be major areas of concern under the Education Reform Act 1988. It will be necessary for every school to develop indicators as a means of measuring performance.' However, the reasoning behind this approach to baseline profiling or screening, with particular reference to the early identification of special educational needs, raises a number of issues which require further exploration. Such methods seem to be much more concerned with institutional accountability and image presentation within the 'market place' of education created by the Education Reform Act, than a sincere attempt to seriously address the individual needs of young children. Moreover, the profiling or screening procedures developed by some local education authorities take a somewhat negative stance in terms of assessing children's achievements as they start school. Accomplishment regarding a child's mathematical, linguistic or scientific knowledge, alongside physical and social skills, are recorded with some sort of grading or scoring process. In other cases early years practitioners are required to circle one of several words which it is felt most accurately describe a child's achievement in these areas, a checklist approach which is not supported by continuous, qualitative observation.

Once again this employs an implicit deficit model of the child, which seems to be an attempt to identify gaps or shortcomings in an individual's character which may in turn be construed as some sort of special educational need. It is important to remember at this juncture Bruce's (1987, p.45) comment in her list of ten principles of early childhood education, '(7) What children can do (rather than what they cannot do) is the starting point in the child's education.'

With increasing numbers of four-year-old children being accommodated in reception classes before statutory school age (Cleave and Brown (1990), Pascal (1990), OFSTED (1993a)), there are also concerns about the timing of baseline profiling or early years screening which have been expressed succinctly by sources such as Curtis (1986, p.139), 'Young children are notoriously changeable and although there are problems inherent in assessing children of any age range they are particularly pertinent to children at the pre-school age.'

The use of profiling or screening of the checklist approach, as the main or sole means for the early identification of SEN, can also give an inaccurate or distorted picture of a child's capabilities because of the enormous variation in the experiences children have before coming to school.

Clark (1988, p.226) highlights the problems illustrated by a number of studies that this type of assessment may produce if certain children are identified as being disadvantaged or having some form of SEN, and this is associated with social class or particular home backgrounds:

> What is also clear is the likelihood that in the more formal test situation or classroom, or on a limited range of tasks, some children will show proportionately less of their competency or creativity, while others from more stimulating homes, of whichever social class, will go beyond the demands of the situation.

Although Clark's comments are in relation to social class and home background, those intending to work with young children in Britain in the 1990s and beyond, also need to bear in mind the cultural bias which may be found in early profiling and screening procedures and the disadvantage at which children from ethnic minority groups may find themselves when encountering such assessment.

All these criticisms create a dilemma for early years practitioners: on the one hand early assessment of a child's special needs is likely to benefit the child; on the other hand, some forms of such assessment can be misleading and even counterproductive. So what is the answer? Checklists of children's ability and behaviour have a place, but to be useful and relevant need to be supported with detailed and in-depth, structured, qualitative and continuous observations in the early years setting. The inaccurate or incomplete picture which may be formed about a child because of an over dependence on this sort of profiling or screening and the inherent flaws in this type of assessment, have been well summed up by Blenkin and Kelly (1992, p.164), 'Thus these forms (of assessment) have stressed the metric rather than the judgmental, the summative rather than the formative, the incremental aggregation of "scores" rather than holistic assessment, and thus attainment rather than development.'

The necessity for, and effectiveness of, assessment and record keeping based on carefully planned and organised observation is more fully discussed by Robson (1989, pp.87–106), Bartholomew and Bruce (1993) and Devereux in Chapter 6 of this book. To enable the early and accurate identification of SEN with young children, it is imperative that the sort of work outlined by the sources mentioned above is undertaken as a team effort within the early years context.

Aspects of team work in relation to addressing SEN in the early years

The newly qualified early years teacher needs to be familiar with three broad areas of team work which facilitate learning and support children identified as having some form of SEN.

Working alongside colleagues in the early years setting on a daily basis

Bartholomew in Chapter 4 of this book has stressed the importance of team work and the commitment required on the part of all team members to work together effectively on a day-to-day basis in order to deliver quality educational provision in the early years context. This is particularly the case in dealing with SEN when the information collated about a child, which will inform decisions about the most appropriate provision, is based upon the collective observations and judgements of the whole early years team.

Cooperating and working with other professional services and agencies

This would include working with colleagues in areas such as the schools psychological service, local education authority inspectorate, support/advisory teachers, portage service, medical and social services. These are just a few examples of other professionals with whom the early years practitioner may come into contact when seeking advice or sharing information about a child's special needs and what progress is being made in meeting those needs. A wide range of other local services and agencies may be involved in working with a family to support individual children depending on the nature and severity of the special need which is being addressed. As a newly qualified teacher working in south

London in the 1970s, it became increasingly clear to me how complex, and in some cases stressful, the lives of children can become when subject to an array of community services attempting to meet the disparate needs of families, which often included the special educational needs of children within those families. Attendance at social services case conferences, as the school representative, to give an account of a child's educational progress against a background of difficult domestic circumstances which a family may be experiencing, is a sobering and thought-provoking occasion. However, this aspect of the teacher's role gives an extremely valuable opportunity to appreciate the work of others in aligned professions. Obviously, not all children experiencing some form of SEN have family difficulties to cope with too. However, if the early years practitioner is required to contribute to the sort of forum mentioned above, two points need to be borne in mind.

Firstly, attending any meeting with other professionals to discuss a child's progress at school is a serious affair, so be well prepared and able to support any opinion expressed with evidence of the child's development in the school context. This may include samples of the child's work, photographic evidence, video or audio tape recordings of the child in the school setting or notes made as part of the observation process undertaken by the early years team.

Secondly, it is important to remember that the purpose of such meetings is to gain the most comprehensive picture as possible regarding the child under discussion. Early years practitioners are in a unique position being able to work with the child on a daily basis. Such familiarity often gives the opportunity to bring a degree of stability to a child who otherwise may be experiencing difficult or unsettled home circumstances. Thus, the early years teacher has a very important contribution to make to any decision which may be reached about the most appropriate form of provision for a child experiencing some form of special need. Such a contribution should be valued equally alongside the views of other professionals involved in the assessment process

Close liaison with and the involvement of parents in the education of their children

In Chapter 5 of this book Robson discusses in detail the importance of establishing an effective partnership between the home and the school as an essential feature of sound, quality educational provision in the early years. What is written here is an unequivocal endorsement of those sentiments since parental involvement takes on a particular significance when supporting a child who has been identified as having special educational needs. Wolfendale (1990) has highlighted the contribution that parents are able to make to the assessment process when working with children experiencing learning difficulties and/or physical disability. Parents are the first educators in a child's life and will have a wealth of information about their child from birth which they can share with professionals working with the child, including the early years practitioner. The involvement of parents in the education of their children has developed significantly over the past 20 years and this has particularly been the case with the setting up of portage services by local health and education services to assist families who have children with SEN.

Portage is a service which usually provides a weekly home visit from a teacher who offers support and guidance to parents, although the visits are not 'one way' with parents learning from the teacher how to work most effectively with their own children. The relationship at its best is reciprocal, a true partnership with the portage teacher learning a great deal about the child in the context of the home as well as helping parents to become skilled observers of their child's growth and development. In this way parents become integral to and active participants in the process of assessing and monitoring their child's progress, as they play an essential part in the individual programme which has been constructed to meet their child's special needs. Parents who have benefited from portage service are thus knowledgeable and well equipped to discuss the needs of their child. They are able to express an informed view as to what would be the most appropriate form of provision to meet individual needs as the child starts school and makes a significant contribution to the learning experiences provided.

As outlined earlier in this chapter, the SEN Code of Practice, set out in the 1993 Education Act, and to be followed by all schools, emphasises the importance of the early and effective involvement of parents in the assessment of children's SEN and in planning the provision to meet those needs. The role of parents and their rights to be fully involved in this process, must be seen by all professionals as being of paramount importance. It is only through trust, confidence and mutual respect between parents and teachers, that a sound, structured and flexible programme will be able successfully to meet the special needs of children in the early years and beyond, as they move into the statutory phase of schooling. The recognition of the part that parents have to play in this way, needs to be clearly set out for all interested parties to see and the most appropriate place for that is in the school policy for SEN.

Whole-school policy and SEN

The whole-school policy addressing SEN will need to meet the requirements of the 1993 Code of Practice and will be drawn up by a cross section of the school community – both teaching and non-teaching staff (representation of the latter group being particularly important where classroom assistants are working alongside teachers supporting children with SEN) and also governors who have a legal responsibility for the oversight of the general work of the school. It is important here to ensure the involvement of parent governors, so that the views of children's first educators are represented from the outset in the policy formulation process. The school may well also draw upon the advice and expertise of other agencies and bodies such as the local education authority inspectorate, advisory teachers, the school psychological service and the experience of colleagues in other schools who are involved in a similar undertaking. The sharing of knowledge and how problems may be overcome is important and can be a valuable time-saving exercise in the policy-drafting process. The purpose of such a whole-school approach to the formulation of an SEN policy is twofold.

Firstly, there is the issue of ownership and possession. As SEN is such an important area which the work of the school has to address, it is crucial that there is the feeling among *all* of those supporting children with special needs – parents, staff, governors, that they are working towards agreed goals with a common purpose for the benefit of all children. Therefore, the development of a whole-school policy has to be a corporate effort and not the responsibility of a select group.

Secondly, the 1993 SEN Code of Practice needs to be viewed as a basic framework of guidance to which the policy of individual schools will bring the finer detail as to how the Code is to be implemented on a termly, weekly and daily basis. The responsibility of the governing body, the headteacher, the SEN coordinator, class teachers and support staff will be clearly laid out, details of in-house assessment and recording procedures will be included and the methods to be followed for communicating with parents and other professionals will be addressed. These are just some of the items a whole-school special educational needs policy will include. As schools are such differing institutions and with over 20,000 primary schools in the state system, inevitably there will wide variation in the format and the amount and type of information contained in SEN policies, which address early years practice, while schools still adhere to the requirements of the 1993 Education Act. However, in addition to all the other information which the newly qualified early years practitioner has to assimilate and internalise as he or she takes up a new post, with the all the exciting (and to some extent daunting) challenges associated with responsibility for the cognitive, social, emotional and physical development of a class of young children, the importance of familiarity with school policy on SEN is a professional responsibility of the highest order.

Conclusion

In bringing this chapter to a close it is hoped that the intending or newly qualified early years practitioner will have gained a greater insight into the complexities of the identification of special educational needs, the importance of sharing information and working closely with colleagues from other professions and the part that parents have to play as the first educators of their children. In supporting children with SEN it has to be remembered that the most productive way forward is with a team effort, that learning for young children is essentially individualistic in nature, and that any special need which may be identified and the support which is initiated to meet that need should not detract from the central tenet that education in the early years should be chracterised by a holistic approach – addressing the needs of the whole child.

Figure 9.1: Further reflection

Think about the questions below in relation to addressing special educational needs, while supporting children and facilitating in the early years context.

- Based on my reading and experience to date, how would I personally attempt to construct a working definition of special educational needs?
- What would I need to consider and take into account about the child, the early years setting in which I am working (or am familiar with), my expectations and those of colleagues with whom I am working?
- How familiar am I with the five stages of SEN Code of Practice as set out in the Education Act 1993?
- Is it possible to identify which stage of the Code may be appropriate to a child with whom I am familiar, and who has been identified as having some form of SEN?
- What is my knowledge of the procedures which have to be followed in identifying and addressing special educational needs in my current school placement or place of work? To whom can I turn for support on a daily basis?
- How familiar am I with the range of support services and agencies which schools can draw upon to assist them in dealing with special educational needs in the early years setting? Try to list as many of these services and agencies that you can think of and what sort of expertise they may be able to provide for the school.
- What are the shortcomings of some forms of assessment used to identify special educational needs in the early years?
- What role do parents have to play and *why* in supporting both the child and the school in addressing special educational needs in the early years context?

Chapter 10

An entitlement curriculum for early childhood

Pat Gura

Introduction

Speaking out on behalf of young children in terms of their educational rights and needs is seen by early childhood educators internationally as both a moral and professional obligation. Stories of individuals and groups who have taken on the established order of the day, defying received wisdom, are part of the lore of early childhood education and care. The present chapter is a salute to that tradition. The early years straddle the non-compulsory/compulsory school age divide in the UK. Children up to age five are officially exempt from the National Curriculum. However, pupils from five to sixteen in state schools have a *legal* entitlement to it. The chapter begins therefore, with a consideration of the dilemmas this poses for those who wish to engage in thoughtful and constructive discussion about curriculum in early childhood, defined here as spanning from birth to eight. In the second part of the chapter, an entitlement curriculum for early childhood is discussed in moral rather than legal terms. The overall position adopted throughout the chapter is summed up in the statements listed in Figure 0.1 (see p.vii), agreed between colleagues in the Early Childhood Centre at the Roehampton Institute, London, as the criteria which guide the planning, conduct and evaluation of our courses. The chapter should be read in the light of these statements.

The dilemma

In the summer of 1994, following the publication of proposed changes to the National Curriculum resulting from the Dearing Review, an article appeared in the *Times Educational Supplement*, written by a highly respected early childhood educationalist. The article (Siraj-Blatchford, 1994a, p.19) was prompted by the bitter disappointment, shared by many in the field, that in merely slimming down the National Curriculum, the Dearing Review, commissioned by the Schools Curriculum and Assessment Authority (SCAA), had left the *structure* of the curriculum unchanged.

The drift of Siraj-Blatchford's comments concern the realities of teaching and learning. She contrasts the ideas of breadth, balance, progression and continuity from the perspective of primary teachers with that from the National Curriculum. For teachers, they serve as dynamic guiding principles in organising for 'the learning and teaching of individual children and groups of pupils'. In National Curriculum terms, they become inert structural features, locked into the fabric of the Subject Orders, i.e., separate subject programmes of study with related attainment targets. The effect of the National Curriculum view is to trap pupils and teachers alike in an unreal world of years, levels and stages.

Siraj-Blatchford emphasises the importance in the early years of relevance and differentiation: the need, in planning for further learning, to take account of pupils' present interests and concerns and what they can relate to from previous experience and achievements. Taken together, the principles of relevance and differentiation inform what she calls the 'localising' of the curriculum by individual practitioners. This requires freedom to exercise professional judgement. The response to these comments from the (then) Chief executive of the SCAA (Woodhead, 1994, p.14) was one of unconcealed impatience. Primary teachers 'from Cumbria to Cornwall' had played important roles in the subject advisory groups, during the twelve-month long Dearing Review.

These facts were widely reported throughout the consultation period. Woodhead therefore concludes that Siraj-Blatchford is speaking to a different agenda. Is it, he wonders, that of turning the clock back to pre-National Curriculum days? If so, she has missed the point of the Dearing Review.

This public spat illustrates the dilemma for critics of the non–negotiable National Curriculum. The cooperation of primary teachers in the Dearing Review is assumed to signal endorsement of the National Curriculum. In reality, the reason many become involved in such exercises is to limit the damage of a fundamentally flawed curriculum model. Reform as opposed to review is not part of the government's agenda.

Commenting on what he calls the 'enduring appeal of subject centred models of curriculum to dominant groups' Goodson says 'they allow endless debate about purposes and parameters ... within boundaries that make any pervasive change all but impossible' (Goodson, 1992a, p.58). In effect, the Chief executive of SCAA was saying that talk of such change is off limits: the only legitimate debate is that which takes place within the frames of reference of the National Curriculum. This would not be unreasonable if the *original* proposals for a National Curriculum had resulted from consultations with primary teachers from Cumbria to Cornwall.

The consultation process

Prior consultation relating to the National Curriculum has been described as a 'scrambled affair' (Maclure, 1988, p.xi). A discussion paper was circulated at the beginning of the 1987 summer holiday season. The Education Reform Bill containing the National Curriculum proposals was to be introduced to parliament in the autumn of that year, giving about eight weeks for the whole consultation exercise. The effect of the holiday timing was to restrict reflective consideration of the proposals between colleagues. Despite the scramble, there were 18,000 replies, according to an unofficial account of the process compiled from documents deposited in the House of Commons Library (Haviland, 1988). These contained overwhelming endorsement for the idea of an *entitlement* curriculum, i.e., a guaranteed minimum for all five to sixteen year olds in state schools. However, Haviland reports, 'I cannot recall one response that endorses without reservation the *structure* for the curriculum which the Government is proposing' (p.viii). Readers will recall that this, in effect, was Siraj-Blatchford's concern.

Entitlement

As we have seen, the idea of an *entitlement* curriculum had very broad appeal, in principle. An entitlement is a right. The National Curriculum grants access to the same minimum curriculum for all pupils between the ages of five and sixteen. The political arguments for a *national* curriculum were couched in terms of the need for a form of education which would transcend time, place and ideology. A *national* curriculum would rise above local politics and the influence of colleges of education. Both were perceived to be driving the education process and often deemed to be at best misguided, at worst subversive. The curriculum, it was suggested, varied within and between LEAs, leading to different educational experiences and outcomes. Pupils moving from one part of the country to another should be entitled to curriculum continuity. There was no guarantee of this under the present system.

The arguments are most laudable and caught many people off guard. Unfortunately, they are not plausible. Three myths are involved.

The myth of falling standards

Firstly, scope for curriculum variation, pre-National Curriculum, was extremely limited from age eleven, due to the public examination system. This suggests the real targets were the primary and early years with their 'progressive' teaching methods, which allegedly swept the country in the 1960s and 1970s. This is a myth.[1] There is a substantial body of evidence, in the form of HMI reports, indicating steady improvements pre-National Curriculum in the teaching of subject content in primary schools dating from the highly critical HMI National Primary Survey (DES, 1978b). Government financial investment in curriculum support and development, combined with the goodwill and professionalism of primary teachers, were responsible for these improvements which could have continued without the imposition of a National Curriculum (Gura, 1994, pp.131–5).

The myth of the New Age pupil
There is also a mythical quality to the idea that we have become a nation of New Age Travellers wandering from school to school. If we had, our thoughts on continuity and progression would undoubtedly be very different from those enshrined in the Subject Orders. No matter what curriculum is in place, moving from one school to another, even once in a lifetime, is probably only the tip of an iceberg. Moving schools does not happen in isolation from other events, often involving major discontinuities, like family break-up and/or moving house. Stress from *multiple* causes interferes with adjustments to a new school, particularly for young children. Schools best able to cope are surely those which demonstrate concern for the whole person through a flexible curriculum. One which accepts that learning in the early years is a feet-on-the-ground business. It is about *living* and occurs in time and place, not suspended above the clouds in an ideology-free zone. This brings us to our third and final myth.

The myth of the ideology-free curriculum
All curriculum choices are made from a value position. The National Curriculum implicitly values inert bodies of knowledge and some more than others. What is left out is just as much a value statement as what is included. Heavier weighting is given to a formally tested/assessed 'core': English, mathematics and science than to the other foundation subjects of: history, art, geography, design and technology, physical education and music. The division into 'core' and 'other' foundation subjects effectively creates what Alexander (1992, p.46) has termed Curriculum One and Curriculum Two. Under pressure, Curriculum Two loses out to Curriculum One. Even post-Dearing this is causing problems.

Evidence of the value laden nature of curriculum choices became increasingly apparent in the arguments which erupted within the various subject groups responsible for constructing each syllabus. Opinions among specialists in the different disciplines about what counts as worthwhile subject content differed widely and sometimes *fundamentally*. On school subjects Goodson comments that 'The school subject is socially and politically constructed and the actors involved deploy a range of ideological and material resources as they pursue their individual and collective missions' (Goodson, 1992a, p.52).

Aims and means

A recurring theme of the replies to the discussion document was the mismatch between the general aims of the proposed curriculum and the means by which these were to be realised. The aims, carried over from the 1944 Butler Act which the new legislation was to replace, were to promote 'the spiritual, moral, cultural, mental and physical development of pupils in the schools and society' and to prepare such pupils for 'the opportunities, responsibilities and experience of adult life'. Support for this position was virtually unanimous. However, the means chosen to guarantee these aims, with no distinction in principle made between the early and later years of compulsory education, was seen to be self-defeating. It consisted of a raft of *binding legislation* detailing every particular of a subject-based curriculum: separate programmes of study for each subject; attainment targets and assessment procedures. The legislative detail was described by the Institute of Economic Affairs as 'a lawyer's dream and a teacher's nightmare' (Haviland, 1988, p.29).

Validation

In the event, the government ignored such concerns and went ahead with its proposals. The subsequent Dearing Review was intended to demonstrate that consultation on the curriculum was a continuing process, but, as we have seen, the terms of engagement are not negotiable. We may react to the 'givens', but we may not propose structural changes. As a consequence of this, the National Curriculum is validated, i.e., viewed as fit for its purpose, merely by usage, i.e., by default. The consequences can be seen in the fact that one definition of high quality in the *non-statutory* education of three to five year olds is increasingly seen as that of linking into the National Curriculum at Key Stage 1. The question of whether this is a suitable curriculum for children from five to eight, let alone the threes to fives, technically ceases to be relevant. A particularly damaging feature of validation by default, is the false sense of continuity with the past suggested by the use in National Curriculum documents of terms which have different meanings from a developmental perspective, as Siraj-Blatchford demonstrated (Kelly, 1994, pp.51–4). Traffic in terms is not one way, however. Nursery education was recently referred to as 'Key Stage Zero' by an advocate for a form of nursery education which nominates love as a core value position, followed by a sense of self-worth, caring for others and learning how to learn (Ball, 1995, pp.45). Nothing could be further from this than the National Curriculum, so why adopt its terminology? The following anecdote may help to throw light on this.

> Two children (four years) were playing with a set of wooden numerals. They were arranging them in novel combinations from one to nine, delighting in the freedom to do that which comes with the confidence of knowing the 'right' way. The adult who was watching drew their attention to the 'zero' lying unused in the tray: what about this one?
>
> First child: We don't want that. It's nothing.
> Adult: I call it zero.
> Second child: Zero, zero zero. Can I have zero?
> First child: That's not fair, you have to share.

Naming it enabled them to see what had formerly been a 'nothing', of no possible interest and to all intents and purposes invisible. Is this the case with nursery education? Is the price of visibility acceptance of 'Key Stage Zero' status and would that make the years from birth to three Key Stage Minus One?

The Children Act 1989

In government guidelines for the interpretation of the Children Act (1989), the right of children up to the age of eight to an 'environment which facilitates development' (Department of Health, 1991a, para.6.28) is discussed with reference to daycare and educational provision. The guidelines argue for children's sense of identity to be included in the definition of development and suggest this involves respect for religious, human, cultural and linguistic diversity. The addition of individual diversity would make the list even more inclusive. Taken together, these dimensions of diversity in our plural society illustrate the richness and complexity of the educational mission in the early years, where the differences between children are greater than in later years. It takes time for the shared frames of reference to develop which make occasional class-teaching a reasonable proposition. An entitlement curriculum for the early years would recognise that to achieve common goals for children, many *different* starting points and pathways are needed as well as many views of achievement. By insisting on *common* starting points and methods of assessment, the consequences for many children of exposure to the National Curriculum will be failure and disaffection from school at an early age (Barrett, 1989a). In the Introduction to this chapter a number of guiding principles (Figure 0.1) were set out to indicate the value position from which the chapter is written. These are the principles by which the arguments put forward must be judged. The National Curriculum is based on different guiding principles, in particular that of 'statutory entitlement'. This must guide our evaluation of it. If there are children who cannot avail themselves of their statutory entitlement, due to lack of relevance and structures which inhibit 'localising', then by its own values, it is failing those children.

Katz (1971, p.104) wonders whether there is an optimum point beyond which an outsider cannot identify with a teacher's classroom perspective, based as it is on real relationships with real children in real situations. She asks whether a researcher whose interest is measurable input/output variables and the curriculum evaluator whose interest is comparing children, put as high a value on accepting children as found, as the headteacher of a school and does the head in turn, value this as highly as the classroom teacher?

The basic problems many early childhood educators have with the National Curriculum are summarised in Figure 10.1.

Figure 10.1 Early childhood educators' objections to the National Curriculum

- The legalistic interpretation of 'entitlement'
- The lack of consistency between aims and means
- The insensitivity to diversity
- The laying down of the law (literally) about what is worth knowing and doing
- The lack of structural differentiation between ages five and sixteen in terms of developmental appropriateness
- The marginalising of professionalism
- The non-negotiability of professionalism
- The threat to the education of birth to five year olds

The blurring of vision

Since 1988, regulations have operated governing the hours student teachers must spend in the study of English, mathematics and science, the 'core' subjects of the National Curriculum. The time remaining is divided between what is left of the 'whole' curriculum. Consequently, preparation for teaching in nursery or primary schools in terms of distinct pedagogies has all but ceased to exist. Not surprisingly, student teachers and practitioners engaged in early childhood education, particularly those involved with pupils between age five and seven, sometimes express impatience when discussion turns to the consideration of alternatives to the National Curriculum. Advice to tutors to 'get real' is not uncommon.

It is true that many problems and moral conflicts have been caused by the imposition of the National Curriculum. In the struggle to survive, it seems all the more important, therefore, that we do not lose our vision. Without a vision, it is not only we as professionals who are diminished, but also the children and families with whom we have chosen to work.

The early years

The view of curriculum offered here is compatible with argument and critique. It is seen as something necessarily open to development and change because of the interaction between schools and society. Openness to development and change is also created through critical review of research findings, of the writings of philosophers and of authoritative commentators on the educational scene. It is committed to participative action research, ideally involving children, parents, practitioners, academics, administrators and politicians. In this context, *assessment* and *evaluation* are seen as integral to the curriculum, providing frameworks for collaborative planning and reviewing on both a daily and longer term basis. It accepts the right of practitioners to engage in continuous revision of the curriculum to meet the daily challenges of teaching and learning, using their theories of practice developed from experience and opportunities to review aspects of their work individually and together with their peers.

Figure 10.2 Further reflection

Adventuring involves:

- uncertainty and risk
- the ability to sense what is going to lead somewhere
- readiness to adapt continuously according to whether a particular route looks promising and to retreat and try another route when it seems pointless to maintain the present course
- acting so as to secure success as personally defined
- developing the ability to make sense of the environment into which we have ventured and confidence to listen to ourselves

(adapted from Raven, 1990, p.244)

To what extent is it possible for you to adventure in relation to the whole curriculum or to aspects of it? What or who helps to make this possible? What could help? What hinders the process?

The dynamic of this view of curriculum is captured in Raven's idea of *adventuring* outlined in Figure 10.2.

Curriculum from birth to eight years

In the United Kingdom *early childhood education* is a relatively recent form of words used to refer collectively to three traditionally separate groupings concerned with organised education and care: birth to three years; three to five years and five to eight years. Like the Children Act of 1989, it recognises the inseparability of education and care for children from birth to eight years. This is expressed in terms of concern for the 'whole child'.

Prior to the National Curriculum, children from five to eight years experienced a distinctive form of 'infant' education which valued flexibility, choice, informality and active engagement with the physical and social worlds. In character, it had more in common with nursery than junior and secondary education. Despite this, the National Curriculum recognises no fundamental difference between pupils from five to sixteen (Blenkin and Kelly, 1994). Justification for a distinctive approach from birth to eight years can be made by reference to what Gardner (1993) terms educational *constraints*: the biological and environmental conditions and forms of understanding accessible to children during this period of their lives. Constraints create possibilities as well as setting limits.

School starting age

Except for state education in the United Kingdom[2] there is a tendency across cultures for the start of formal, compulsory education to be set at between six and eight years of age. This may be explained by what Tucker (1977) found to be a historically enduring perception of change in the pattern of children's thinking, around the age of seven, towards increased facility for abstract thought. This appears to signal that more formal learning can begin which relies less on concrete experience and personal forms of communication than in the previous period and more on public forms.

This view has support from many researchers, with that of Gardner (1993) being particularly persuasive. The years from birth to between seven and ten years form what Gardner terms the *intuitive* or informal stage of learning, where processes *within* the individual play a key role in determining the forms of understanding accessible to children *without formal instruction.*[3] This is not to say that they cannot benefit from appropriate educational experiences as we shall see later.

The setting of school starting age at five years in the UK has tended to lead to the assumption in the public mind that this is a developmental benchmark signalling 'readiness'. According to an account by Szreter (1964), the setting at five rather than six in 1870, as the age of admission, was the result of impatience on the part of a senior member of parliament over a time-consuming amendment in favour of age six. Given this whimsical background, it is alarming to note the present trend towards an arbitrary, but this time non-statutory, further lowering of the age of admission to four years.

Beginning in the 1980s this accelerating trend was initially a response to a combination of falling primary school rolls and under-provision of nursery education for three to five year olds. Some local authorities adhere to high nursery education standards for what are sometimes termed 'early reception' classes, with appropriately qualified staff and higher adult to child ratios than for older children. During the past decade, we have seen the 'normalising' of age four in the public mind as school starting age. 'Summer born' children may enter classes in September, at the start of the academic year when just turned four years old, where the National Curriculum is being taught to five, six and sometimes seven year olds. The quality of education of these children gives rise to much concern, despite the Dearing Review. Play in school has been a noticeable casualty which particularly affects these younger children. Pressure on teacher time allows little scope for play-partnering between adults and children. For the older children, play is virtually non-existent (Cox and Sanders, 1994). Play has an important role in early childhood education as a means of exploring, sharing, reflecting on and integrating ideas. Learning without play is hurried learning and must inevitably be less thorough and secure (Elkind, 1981).

A further by-product of admitting four year olds to school is to deprive younger children in nursery settings of the companionship and stimulus of being with older children and the four year olds of 'senior' nursery status – a significant rite of passage. Instead they become the 'little ones' again.

Birth to three year olds

The inclusion of children from birth within the scope of the definition of early childhood education is prompted by Winnicott's notion of the baby as a 'going concern' whose growth and development is 'inevitable and unstoppable' (1964, p.29). Too many adults, according to Winnicott, feel responsible for shaping and forming children without being aware of the existence and persistence within children of processes of growth and development. Consequently, they make life difficult for themselves and the children they so wish to help. This view has had much additional support in recent years from studies of newborns, which demonstrate their active engagement with the physical and social worlds.

Very young babies have demonstrated awareness of themselves as causes, controlling and shaping some of the events in their world (Guha, 1988, pp.64–7). Gardner reports (1993, pp.48–9) that under experimental conditions, babies are able to differentiate colours, linguistic sounds and musical patterns; they have expectations about the properties and behaviour of objects and seem to recognise that events may be caused by sources external to themselves. They also demonstrate the makings of a sense of number. Other studies show that babies are deeply interested in other human beings and can hold conversation-like interchanges with supportive adults (Bruner, 1983). Gender role studies indicate that from birth children are learning the *values* of the social groups in which they live (Lloyd, 1987). This has wide-ranging implications for early childhood educators. Values pervade every aspect of our lives and determine the decisions we make about every aspect of the curriculum. Drummond *et al.* (1992) recommend that we ask ourselves *why* we do what we do, in order to uncover the value positions they represent. Figure 10.3 suggests such an exercise. Despite the topic, it is not aimed at those who work with babies and toddlers but at illuminating the pervasiveness of values.

Figure 10.3 Further reflection – values

The town of Reggio Emilia in northern Italy is internationally renowned for the excellence of its approach to the education of children from birth to age six. Babies who have reached the stage where they can crawl about are provided with individual sleep nests, resembling large dog baskets which they can crawl in and out of as they choose. This tells us a great deal about the staff attitude to babies, which in turn affects the way the babies view themselves.

- Can you suggest what these might be?

By way of contrast, visualise the traditional raised cot:

- What does it remind you of?
- Does it suggest anything about the status of babies?

We can use this questioning approach to look at our relationships with families; with children; our choice of equipment; the arrangement of space and time; decisions about content and ways of addressing it; as well as our methods of assessment and evaluation

According to Leach (1994, p.11) research findings in the fields of molecular biology, neurology and biochemistry indicate the years from birth to three are the optimum period for the making, developing and refining of neural connections between brain cells. The process is activated by engagement with the physical and social environments. Along with experts in North America and Japan, Leach feels there is a risk of such findings being used to press for 'formalised' curricula for babies and warns that the processes described can be inhibited by stress.

Given the many indications of the crucial importance of the earliest years for future attitudes to and potential for learning, it is important that the *present* well being and concerns of babies and toddlers are given priority in educational settings. The principle of 'the loving use of power' applies here as throughout early childhood and is non-negotiable (Drummond *et al.*, 1992, p.9).

Three to five years

Children between the ages of three and five years are in a period of transition from dependency to increasing independence. Independence involves risk and this means being allowed to make mistakes and to learn from them. It involves inventing alternative and sometimes extraordinary ways of doing ordinary things. It may involve putting a good result at risk for the possibility of a better one.

It involves making, revising and sometimes breaking rules and endless negotiation; risk of criticism and possibly rejection by peers. Gaining optimum physical, emotional and intellectual independence requires optimum freedom for children and sensitivity on the part of adults about how and when to help and when to stand back. Adults who make premature demands on children at this stage, to attain arbitrary behavioural objectives, put at risk the delicate balancing act which children perform between advancing and withdrawal. Although withdrawal is part of the process, the general trend should be towards increasing responsibility for the self both as an individual and as a member of the group.

Optimum freedom is *freedom within clearly defined limits.* Without the opportunity to try their wings, children become fearful of the unknown, less curious, less resourceful, less creative, less ready for the challenges ahead and more compliant.

Winnicott suggests that children's 'most sacred attribute' is doubt about the self (1996, p.204). If our goal is the liberation of children's minds rather than control of them, then we must permit them to adventure at this time.

Five to eight years

Many early childhood educators share the belief that children have the right to an education which enables them to live their present lives to their fullest human extent. Added to this, in the light of research into the experience of starting school (Barrett, 1986; Woodhead, 1989), the years from five to seven are increasingly seen as a period of adjustment to the culture of school, of becoming a pupil, with the nature of the adjustments changing throughout the period. The initial stages are known to be particularly stressful for many children. Learning to 'be' in school in the early years takes place against a background of continuous negotiation between personal meaning-making systems and the public languages of formal discourse.

Research into children's views of school indicates the overwhelming importance for children of other children in school.[4] Teacher–researcher Vivien Paley suggests that from children's perspectives the core curriculum consists of 3Fs: friendship, fairness and fantasy.[5]

Making, having and keeping friends must be planned for as part of a whole curriculum in the early years. Collaboration rather than competition is therefore an important guiding principle.

The mechanistic structures of the National Curriculum, especially in terms of assessment, combined with publication of test results, suggests that the induction aspect of early childhood education has become a victim of pressures to get children on target, not only for tests at seven, but increasingly, through *baseline* testing, at five years.[6]

In this section, the proposition that the early childhood curriculum should concern itself with the educational rights and needs of children from birth to eight has been examined. It is seen as offering protection to children from inappropriate experiences while at the same time projecting what might be termed the special mission of each age group within the larger group. Continuity and progression within and between the age groups is seen in terms of ever-expanding horizons.

In the next section, we take a closer look at common features of the curriculum from birth to eight years. Children are viewed as *going concerns* and *meaning makers* and education is seen as the process which supports and furthers their meaning-making in all areas of experience and learning: linguistic; aesthetic and creative; human and social; mathematical; moral; physical; scientific; technological and spiritual (DES, 1990, para.71).

Active learning

The idea of 'active learning' and the roles played in this by concrete or 'hands on' experience and learners' interests, are familiar aspects of many early childhood curricula and were characteristic of the thinking of Montessori, Isaacs, Pestalozzi and Piaget.[7] In the late 1950s, under the influence of Piagetian cognitive psychology, a curriculum approach began to emerge which was shared by schools in both the primary and nursery sectors in the UK. Its most significant feature was the view of learning as a continuous and active mental process of meaning making.[8] According to the theory, learning is not a linear input–output process. Information is not simply absorbed or added whole to a memory store, but worked on until it makes sense in terms of the learner's existing frames of reference: 'Deliver us from evil' becomes 'Deliver us from eagles' because it makes sense to the listener.[9] This is a *constructive* error, indicating the active nature of meaning making. Classic examples of constructive error are 'foots' and 'sheeps' caused by over-generalisation of the add-an-s rule to make the plural form. In making sense, it is sometimes the existing frames of reference, within the learner which have to be adapted. Each of the above errors may eventually be corrected internally as a result of further learning. Here is another example of an existing understanding being updated:

> Lucy (three +) was asked to go next door to borrow an egg to put in a cake. She set off, reappearing seconds later with a query 'What are you going to do with it?' After several minutes of talking at cross purposes centred on the meaning of 'borrow' the errand was successfully negotiated. The business of 'borrowing' had great salience for her at the time, due to property disputes involving best friends and favourite toys. Essentially, for her, borrowing involved not only the eventual return of an item, it must also be *intact*, ergo can one 'borrow' an egg which is to be broken into a cake mix, baked and eaten? Adjustments in understandings took place on both sides of the discussion.

To tell or not to tell

Early childhood educators are reluctant to spend precious time telling children about the world because there is very little that can simply be 'told'. That which can be, tends to make very little difference to the learner, particularly if the information was not sought. Ideas are not freestanding 'things' which one has or has not in one's grasp at a given moment.

One early childhood educator struggled to discover how she might teach Attainment Target 2, Level 1 of history in the National Curriculum. This states that children should be able to: understand that stories may be about real people or fictional characters. As an example it suggests that they should be able to recognise the difference between a fairy tale and a story about the past. The teacher, Gill Crowley (personal communication), elected to follow up the example in a small-scale study, with a group of five to six year olds. The children were uninterested in genre. They enjoyed the stories, although not all of them equally. Each child engaged with each story in a personal way. Academic concerns and categorisations were their teacher's problem, not theirs and they were puzzled by her questions, despite the sensitivity with which they were put and the active struggle of both children and adult to make sense to each other. A sample of dialogue follows relating to a folktale about a hen who dreamed of saving the world. The teacher is probing the children's understandings, in the hope of steering them towards a definition of make believe:

GC: Can hens dream?
S: No
C: No
N: Yes
GC: Hens can dream?
K: Seals cry
J: You can see their tears
S and C are swayed by the seal evidence and now agree that hens can dream

Would *telling* them make the slightest difference to the lives of these children? Discussion can be a very powerful means of making sense but only where control is shared. Teachers of five to eight year olds have little control of the curriculum. This in turn decreases the scope for sharing control with children. An unanticipated variable in this study was the books from which the stories were read. As physical objects they were used by the children as a source of clues in coping with the topic of fact and fiction. Worn looking books were deemed to be old and therefore about the past. Illustrations were proof of reality. Black and white photographs represented real past events; colour photographs, real contemporary events. It is difficult not to be awestruck by the tenacity, not to say courtesy, of children as meaning makers and all the more important that we think before and after we teach.

Matching and motivation

The understandings which learners already have determine what can be learned from new experiences. This is the basis of the pedagogical principle of starting 'where the child is'. Consistent with this is the idea of using children's interests, beliefs, aspirations and concerns as necessary starting points to further learning.

Observation is the preferred means by which children's present understandings and interests are assessed and these are used as the basis for planning experiences for learning. This does not mean, as is sometimes suggested, that an individual curriculum is planned for each child. Within any age group, and even mixed age groups which have a shared history, there will be common interests and concerns. This is one reason that an approach based on *projects* is regarded as an important and powerful structure for the framing of content (Katz and Chard, 1989; Edwards *et al.*, 1995).

Post-Piagetian research gives the project approach a boost by suggesting that it is better for young children to become experts on a few topics which they find intrinsically absorbing, than to be uncommitted novices at everything. Inagaki, a science educator, describes a study of five to six year olds who were engaged in the care of goldfish over a period at home. As might be expected, these children demonstrated their greater knowledge and understanding of goldfish than others who had not been involved. What is more interesting is that they also tended to extrapolate from the knowledge acquired through caring for goldfish in speculating about the reactions of creatures like frogs to a variety of situations. Inagaki concludes that knowledge gained in the pursuit of a keenly felt interest, may be used as frames of reference for reasoning and gaining knowledge in related areas (1992, pp.127–8).

Children's consuming interests outside as well as inside school offer important clues to the kinds of experiences to which they will be able to relate.

The two contexts of learning

Piagetian theory locates the processes of making sense within the individual mind. Vygotsky[10] suggests this is only half the story: we are social creatures and our individual meaning making is mediated by the meanings we encounter in the social world. The examples offered in this chapter would support the Vygotskian view. In private we may call a spade anything we like, but to understand and be understood by others we must learn to call a spade a spade. Vygotsky proposes a two-way trade relationship between individual minds and the minds of others. In early infancy 'others' will be particular people, like family members. The category 'others' gradually extends to friends and wider cultural groupings in the community and further afield. 'Others' represent the *outer* or social context of learning, the individual represents the *inner*. Outer and inner trade with each other continuously, with each helping to transform the other in the process. Nothing stands still. In this way, individuals and others come to resemble *and* differ from each other.

Time and space

Curriculum arrangements must acknowledge both contexts of learning, otherwise we waste one half of our human potential, whether this is the individual or social half. Space must be allowed for freedom of movement and assembly. Generous blocks of time must be allocated for total immersion in activities which are agreed to be relevant and worth doing for their own sake. There must also be time and space for being alone, for communicating with the self.

Our arrangements of time and space send messages to children about the valuing of self and others.[11] The inner and outer contexts of learning are not alternatives. They interpenetrate and together make up the human experience of learning.

Symbolic representation

The power of children's thinking is often concealed by a restricted adult view of language and literacy. The liberation of children's minds so that they can participate fully in the making of personal and social meanings involves the right to be understood in what Malaguzzi (1995, p.vi) refers to as the 'hundred languages of children'. This is a reference to the infinitely varied ways in which children search for, secure and express meanings in the early years: exploration and investigation of the world as it is and as it might be through play; dreaming; talking; listening; drawing; writing; painting; three-dimensional modelling; collecting, patterning; music-making, moving, dancing and singing; creating, inventing, designing; numbering and counting; wondering and contemplating; laughing and crying, loving and hating; caring and ... on and on.

The languages of early childhood contain the seeds of the more culturally determined languages which will, in the years to follow, structure their development in the areas of experience and learning listed earlier: linguistic; aesthetic and creative; human and social; mathematical; moral; physical; scientific; technological and spiritual. A fast-growing area of research is the identification of points of contact between the intuitive theories of mind, matter, time and space, cause and effect and the rule-governed disciplines of formal education.[12] There is no easy and obvious passage from one to the other. This flies in the face of the National Curriculum view which suggests a seamless continuum. Gardner (1993) suggests that only by recognising the qualitative difference between intuitive and culturally determined ways of making sense will ways forward be found. In the meantime, we can support and encourage children's playful appropriation of public forms of making sense, as they do with the writing and number systems encountered in their everyday world:

> A small group of three to six year olds are discussing their ages and finding the appropriate matching numeral from the assortment in the tray. Sean says he is three and a half and places a three on the magnetic board.
> Adult: 'Three. That's good. Now what about the half? Shall I show you how to do that?' (Sean nods. Andrew and Joshua move closer.) Next to Sean's three, the adult creates the symbol for 'half' with three pieces: 'There you are, Sean. Now it says three and a half.'
> Sean is very pleased but Joshua is enthralled. He promptly copies the three and a half, telling anyone who cares to listen: 'That says three and a half.' Then, announcing each one as he goes along, he makes four and a half, eight and a half, nought and a half, nine and a half, two and a half. At this point he stops and reads them all back.
> (personal observation, PG)[13]

Play and games

Play is a form of adventuring. Games have socially defined rules which impose limits on the extent to which players may adventure. Eisner (1990) suggests that a balance needs to be struck in education between playful and gamelike experiences; between invention and exploration and operating within social conventions, such as academic disciplines. He contrasts the incidental discovery that a dining fork can be used for flicking peas, with the conventional use of the fork as an eating utensil. Under social pressure, the playful use is sacrificed to the conventional. An entitlement curriculum will therefore be one which values both playful and gamelike experiences for the contribution both can make to the development of the individual and society.

Summary and conclusions

In this chapter, two views of entitlement have been examined: the legalistic and the moral. The legalistic, represented by the National Curriculum, was based on the acquisition of inert bodies of knowledge; the moral on people and meaning making.

These two positions represent fundamentally different value systems. Given such differences, common ground is hard to find. Early childhood educators struggle to create it, at the risk of seeming to endorse the knowledge-based curriculum.

The irony of the legal structuring of the knowledge centred view is that it is designed to ensure access. By legislating for the 'delivery' of the same content for everyone of the same age, at the same time, regardless, many children will inevitably be disenfranchised.

The legal view handicaps educators and children by inhibiting, if not prohibiting 'localising' of the curriculum, to take account of diversity. The moral view recognises individual and cultural diversity in organising for many points of entry and pathways to common goals. Arguments in favour of a curriculum for children from birth to eight have been offered in terms which seek to protect children from inappropriate experiences. The impression that the influence of the National Curriculum is bearing down on children before the age of five is inescapable. Diagnostic baseline testing of five year olds is on the increase. The frames of reference for these are the National Curriculum core. How long will it be before nurseries are expected to teach to the test? Leach (1994) is surely right, given this downward creep, to be concerned about formal curricula for babies and toddlers.

In addition to protection of their rights, a positive alternative to the National Curriculum has been put forward which values young children's minds and concerns and seeks to liberate not control them.

Rather than suggest that early childhood educators adopting the moral position have all the answers, a dynamic, searching, critical view of the curriculum has been proposed with all participants having a voice. The objections to the National Curriculum on behalf of young children have not been about knowledge, as such. That would be nonsense. They have been about the premature introduction of formal, rule governed ways of making sense to people who have no use for them, yet. They have urgent business of their own to attend to and ways of going about it. This is what early childhood educators must compete with in order to impose unsolicited bodies of knowledge. Instead of working with the grain they are required to go against it. In the absence of relevance, they have to think of ways to motivate children. This makes them less, rather than more responsible for their own learning.

The crowning irony is that the intuitive theories of mind, matter and such which young children develop informally will, according to Gardner (1993), still be influencing their thinking, long after they have forgotten everything they ever learned from the age of ten or so – unless something is done about the education of older pupils.

Notes

1. Bennett (1976): although Bennett was critical of aspects of teaching in junior schools, he is mistakenly (or mischievously) credited with confirming rampant progressivism in the 1960 and 1970s. He records finding little evidence of permissiveness taking over our primary schools.
2. New Commonwealth countries also tend towards age five – a legacy of former colonial rule and former ties with the UK.
3. According to Gardner, intuititive ways of making sense remain throughout our lives as part of our thinking repertoire, often reasserting themselves after the end of formal schooling, as our dominant mode. This may occur, even where adults hold degrees in one or other of the academic disciplines, if their learning after the early years has been without understanding.
4. Langsted (1994) offers revealing insights about school from children's perspectives.
5. Paley (1988, p.12) fantasy refers to make believe play which has a dreamlike quality.
6. Bosely (1995) describes baseline testing in Birmingham.
7. See Kamii (1975, pp.84–6) for brief review of active approaches.
8. This view of learning is sometimes referred to as 'constructivist'.
9. Dixon (1989) warns against making assumptions about the meanings children are making of common experiences and offers this line from the Lord's Prayer of the Christian faith as an example.
10. Vygotsky (1978) was a Soviet psychologist whose work was published and disseminated in the West, posthumously. Interpretations of his work can be found in Bruner and Haste (1987a) and Wood (1988).
11. McAuley and Jackson (1992) discuss a range of 'learning structures' in terms of the implicit value systems they represent.
12. Taken together, the following texts give an overview of work in this area: Aubrey (1994), Coghill (1989), Gifford (1995), Goldsmiths' Association for Early Childhood (1994), Haste (1987), Inagaki (1992) and Whitehead (1990).
13. Gifford (1995) review of research into early number and progress report of an action research project directed by Gifford, based at the Early Childhood Centre, Roehampton Institute, London.

Chapter 11

The physical environment

Sue Robson

Introduction

> Until this matter of environment is settled no method can save us.
>
> (McMillan, 1930, p.2)

The nursery and school classroom environments within which we 'live' (McLean, 1991) have an effect upon us all. Underlying the ways in which these spaces are organised are the philosophies of schools and teachers, and their beliefs about care and learning, and the most effective ways of organising for them. Many early years settings will inevitably contain much similar apparatus, and may be organized in what seem to be physically quite similar ways. Any similarities may, however, end there. The provision we make comes to life through the ways in which it is used, and it would be very wrong to equate *provision* with *curriculum*. It is what we *do*, or, more importantly, what the *children* do, with the environment and materials in it which matters. As Hartley demonstrates, things have the potential to be used in very different ways, depending on our beliefs, and the ways in which those beliefs are enacted in our planning. He describes two nurseries, each containing much the same basic equipment, and each espousing broadly similar reasons for the physical organisation they favoured: 'To be structured so they [the children] can be unstructured' and 'The freedom to control themselves' (Hartley, 1987, p.63). In practice, their appearance, and what went on in both, was quite different.

It is this *difference* which is crucial. Blenkin and Whitehead suggest that the creation of an environment or setting is 'the most neglected and misunderstood dimension of the planned curriculum' (1988, p.36) because it is often seen as peripheral to the *real* task of curriculum planning. In reality, attention to the environment in which we live and work is central to the task of teaching, providing the physical context to working with young children. Clarke-Stewart (1991) has identified several indicators of quality that impinge upon children's development, among which is a well organised and stimulating physical environment. The potential exists, then, for the physical setting to have a positive impact upon the children in it. By implication the converse is also possible: that the physical features of the places in which young children are expected to live and learn can lead to poorer quality for them (Stephen and Wilkinson, 1995).

Undoubtedly (and unfortunately) some aspects of these environments can be beyond our power to change. You may be working in a purpose-built centre with sufficient indoor and outdoor space, good equipment and appropriate furnishings. On the other hand, many more of us may find ourselves in spaces less suitable: classrooms converted for use with young children, no outdoor space, toilets a long trek away from the classroom, little appropriate equipment and furnishings which have all the appearance of having been collected by a committee at a jumble sale. As Goldschmied and Jackson (1994) point out, commercial organisations often spend huge sums of money in order to create an attractive environment for customers during their brief stay, while children are often condemned to pass their most formative school years in less than ideal surroundings.

A seemingly poor environment, though, can never be used as an excuse for offering poor quality to the children. A preliminary finding of the research project 'Principles into Practice: improving the quality of children's early learning' is 'that quality is a matter of well-qualified professional people and their commitment to young children; it is not simply appropriate resources, and it is certainly not bureaucratic structures' (Whitehead, 1994, p.28). In this chapter I want to look at the ways in which we, as 'professional people', can make the most of the spaces we do have, to provide an environment in which adults and children alike can live and work happily, and which has a positive impact upon each child's development. We shall consider why it is so important to plan our environment, and how this can contribute to our aims for young children, and then look at some aspects of this organisation. While you are reading, you may find it useful to think about classrooms with which you are familiar, looking particularly at what seem to be the underlying assumptions and beliefs about teaching, learning and the care of young children.

Why do we need to plan our environment?

Perhaps the chief reason we need to consider how the classroom, unit or centre is physically organised is one which underpins all aspects of working with young children, that what we do should never become 'a standard practice beyond ... reflection' (Hartley, 1987, p.66). This is particularly important when considering the organisation of space and resources, because the 'givens' (Wood *et al.*, 1980) are so many. Opportunities to alter the physical construction of buildings, removing walls, for example, are rare, and we cannot just go and buy whatever equipment we think we need because money is often very limited. All of this can lead us towards focusing on limitations rather than possibilities: 'I can't do that, because ...', rather than 'how can I do that with what I've got, or what I can get hold of?' While this should not be taken to mean that working with young children is about 'make do and mend' (for it certainly is not), it does imply the importance of continued reappraisal of the environment, and its appropriacy for the children concerned and their needs and interests. The needs of four-year-old children in a nursery or reception class may be very different to those of one year olds in a nursery centre, or six year olds in an infant class, and organisation must reflect these differences.

Some features of learning and young children

What must always drive this reappraisal are our aims for the children in our care, our beliefs about what will be most appropriate for them, and about the nature of learning. Concern for the physical dimension of the classroom is a means to these ends, and not an end in itself. What, then, do we know about how young children learn? Pat Gura, in Chapter 10, described what she called 'the two contexts of learning', commenting that curriculum arrangements must acknowledge both the inner, or individual context, and the outer, or social context of learning: 'They interpenetrate and together make up the human experience of learning' (p.149). This emphasis, supported by much research and writing in recent years,[1] suggests the need for an environment which facilitates and supports children's efforts as social beings, and the idea of learning as a social process. Alongside this, Blenkin and Whitehead suggest that 'The underlying principle which should guide the establishment of such an environment is that it must enable the children to be active in learning' (1988, p.47). Taken together, they imply a need to ensure that young children have opportunities to be physically and mentally active,[2] in an environment which allows them to collaborate with others, both adults and children, as well as offering them opportunities to play and work alone.

Tizard and Hughes (1984) suggest that what characterises young children is their relative ignorance and a limited conceptual framework with which to organise their experience and thought. Part of our energies, then, will need to be directed towards providing a wide range of worthwhile experiences for them, which reflect children's own interests, and acknowledge their importance for them. In so doing, it is worth bearing in mind that young children seem to learn most from self-chosen play activities, and opportunities for children to choose and develop those experiences for themselves will be of particular importance. There is now considerable consensus (Clark, 1988), supported by HMI (1989b) and OFSTED (1993a), that the quality of opportunities young children have for both play and talk will be crucial to their development, and that these two are the chief vehicles by which young children learn. The environment, then, must offer high-quality opportunities for children to be playful and engage in play, alone and with others, and to develop their linguistic skills with a range of talk partners. We shall look later at how this may happen in practice.

All of these aims are, so far, essentially cognitive ones related to young children's intellectual growth. Others are also central to their development. The social, emotional and physical development of young children are all concerns for the professionals working with them, and will be reflected in the provision made. Socially, for example, the aim of developing children's capacity to share and to collaborate with others, will affect the organisation set up. Other aims may be more particular to individual centres or places. Karrby and Giota, for example, commenting on Swedish day-care centres, stress the goal of creating 'a stimulating social environment for the children in which democratic values are expressed in the practice and relationships within the preschool' (1994, p.4).

Planning and provision

What kinds of experiences, then, is it appropriate to plan for young children? HMI (1989b) suggest the appropriacy of nine areas of learning and experience: linguistic; aesthetic and creative; human and social; mathematical; moral; physical; scientific; technological; and spiritual. This framework is also used throughout the Rumbold Report, *Starting With Quality* (DES, 1990). These 'areas' are conceptual rather than physical, but they can help us to organise our thinking about the kind of provision we make. Similarly, Athey's work on schemas (Athey, 1990) can provide much invaluable information about the patterns and commonalities in young children's actions and thinking, and the ways in which provision can meet their interests.

The New Zealand Draft Guidelines for Developmentally Appropriate Programmes in Early Childhood Services, that is, from birth to school age, (Ministry of Education (New Zealand), 1993) set out five aims, which are there to inform planning and activities:

1 *Well-being.* The health and well being of the child is protected and nurtured.
2 *Belonging.* Children and their families feel a sense of belonging.
3 *Contribution.* Opportunities for learning are equitable and each child's contribution is valued.
4 *Communication.* The languages and symbols of their own and other cultures are promoted and protected.
5 *Exploration.* The child learns through active exploration of the environment.

(Ministry of Education (New Zealand), 1993)

Each aim is elaborated through a series of goals, all of which are prefaced by the need to ensure that children will experience an environment in which the goal can be met. This close relationship clearly demonstrates the way in which aims and provision must function together in early childhood services.

How do children 'read' the environment?

What of the children themselves? Pat Gura (Chapter 10) has commented on the way in which arrangements of time and space send messages to the children.

These messages may be about a range of issues. As she says, they will be about the valuing of self and others, they may also tell children much about what is sanctioned and prized in the classroom. The space given to particular types of activity, the presence or absence of adults in particular areas of the room, the proximity of different areas and materials, all say much to children about what has value and status in a particular unit. Jackson (1987) makes a strong case for suggesting that children's capacity to make sense of these messages and to grasp the organisational procedures of the classroom will condition their access to the learning opportunities within it. Not only that, but if they fail to do so and remain unaware of classroom routines and expectations, they may be regarded as unsuccessful by the adults concerned, with all that this can imply for those adults' future expectations of them. There surely can be no need for further justification of the importance of considering how we organise the environment.

Settings, and the ways in which we organise them, then, have an effect on all of those within them. Dowling (1992) maintains that they affect the ways in which we work, and the evidence of Sylva *et al.* (1980) and Smith and Connelly (1981) suggests that the quality of children's play is affected by design and layout of space. Pascal provides a poignant reminder that it can affect not just what children do, but, importantly, how they feel, in her record of a teacher's comment:

> I have just moved with a group of children from the nursery class to the reception class and the difference was so dramatic. Gone was the wonderful space, the large apparatus, jigsaws, construction toys ... I felt frustrated and disappointed – can you imagine how the children felt?
>
> (Pascal, 1990, p.23)

How can these underpinning principles and beliefs be reflected in the ways in which the environment is organised? The environment is, of course, ultimately the totality of children's experience at school,[3] but in order to look closely it can be considered in particular areas, beginning with basic structure and organisation.[4]

Fitness and flexibility

In considering the way in which the space is to be used, it is worth borrowing a phrase given prominence in Alexander *et al.* (1992),[5] that of 'fitness for purpose'. In the present context this means thinking about developing spaces appropriate to the ages and stages of the children who are to use them. This involves a recognition of the differing needs of young children. Provision appropriate for the under threes will differ, for example, for that we make for four year olds. Pat Gura, in Chapter 10, commented on the fact that it takes time for the shared frames of reference which make occasional class teaching appropriate to occur (p.141). What need, is there, then, to think about designing a space in which the whole class or unit can be 'taught' at the same time? Similarly, if one of our intentions is for children to develop a disposition to work and play collaboratively, we shall need to reflect this in aspects such as seating arrangements.[6] In setting out room arrangements for the youngest children, Whalley (1994) and Goldschmied and Jackson (1994) put forward cases for two different types of organisation. Whalley documents the decision made by staff at Pen Green Family Centre, not to separate the under and over three year olds, and to have family groups rather than a baby room, toddler room and preschool room. Their decision was based on ideological as well as physical grounds (p.36). By contrast, Goldschmied and Jackson suggest the desirability of age grouping in day-care centres (p.19). This well illustrates that, ultimately, there are no universally applicable answers, only solutions that are right for a particular situation, at a particular time.

Appraising the environment

Above all, it will be necessary to be very familiar with the space available, and with all that it contains. We will need to be clear about the possibilities it holds, and to appraise the worth of equipment. In the end, the only way to do this is to have first-hand experience of using the space and its contents, relying neither on the fact that it is already there, nor on an idea that something is so much a part of the early years 'tradition' that we cannot *not* have it. At Redford House, for example, discussed in Chapter 4, a billiard table, not always seen as an essential piece of nursery equipment, is there for those children in a trajectory schema, and whose interests are in straight lines, stripes, hitting and throwing.[7] This illustrates well how the provision you make can be varied and unusual, while supporting your aims and beliefs. Goldschmied and Jackson suggest that it can be worthwhile holding a meeting for all who use a particular space (and I would suggest that this could be adults and children alike) where the theme is 'What I would like to keep in this room and what I would like to get rid of' (1994, p.22), as a way of really appraising the fitness for purpose of materials, equipment and spaces, as well as it being a mechanism for avoiding visual chaos.

Arranging space

In many schools, classrooms for older infants and junior age children are arranged in areas with a distinct curriculum focus – a maths area, an art area, a writing area and so on. A development on this is to think in terms of learning centres, which combine subjects, for example bays for Investigation (essentially science, maths, technology), Language (mainly English, history, geography) and Creative (mostly art, design, music) (Moyles, 1992, p.45). Is such a form of organisation similarly appropriate for younger children, too? Nash (1981) compared the experiences of four- and five-year-old children, working in classrooms organised in two different ways, nineteen so-called 'spatially planned' rooms, and nineteen 'randomly arranged'. Decisions about how to arrange materials in the randomly arranged rooms were made on what Nash calls 'housekeeping criteria less relevant to learning objectives' (p.147). That is, considerations such as noise and availability of water, and, in some cases, no stated criteria at all. The spatially planned classrooms had areas for Oral Language, Number and Science concept development, Fine Motor and Visual and Auditory Readiness, Creative Skills and

Ideas, and Gross Motor. The conclusion of the research was that, on a range of measures, the teachers' planned 'desired learning outcomes' (p.154)[8] were best fulfilled in the spatially planned classrooms. Nash is keen to point out that the randomly arranged rooms were 'no less powerful in producing learning' (p.154), but that this was not the learning intended by the teachers.

Nash's study seems to demonstrate clearly that the balance and distribution of space, materials, people and time can influence children's development and the fulfilment of staff's aims (and thus, by implication, also make it less valuable for children in 'random' or unconsidered arrangements). However, the strong emphasis on the adult having identified and pre-specified learning objectives for all of the child's activities could lead us to take less account of children's own competence in expressing their own needs and interests, and taking some control of their own learning. Children, in Nash's study, were encouraged by the arrangement of the room to use the variety of materials *within* an area, thus making worthwhile connections in that way, but not to make connections *across* areas, for example, by using equipment from the Creative Skills and Ideas area in their Gross Motor play. One child cited by Nash talks eloquently of what you can (and cannot do) in various classroom areas. As McAuley and Jackson (1992) point out, he is 'a Mozart, except that for "music" read "pigeonholes"!' (p.64).

The major disadvantage of what Nash suggests is that it may lead us to view equipment, spaces and materials as having specific purposes and distinct characteristics, which may preclude both adults and children thinking of their use in novel ways, and ways in which meaningful and worthwhile connections can be made. One feature of successful learning is the capability to transfer knowledge and understanding from one area to another, and the making of useful connections between ideas. If we wish to develop such competence in young children, a material provision which reflects this flexibility is vital.

What may be most useful is to consider the space available as a range of clearly defined different areas, ordered partly according to necessary 'housekeeping' criteria (there are, after all, very good reasons for siting art areas near a sink and on an easily cleaned floor surface, and similarly books and construction areas may not be good neighbours), and partly with a view to facilitating interesting associations and creative transformations of materials. Thus, physical proximity of areas, for example, home corners and block play areas, may enrich children's play through the combination of materials from both, but children can also be encouraged to feel able to move a whole range of materials and equipment about, to suit their purposes. Cleave and Brown illustrate this well:

> A group of children observed playing in the home corner first kitted themselves out with shoes from the 'shoe shop'. They made a vehicle from the large construction blocks and went on a journey. It was a hot day so the children used paper provided from the painting and writing tables to make a fan to cool themselves. They returned to the 'vehicle' fanning themselves as they travelled back to the home corner for 'lunch'.
>
> (1991, p.151)

Of course, there are practical considerations here, as I have noted elsewhere (Robson, 1992). The emptying of paint into the water tray by a child may be seen more as a nuisance and a disruption to the play of other children than as an interesting transformation for one child. It can, though, surely be accommodated – a bowl for experimentation and a discussion about the implications of their actions may be what is required. The Froebel Blockplay Research Group point to the dilemma sometimes posed by particular pieces of equipment such as blocks: transporters 'can transport anything, 'whereas builders *need blocks*' (their emphasis) (Gura, 1992, p.161). But this too, can be a subject for discussion and negotiation, and can also be about another important aspect of nursery life, that of caring for the environment, and carefully restoring apparatus to its original place once you have finished with it.

All of this leads me to conclude that a 'transparent structure' (Hutt *et al.*, 1989, p.230), which encourages neither the children nor the adults involved to view the nursery spaces in rigid terms may be most desirable. Hutt and his colleagues concluded that, where such rigidity was a feature, children's play tended to be more stereotypical, and less innovative. The dry sand and water trays, for example, they found to be places where children could, essentially, be alone. Play was usually in parallel, and 'one can shut out some of the hustle and bustle endemic to nurseries' (p.98). There is, of course, a need for quiet niches in the nursery, where children can be alone if they so choose. However, to see an element of provision such as the dry sand as a haven of solitude may not be using it to its full potential. There is a need for different 'micro-environments' (p.98) in the nursery, but, as McAuley and Jackson conclude: 'Adult involvement together with reflection on the purpose and value of all areas of provision should enhance the quality of *all* "micro-environments"' (1992, p.68).

Freedom of access

Implicit in this sort of organisation is freedom of access for children, with opportunities for them to develop autonomy and a sense of control. Pat Gura has commented (Chapter 10) on the provision in some Italian nurseries of low 'sleep nests' for babies and toddlers, containing their own belongings, and into which they can crawl, by themselves, to take a nap. Traditional, high-sided cots obviously require adult help for this. Older children in the nursery can be helped to take responsibility for themselves, making decisions and selecting resources as they need them. So, materials, equipment and all areas of the nursery, both indoor and out, need, as far as possible to be freely accessible to children at all times.'Children need opportunities in becoming proficient when they are ready, not when teachers are ready' (Bruce, 1987, p.59). What messages might we be giving to children, and how much more dependent upon us are we making them if we have decided beforehand everything that can be out for them to use, with other things kept behind closed doors to which they have no access? Pragmatically, too, such a system will increase the number of low-level demands made upon adults, to service requests for materials (McLean, 1991, p.168).

In practice, staff attitudes will condition children's feelings of 'permission' to use equipment, the timetable will need to ensure that children can have access, and materials and equipment will need to be stored in such a way that children can not only retrieve what they need when they need it (and not when an adult can reach it for them) but they can also put it back ready for someone else. Shelves and containers clearly labelled (with words and pictures), at child height can contribute to this independence. Some nurseries and classrooms have silhouetted shapes of equipment stuck on walls and shelves, which readily identifies not only where a tool goes, but also if something is missing. The attitudes of adults, in giving children responsibility, and in helping them to take on some of the routines which assist this independence, will be crucial to its success as a strategy. Tidying up times also then have the potential to be occasions for real conversations between adults and children, discussing where materials are kept, resolving problems, and sharing responsibilities. Children are capable of taking on much of this responsibility for caring for their environment, particularly if they are shown how to, and are provided with the right cloths, mops, brushes and pans for doing so. It is also a far more satisfactory experience for a child to have been responsible for getting their own paper out, clipping it to an easel, painting, putting the finished painting to dry on a rack or line and then cleaning the easel ready for the next child than to have their part of the process limited to the act of painting itself.

Organising time

Time itself is an important resource in the classroom, which needs to be organised with the same care as any other aspect of provision. Children's time in school is often fragmented by organisational aspects outside their (and sometimes their teachers') control. Timetabling the use of shared facilities, assemblies, lunch breaks and the deployment of specialist staff can all contribute to a day punctuated by interruptions: 'I just got to the interestin' bit ... I don't care about the time ... that's plain stupid ... time's as long as it takes' is the grumble Cousins overhears one boy making about the interruptions to his day (1990, p.31). Other children may not start an activity, knowing, from past experience, that they will not have the chance to complete it because of the restricted time available. What need, then, is there to break up the time available in the classroom or unit any more than is necessary? Too much dependence on the routine of a strict timetable may not be good for adults either. Suransky (1982) quotes the following exchange in a nursery: 'Samantha approached teacher Sally and said she was hungry. Teacher Sally looked at her and said,"It's not hungry time yet!"' (p.60).

If children are to feel enabled to take on challenges, and to sustain their interest over a long period then they will need to have the opportunity for continuous uninterrupted activity, and to know that this will be the case. This includes opportunities to carry on with an activity or project from one day to another, so space for storing these will also be important. The Froebel Blockplay Research Group comment on the way a 'hit and run' approach to block play can occur in children where lack of time prevents them from embarking on the sort of blockplay that develops over a sustained period (Gura, 1992). They suggest that such a description may apply in many situations where insufficient time is allowed for play to develop. So, a flexible approach to timetabling and daily routines, where children have opportunities for sustained activity, can take breaks for snacks and drinks as they need, while also knowing what time constraints there are, will be most appropriate for young children. At the same time, thought will need to be given to ensuring that events are not so unstructured as to leave children feeling confused and uncertain.

As a final note here, this flexible approach is also useful for adults in appraising the use of the nursery space. Careful observation of what children are taking where, of how they are using and transforming materials, and to what purposes they are putting equipment, can be invaluable in deciding future provision, and in making adjustments to space.

Equal opportunities: access to the classroom

The obligation all professionals working with young children have for ensuring equality of opportunity is looked at in Chapters 8 and 9 in this book. One of the factors which will condition the ways in which such aims can be realised is the quality and type of material provision made, to ensure that all children have access to the events of the classroom, and to counter stereotyping and prejudice. A wide range of resources, representing many cultures and not supportive of stereotypes of race, gender, class and disability is one element of this provision, but it must be complemented by the ways in which that provision is used. Much research[9] points to the attraction of different types of activities for boys and girls in the classroom, with consequent effects upon teachers' perceptions of their maturity, adjustment to school, and behaviour. Davies and Brember (1994) comment on boys' attraction to blocks, climbing areas and the outside, contrasting this with girls' apparent preference for table-top activities and domestic play. As a result, girls, involved in activities with more stable social groupings, and certainly less physically active play, may appear calmer and more settled. Added to this, Hutt *et al.* (1989) observed that girls tended to be attracted to activities where adults were present, whereas boys were more oriented towards objects, and not people, but that in all areas adult presence lengthened children's attention spans at an activity. Within the nursery there is often a tendency for adults to become involved in some areas much more than others. Creative and collage tables, for example, tend to have high levels of adult involvement, construction areas much less so. In practice, then, girls will often be the ones who benefit most from adult support and extension, and both sexes will tend to persist in a narrower range of activities.

What can be done about such a situation? Various approaches have been tried, including timetabling the use of equipment, although, as Judd (1988) points out, this is not a straightforward solution. A girls-only block play session ended in boys attacking the girls' structure when she was called away, and the girls fled. One important way of effecting change would be to ensure that adults become involved in all areas of the nursery, encouraging boys and girls to experience a wider range of activities. Similarly, facilitating mixed-age play may also be beneficial for children.

One undoubted fact which may also influence children's access to the classroom is the predominance of women in primary and early years settings. Michael Annan, a black male primary teacher, draws attention to the way in which 'even key elements in good practice – home corners, a particular approach to display – seemed to reflect a predominantly female culture' (1993, p.100), and generally a white middle-class one at that. As a professional, he describes the way in which he had to find his own way in establishing a place for himself, something children also need to do. The culture of the classroom will, then, need to encompass many viewpoints and experiences if all children are to derive most benefit from it.

Take a long hard look ...

None of us ever has what we might think of as the 'perfect' space, so using what we do have to the very best advantage is vital. Before thinking about what you are going to do with the furniture and equipment, look long and hard at the basic space, indoor and out, and think about its possibilities and its constraints. Why *did* the teacher who had the room before you put the computer where people had to squeeze past it to get in? – because it was near the only electric socket in the room. The only way you will find this out, however, is to explore the space and its contents. Making a note of all of the equipment, and a plan of the space, can be a very useful activity, and gives you the opportunity to explore possible arrangements on paper – rather than at five o'clock on a Friday afternoon, with everything piled in huge heaps around you in the classroom.

Figure 11.1 Activity – looking at space

Make a plan of the space available, indoor and outdoor.

Note:
- the positions of windows, doors, gates
- other fixed points such as sockets, taps, floors and ground surfaces
- all of the equipment

Consider:
- your aims for the children
- your views on learning
- the range of experiences you want the children to have

Now try to draw up plans for the space which take account of these factors

The first consideration in looking at the space available is to ensure children's safety and security. Outside, for example, are all exits secure, with latches on gates placed so that children inside cannot undo them? Is large climbing apparatus safe? Where are the fire exits? Inside, are electrical sockets covered? Do radiators have guards on them? Is all of the equipment in good repair? Ultimately, many of these issues are the responsibility of the school as a whole, but on a day-to-day basis it is important to feel sure that you have kept a check on all possible hazards, as well as ones you have not even thought of! Young children are curious and keen to explore their surroundings, while also being unaware sometimes of the dangers it poses. (Helping children to develop the skills they need to use things in the nursery is also, of course, an important responsibility for all adults working with them, and their competence in handling woodwork tools, for example, often surprises those working with older children. As a message about the capabilities of young children it is hard to beat.)

An examination of the space for its working and playing potential needs to come next. Are there different surfaces on the floor inside and the ground outside? Is there a sink? Where are doors and windows, and what are the issues of access and light? In one hutted classroom a teacher had imaginatively made more space by converting the windowless storeroom into a quiet space. All went well until two children took calculators in there to use. They kept coming out to tell her that the calculators were broken. Nonsense, she said, trying them out and finding that they worked perfectly. It was some time before she remembered that they were solar powered...

These questions need to be explored at the beginning of the year, before the children have come in. Once they have, there is no reason why they cannot also be involved. It is their space, and they need to 'own' it just as much as the adults do. During the year furniture, equipment and materials, both indoor and out, may often be moved, as the children's needs and interests change. The room arrangement should reflect these changes. There is a school of thought that furniture and equipment should stay in the same place, so that children feel secure and always know where things are. The analogy that has been made (Goldschmied and Jackson, 1994) is that, as adults, we become frustrated and confused when our local supermarket rearranges itself. While a certain degree of stability in the environment is desirable, particularly for younger children, there are some important qualitative differences – my local supermarket did not consult me when they decided to put the meat counter in the corner previously occupied by washing powder, and I had no power to do anything about it. In rearranging our working spaces in school, useful and important discussions can occur, where children have the opportunity to solve real problems, to see things how others might, and to have an impact on their surroundings. Home corner areas, for example, are often transformed into cafes, opticians, hospitals, shops, etc. They are most effective when children and adults have planned and worked together to organise and resource such areas, with the provision made developing over time, as people contribute both ideas and items for use. It may also become apparent that some areas of space are in better, more active use than others, and careful observation can help us to think about what changes could be made for all space to be used most effectively.

In and out of doors

In their study of four year olds in reception classes, Cleave and Brown (1991)[10] are adamant that young children need space both indoors and out. Sadly, this is not always a possibility, perhaps because no appropriate outdoor space is available or occasionally because it is not considered necessary by the school as a whole. In this section, then, indoor and outdoor spaces are considered separately in recognition of this, rather than because they should be looked at as separate spaces. Indeed, the space, both indoor and out, should be viewed as a whole, and all as a learning environment.

The nine areas of learning and experience looked at earlier (HMI, 1989b) provide one starting point in offering some guidance on decisions about the range of spaces to set up, and also what to put in those spaces. They can be coupled with Dowling's (1992) reminder about providing sensory and physical experiences and opportunities for children to represent their experiences. It is also useful to remember the aims of the *Te Whariki* document (Ministry of Education (New Zealand) 1993) that the environment should support the development of children's sense of well being and belonging, and ensure opportunities for them to contribute, communicate and explore. The physical organisation, then, will need to provide opportunities for activity in all of those areas, in ways which truly reflect principles and beliefs about young children's learning.

Figure 11.2 Further reflection – looking at your environment

Does the environment support children in their efforts

- to feel a sense of belonging, and to feel safe
- to represent their experiences in as many ways as possible
- to develop linguistically through talk with other children and adults in small or large groups. To listen to others. To develop as emergent writers and readers, through provision in writing areas, home corners, book corners.
- to develop aesthetically and expressively through sensory experience, role play, painting, drawing, model making, and use of a wide variety of different media such as fabric, junk, clay. To experience music, through making and listening, to use movement and dance.
- to develop as social beings, through interaction, playing alone and with others, being active, quiet, noisy. To work collaboratively and singly, cooperating with other children and adults.
- to develop morally and spiritually, respecting themselves and others, and gaining knowledge and experience of the beliefs and customs of all people.
- to learn about the world around them, and the people, places and events that make up the world.
- to develop mathematically through experience with small and large apparatus, and through exploration and use of their environment.
- to develop physically, both fine and gross motor skills, through the use of tools, apparatus, and active play experiences.
- to develop scientifically, exploring the natural environment and all aspects of the physical world.
- to develop technologically, constructing and problem solving, investigating objects and machines, and using computers, calculators and other electronic devices.

Indoor space

Furniture, and its placing, is the chief means of creating defined areas indoors, but it also, at the same time, acts to condition children's access to these areas. Chairs, tables and storage facilities all need to be at child height if children are to be able to operate independently. Just as importantly, the amount of furniture needs very careful consideration. The assumption that all children will need a chair *at the same time* needs to be questioned in classrooms and units where class teaching is inappropriate or, at least, most unusual, and where space may be at a premium.[11] In some instances, chairs and tables could be removed and stored elsewhere, and the space thus generated used to create areas. Screens, storage trolleys and other equipment can be used for this, creating areas to suit a range of purposes. In many instances, it will be appropriate for such areas to be places where children can 'be themselves' (Hartley, 1993, p.88), and spaces where children can be quiet and private are essential. In some cases too easy adult surveillance may mean that children actually make less use of the space available (Hartley, 1993, p.91). In others, however, it may mean that some children are effectively denied access, by not giving them the chance to stand back, observe from afar, and enter an activity at their own pace. Barriers and room dividers, then, should be placed with all of these needs in mind.

McLean (1991) describes the consequences of two teachers' different approaches to the management of space. One 'used the physical environment as a preventative approach to peer conflict' (p.93), providing materials and space for activities to minimise the potential for disputes. By contrast, the second teacher, who had positioned the block area next to a major traffic way for the children, often had to intervene to resolve such conflicts. Such examples highlight how the organisation of space can affect the quality of relationships as well as the ways in which children work. Some types of activity will, of course, need more space than others, and it is important to be realistic in creating spaces for them. Too small a construction area, for example, will limit the kinds of large constructions children can make, as well as causing conflict when they encroach on other spaces. The Froebel Blockplay Research group also found that 'Where space is restricted, impromptu partnering of any kind occurs less often than when children circulate more freely in the block area' (Gura, 1992, p.175). They suggest that the need to take turns more often in restricted space situations led to children tending to opt for 'best-friend' or same-sex play partners more often. This is something which may be generalisable to more situations than just block play, and, whereas playing and talking in pairs with a firm friend can be a powerful mechanism for learning (Bruner, 1980; Murray, 1988), the opportunity for children to develop socially through a range of partnerships is an important role of the school.

Resources

Having created a spatial framework in the class, the picture is completed with a consideration of the resources and equipment, their use and storage. Good quality, well-maintained, appropriate equipment allows children to satisfactorily undertake and complete a task. There can be few things more frustrating than trying to cut with blunt scissors, particularly when you are a relative novice at cutting to begin with! Similarly, it is disappointing for anyone to put the effort required into completing a puzzle, only to find that the last piece is missing, or for a group of children to have difficulty sharing equipment because there is not enough to go round. In other cases, of course, poorly maintained or inappropriate equipment may even be dangerous: woodwork tools not designed for repeated use, and unstable or damaged climbing apparatus, for example. Blenkin and Whitehead's view, that the room should be seen as a workshop 'resourced with all the appropriate tackle and gear' (1988, p.47) is a useful guiding principle, and points to another important aspect of resourcing, that, as far as possible, real objects, rather than toy imitations, should be used. Home corners provide more meaningful experiences for children when the pots and pans are real rather than the plastic variety often found in toy catalogues. Real woodwork and gardening tools are both better designed for the job than their toy counterparts, and more robust in use. McLean describes an Australian preschool where 'one corner resembled an artist's studio ... this work area looked like "the real thing"; not a place where children "played" at being artists' (1991, p.71). Such spaces not only give children the appropriate tools for the job, but are also far more inviting.

Such resources can be collected from a wide range of sources, not the least of which can be the children and their families themselves. Setting up an area as, for example, a hairdressers or a garden centre, or for a project or topic, can be done *with* the children, not *to* them. Planning activities and provision with children gives them the opportunity to contribute ideas and materials, bringing in things from home and elsewhere, and ensuring that they see the activity as theirs from the very beginning. The alternative, that of presenting a finished package of an idea to the children, effectively puts them in the position of starting an activity half way through.

Display

Display in the nursery needs to be viewed in a similar way. As a new teacher I put much time and effort into constructing elaborate wall displays, based around a particular story, for example. The children were deployed like footsoldiers to 'paint a cow' or 'do a picture of the hungry wolf'. Like a general overseeing the scene of battle, only I knew how all of their efforts were designed to come together. The finished product was invariably attractive and elicited favourable comments from other adults. What it did not have, I began to realise, was very much to do with the children themselves. The impetus for the work came from me, and not them, and their part in the process was limited to painting to order pictures which I then often butchered by cutting around them to create my desired effect. There is a place for large displays, of course, but the children themselves can take much more responsibility than I was prepared to give them, and they can make the decisions about what goes on such a display, and how it can be carried out. A more common type of display, however, must be of children's individual efforts. Again, children, with adult help and guidance, can mount their own work, and put it up on walls or out on shelves and tables. Like a project or topic, displays develop over time, and new models and pictures can be added or taken away as appropriate.

The displays themselves serve a range of purposes. Clearly, one aspect is to make the nursery an attractive place in which to be, hopefully for adults and children alike, but primarily for the children themselves. In addition, they act as a public acknowledgement of children's efforts, and as a way of sharing their activities. Most importantly, they can be used to both stimulate children's interest and awareness, and consolidate their understanding. If they are to do so, however, the displays themselves need to 'live', with adults drawing children's attention to them and using them to stimulate discussion and enquiry. Too often displays are mounted, and then forgotten about until it is time for them to be taken down and changed. Apart from anything else, this represents such a wasted opportunity.

Outdoor space

By the time children are six or seven years old, outdoor play at school has invariably become a way of 'letting off steam' rather than an opportunity for learning and development. In the early years, at least, the indoor and outdoor environments can, and should, both be seen as central to children's use, with 'no firm distinction between indoors and out' (McLean, 1991, p.71). Sadly, not all early years classes have dedicated outdoor areas, particularly at reception level and later,[12] but where they do, the space can be planned to provide a complete learning environment, where children have opportunities for gross motor play, for investigations, for gardening, and using much of the equipment from indoors. In short, the vast majority of activities that take place inside the nursery can easily occur outside, alongside others, such as running, jumping, bicycle riding, environmental studies and digging, which may be impossible inside. In talking to children throughout the primary age range, Titman (1994) found that children of all ages sought a broadly similar range of opportunities from the school outdoor environment: 'a place for *doing* ... a place for *thinking* ... a place for *feeling* ... a place for *being*' (her emphasis) (p.58). She adds one other quality, too: 'In addition, and of overriding importance perhaps, was the need for school grounds to be "a place for fun"!' (p.58).

Alongside the potential of outdoor spaces for young children's development, there are other reasons why opportunities for them to play outside at school may be important, more now perhaps than ever before. Many children now live in densely populated urban areas, with perhaps little access to gardens and outdoor spaces at home. Increased fears about traffic and danger from strangers mean that parents are reluctant to allow their children to play outside. A recent survey (McNeish and Roberts, 1995) found that the great majority of parents perceived their children to be at far greater risk from these dangers than they had been when they were children themselves. As a consequence, children are often obliged to play indoors, with activities such as watching the television and playing board games featuring high on the list. While in themselves these are not bad ways for children to spend their time, if they predominate then children are clearly getting less opportunity for physical exercise, for learning about their environment and for social interaction. These same parental fears have led to even less independence for children, as more and more are taken to and from school and other activities, by their parents, and often in cars. The consequent implications for their future health (and their present development and enjoyment) are clear. So, the availability of richly provisioned, challenging outdoor space in school is a real priority.

Principles in organising outdoor space are similar to those guiding the provision made indoors. Children need opportunities to experience a wide range of activities, to play alone and with others, to be private, to be active, to make choices and decisions for themselves. Again, as with indoor spaces, this necessitates seeing the space as a series of 'micro-environments', where what is on offer is easily accessible to the children, without adult help, and where children feel able to move materials from one place to another, as it suits their purposes. McLean describes an Australian preschool where each day 'the "Telecom boys" worked diligently, using a collection of props that included ladders, shovels, a very thick rope, hard hats, a box of discarded telephone equipment and porter's trolleys' (McLean, 1991, p.167), or another group of children excavating a 'mine' in the digging area, which grew to a considerable size, as they returned to it over a period of weeks (McLean, 1991, p.167). By contrast, another preschool setting in her study reveals the difficulties of an outdoor area with little equipment, where children seemed to end up fighting and chasing each other because there was little else for them to do (p.133). Such scarcity may tend 'to facilitate children's play activities as "users" rather than as "creators"' (Papatheodorou and Ramasut, 1994, p.67), as well as leading to a less harmonious time for children and adults alike. It is useful to look at the table compiled by Titman (see Figure 11.3) of children's own views about what they saw as positive and negative in outdoor spaces.

Figure 11.3: How children view their environment

Positive elements	**Negative elements**
Colour (natural)	Dirt
Trees	Pollution
Woods	Rubbish
Places with different levels	Litter
Shady areas	Damaged things
Leaves	Colour (unnatural)
Big grassy areas	Tarmac
Animals	Animals
Places you can ... climb/hide/explore/make a den	Places where you can't ...
Places that challenge you	Nowhere to sit/hide/shelter
Places that have 'millions of bits'	Places that are 'boring'
Places that have wildlife	Places that are too 'open'

Source: Titman, 1994, p.25

This list, while providing useful insights into children's own views about their environment, also demonstrates a point made earlier, that solutions are ones right for particular people and places. 'Animals', as a category appears in both negative and positive lists. Children from rural areas, for whom farm animals were a part of their usual experience, responded positively to them in school grounds, whereas children from urban areas, for whom they tended not to be a part of their usual cultural context, viewed them more negatively. As with indoors, provision grows and develops in response to the children's needs and interests, and provides a vital context for shared experiences, between adults and children as they work together in it.

Summary and conclusion

This chapter has stressed the importance of consideration of the physical environment in school, in particular as a means of enacting professionals' beliefs about young children's learning and development, and their aims for the children in their care. The message of research seems to suggest that some forms of organisation can be facilitatory of those aims, while others can be de-skilling, even to the point of fostering a 'learned helplessness' in children where their opportunities for taking responsibility for themselves are limited. Bilton, citing the work of Gura (1992) and Moyles (1992), suggests: 'it would appear that the most effective learning comes from simple yet versatile materials and environments which extend the child's imagination and not the designer's and can be adapted by the child to suit their level of understanding and learning needs' (Bilton, 1994, p.36). A structure and organisation which allows children to view things with flexibility, and in which messages about a hierarchy of values attached to particular activities are not conveyed by the presence or absence of adults at them is advocated here, as a way of fulfilling our intentions.

Only by providing a quality environment for children can we hope to ensure a quality experience for them, and thus have high-quality expectations of them.

Notes

1 See, for example Bruner and Haste (1987a), Vygotsky (1978) and Wells (1986).
2 This has its roots in the thinking of Piaget, and, perhaps unlike some other aspects of his work, there seems very good reason to suppose that it still holds true.
3 The Harms and Clifford *Early Childhood Environment Rating Scale* (1980), for example, has the following categories: personal care routines; furnishing and display for children; language-reasoning experiences; fine and gross motor activities; creative activities; social development; adult needs.
4 It is important to bear in mind that the needs of young children are unique, and different, and that appropriate practice for children at various ages will, likewise, differ. While considering all ages, following sections in this chapter are centred more around provision for the over-threes, that is, children in nursery schools and infant and first schools. Provision for the education and care of children under the age of three years is looked at in more detail in Goldschmied and Jackson (1994), National Children's Bureau (1991), and Rouse and Griffin (1992) and these are useful reference points.
5 Sometimes referred to as the 'Three Wise Men' Paper.

6 It is interesting to note the comments of researchers such as Galton *et al.* (1980) in *Inside the Primary Classroom* and Bennett *et al.* (1984) in *The Quality of Pupil Learning Experiences* that, in many classrooms, tables grouped together, ostensibly in a social setting, occur often in classrooms where the expectations are that children will, despite these material signals, nevertheless be expected to work individually, and not to collaborate with their neighbours.
7 For a rationale and description of schema see, for example, Athey (1990) and Bartholomew and Bruce (1993).
8 It is interesting to note the similarity of terminology here with the School Curriculum and Assessment Authority's *Desirable Outcomes for Children's Learning*, concerning provision for pre-statutory aged children in England and Wales.
9 See, for example, Davies and Brember (1994), Gura *et al.* (1992), Hutt *et al.* (1989), Tizard *et al.* (1981).
10 This book is a very useful reference for thinking about appropriate provision in all areas, including classroom plans, space, equipment, resources, furniture and storage.
11 Pascal (1990, p.22) found that, in nearly nine out of ten of the Reception classrooms she visited, tables and chairs took up most of the available space, dominating other facilities and equipment, and often leaving so little space that adults and children alike had to squeeze between the furniture just to move around.
12 Cleave and Brown (1991) have some useful examples of ways in which schools have adapted spaces in order to overcome some of the constraints they had in providing outdoor space.

Bibliography

Adams, R. (1983) *I'm Not Complaining*. London: Virago. First published 1938.
Adelman, C. (1989) 'The Context of Learning: an historical perspective', in G. Barrett (Ed) (1989a) op. cit.
Alexander, R. (1992) *Policy and Practice in Primary Education*. London: Routledge.
Alexander, R., Rose, J. and Woodhead, C. (1992) *Curriculum Organisation and Classroom Practice: a discussion paper*. London: DES.
Annan, M. (1993) 'From a Different Perspective', in M. Barrs and S. Pidgeon (Eds) *Reading the Difference*. London: Centre for Language in Primary Education.
Anning, A. (1991) *The First Years at School*. Milton Keynes: Open University Press.
Astington, J.W. (1994) *The Child's Discovery of the Mind*. Cambridge, USA: Fontana/Harvard University Press.
Athey, C. (1990) *Extending Thought in Young Children*. London: Paul Chapman.
Atkin, J. (1991) 'Thinking About Play' in N. Hall and L. Abbott (Eds) *Play in the Primary Curriculum*. London: Hodder & Stoughton.
Aubrey, C. (Ed) (1994) *The Role of Subject Knowledge in the Early Years of Schooling*. London: Falmer Press.
Bain, R., Fitzgerald, B. and Taylor, M. (Eds) (1992) *Looking into Language*. Sevenoaks, Kent: Hodder & Stoughton.
Ball, Sir C. (1994) *Start Right: the importance of early learning*. London: RSA.
Ball, Sir C. (1995) 'Key Stage Zero', *Guardian Education*, 3. 7, pp.4–5.
Ball, S. J. and Goodson, I.F. (Eds) (1985) *Teachers' Lives and Careers*. Lewes: Falmer Press.
Barrett, G. (1986) *Starting School: An Evaluation of the Experience: final report of an evaluation of responses of reception children to school, commissioned by the Assistant Masters and Mistresses Association*. Centre for Applied Research in Education, School of Education University of East Anglia.
Barrett, G. (Ed) (1989a) *Disaffection from School*. London: Falmer Press.
Barrett, G. (1989b) 'Teachers' perspectives', in G. Barrett (Ed) op. cit.
Barratt-Pugh, C. (1994) 'Language Development in a Multilingual Context', in L. Abbott and R. Rodger (Eds) *Quality Education in the Early Years*. Buckingham: Open University Press.
Barrs, M., Ellis, S., Hester, H. and Thomas, A. (1990) *Patterns of Learning*. London: CLPE.
Barth, B.M. (1995) 'The Role of Context and Interactions in the Child's Construction of Knowledge', *European Early Childhood Educational Research Journal*, **3**.
Bartholomew, L. and Bruce, T. (1993) *Getting to Know You*. London: Hodder & Stoughton.
Bastiani, J. (1989) *Working With Parents*. Windsor, Berks: NFER-Nelson.
Beard, H. and Cerf, C. (1992) *The Official Politically Correct Dictionary and Handbook*. London: Grafton.
Becher, R.M. (1986) 'Parental Involvement: a review of research and principles of successful practice', in L. Katz (Ed) *Current Topics in Early Childhood Education*, Vol VI. New York: Ablex.
Bennett, N. (1976) *Teaching Styles and Pupil Progress*. London: Open Books.
Bennett, N. and Dunne, E. (1992) *Managing Classroom Groups*. London: Simon & Schuster.
Bennett, N. and Kell, J. (1989) *A Good Start? Four Year Olds in Infant Schools*. Oxford: Blackwell.
Bennett, N., Wood, E. and Rogers, S. (1995) 'Play and Pedagogy: the relationship between teacher, thought and action'. Paper presented at EECERA Conference, Paris, September.
Bennett, N., Desforges, C., Cockburn, A. and Wilkinson, B. (1984) *The Quality of Pupil Learning*

Experiences. London: Lawrence Erlbaum.

Beveridge, S. (1992) ' "This is Your Charter...": parents as consumers or partners in the educational process?', *Early Years,* **13**(1), pp.12–15.

Bilton, H. (1994) 'The Nursery Class Garden. Designing and building an outdoor environment for young children', *Early Years,* **14**(2), pp.34–7.

Bird, M. (1991) *Mathematics for Young Children: An active thinking approach.* London: Routledge.

Blatchford, P., Battle, S. and Mays, J. (1982) *The First Transition.* Windsor, Berks: NFER-Nelson.

Blenkin, G.M. and Kelly, A.V. (Eds) (1992) *Assessment in Early Childhood Education.* London: Paul Chapman.

Blenkin, G.M. and Kelly, A.V. (Eds) (1994a) *The National Curriculum and Early Learning: an evaluation.* London: Paul Chapman.

Blenkin, G.M. and Kelly, A.V. (1994b) 'The Death of Infancy', *Curriculum 3–13,* October, pp.3–9.

Blenkin, G.M. and Whitehead, M.R. (1988) 'Creating a Context for Development', in G.M. Blenkin and A.V. Kelly (Eds) *Early Childhood Education. A Developmental Curriculum.* London: Paul Chapman.

Bosely, S. (1995) 'Early Learning', *Guardian Education,* 23.5, p.2.

Bradley, B. (1989) *Visions of Infancy.* Cambridge: Polity Press.

Braun, D. (1992) 'Working With Parents', in G. Pugh (Ed) *Contemporary Issues in the Early Years.* London: Paul Chapman/National Children's Bureau.

Bridges, A. (1995) 'Planned With Precision: Perceived With Confusion'. Unpublished MA Dissertation, University of Surrey.

Brierley, J. (1987) *Give Me a Child Until He is Seven: brain studies and early childhood education.* Lewes: Falmer Press.

Britton, J. (1972) *Language and Learning.* Harmondsworth: Penguin.

Britton, J. (1977) 'The third area where we are more ourselves', in M. Meek *et al.*, op. cit.

Brown, I. (1988) 'Who were the Eugenicists? A study of the formation of an early twentieth-century pressure group', *History of Education,* **17**(4), 295–307.

Brown, J.R. and Dunn, J. (1991)'"You can cry, mum": the social and developmental implications of talk about internal states', in G.E. Butterworth *et al.* op. cit..

Browne, N. and France, P. (1985) '"Only cissies wear dresses": a look at sexist talk in the nursery', in G. Weiner (Ed) *Just a Bunch of Girls.* Milton Keynes: Open University Press.

Browne, N. and France, P. (1986) 'Unclouded minds saw unclouded visions': visual images in the nursery', in N. Browne and P. France (Eds) *Untying the apron strings. Anti-Sexist Provision for the Under Fives.* Milton Keynes: Open University Press.

Browne, N. and Ross, C. (1991) '"Girls' Stuff, Boys' Stuff": young children talking and playing', in N. Browne (Ed) *Science and Technology in the Early Years, an Equal Opportunities Approach.* Milton Keynes: Open University Press.

Bruce, T. (1987) *Early Childhood Education.* Sevenoaks, Kent: Hodder & Stoughton.

Bruce, T. (1992) 'Children, Adults and Blockplay', in P. Gura (Ed) op. cit.

Bruner, J. (1980) *Under Five in Britain.* London: Grant McIntyre.

Bruner, J. (1983) *Child's Talk: learning to use language.* Oxford: Oxford University Press.

Bruner, J. (1990) *Acts of Meaning.* Cambridge, Mass.: Harvard University Press.

Bruner, J. and Haste, H. (Eds) (1987a) *Making Sense.* London: Methuen.

Bruner, J. and Haste, H. (1987b) 'Introduction', in J. Bruner and H. Haste op. cit., pp.1–25.

Burgess, H. and Carter, B. (1992) '"Bringing Out the Best in People": teacher training and the "real" teacher', *British Journal of Sociology of Education,* **13**(3), pp.349–59.

Burgess-Macey, C. (1993/4) 'Quality and Equality in the Early Years', *Language Matters,* **1**, pp.18–21.

Butterworth, D. (1991) 'Gender Equity in Early Childhood: the state of play', *Australian Journal of Early Childhood,* **16**(4) pp.3–9.

Butterworth, G.E., Harris, P.L., Leslie, A.M. and Wellman, H.M. (Eds) (1991) *Perspectives on the Child's Theory of Mind.* Oxford: Oxford University Press.

CACE (1967) *Children and their Primary Schools* (Plowden Report). London: HMSO.

Cameron, D. (1992) *Feminism and Linguistic Theory.* Basingstoke: Macmillan.

Casey, K. (1990) 'Teacher as Mother: curriculum theorizing in the life histories of contemporary women teachers', *Cambridge Journal of Education,* **20**(3), pp.301–20.

Cazden, C.B. (1988) *Classroom Discourse: the language of teaching and learning.* Portsmouth, NH: Heinemann.

Chukovsky, K. (1968) *From Two to Five.* Berkeley, California: University of California Press.

Clark, M.M. (Ed) (1987) 'Roles, Responsibilities and Relationships in the Education of the Young Child', *Educational Review*, Faculty of Education, University of Birmingham.

Clark, M.M. (1988) *Children Under Five: educational research and evidence*. London: Gordon & Breach.

Clarke-Stewart, A. (1991) 'Day Care in the USA', P. Moss and E. Melhuish (Eds) *Current Issues in Day Care for Young Children*. London: HMSO.

Clay, M.M. (1979) *The Early Detection of Reading Difficulties: a diagnostic survey with recovery procedures*. Auckland: Heinemann

Cleave, S. and Brown, S. (1989) *Four Year Olds in School: meeting their needs*. Slough: NFER.

Cleave, S. and Brown, S. (1991) *Early to School. Four year olds in infant classes*. Windsor, Berks: NFER-Nelson.

Cleave, S., Jowett, S. and Bate, M. (1982) *And So To School – A Study of Continuity from Pre-School to Infant School*. Windsor, Berks: NFER-Nelson.

Clift, P., Cleave, S. and Griffin, M. (1980) *The Aims and Deployment of Staff in the Nursery*. Windsor: NFER.

Cockburn, A. (1992) *Beginning Teaching, an Introduction to Early Years Teaching*. London: Paul Chapman.

Coghill, V. (1989) 'Making and Playing, the Other Basic Skills: design education for the early years', A. Dyson (Ed) *Looking, Making and Learning*. The Bedford Way Series, Institute of Education University of London, pp.56–69.

Cohen, D. and MacKeith, S. (1991) *The Development of the Imagination: the private worlds of children*. London: Routledge.

Coopersmith, J. (1967) *The Antecedents of Self Esteem*. San Fransisco: W.H. Freeman.

Corsaro, W. and Schwartz, K. (1991) 'Peer Play and Socialisation in Two Cultures', B. Scales *et al.*, op. cit.

Coulter, R.P. and McNay, M. (1993) 'Exploring Men's Experiences as Elementary School Teachers', *Canadian Journal of Education*, **18**(4), pp.398–413.

Cousins, J. (1990) '"Are your little Humpty Dumpties floating or sinking?" What sense do children of four make of reception class at school? Different conceptions at the time of transition', *Early Years*, **10**(2), pp.28–38.

Cox, T. and Sanders, S. (1994) *The Impact of the National Curriculum on the Teaching of Five Year Olds*. London: Falmer Press.

Curtis, A.M. (1986) *A Curriculum for the Pre-school Child: learning to learn*. Windsor, Berkshire: NFER/Nelson.

Curtis, A. and Hevey, D. (1992) 'Training to Work in the Early Years' in G. Pugh (Ed) *Contemporary Issues in the Early Years*. London: Paul Chapman.

Davies, A., Holland, J. and Minhas, R. (1990) *Equal Opportunities in the new ERA*. London: Tufnell Press.

Davies, B. (1982) *Life in the Classroom and Playground: the accounts of primary school children*. London: Routledge and Kegan Paul.

Davies, B. (1989) *Frogs and Snails and Feminist Tales*. Sydney, Australia; Wellington, New Zealand; Winchester, Mass.; London: Allen & Unwin.

Davies, J. and Brember, I. (1994) 'Morning and Afternoon Nursery Sessions: can they be equally effective in giving children a positive start to school?', *International Journal of Early Years Education*, **2**(2).

Delamont, S. (1994) 'Sex Roles in the Formative Years', in A. Pollard and J. Bourne (Eds) *Teaching and Learning in the Primary School*. London: Routledge in association with the Open University.

Department of Education (1985) *Reading in Junior Classes: Ready to Read*. Wellington: Department of Education.

Department of Education and Science (1977) *A New Partnership for Our Schools* (Taylor Report). London: HMSO.

Department of Education and Science (1978a) *Special Educational Needs*. (Warnock Report). London: HMSO.

Department of Education and Science (1978b) *Primary Education in England: a survey by HM Inspectors of Schools*. London: HMSO.

Department of Education and Science (1985) *The Curriculum from 5–16: curriculum matters 2*. London: HMSO.

Department of Education and Science (1988a) *Four Year Olds in Infant Classrooms.* London: HMSO.
Department of Education and Science (1988b) *Local Management of Schools: a report to the Department of Education and Science.* London: HMSO.
Department of Education and Science (1989) *Discipline in Schools* (Elton Report). London: HMSO.
Department of Education and Science (1990) *Starting with Quality* (Rumbold Report). London: HMSO.
Department of Education and Science (1994a) *Our Children's Education. The Updated Parent's Charter.* London: HMSO.
Department of Education and Science (1994b) *Statistics of Education. Schools in England.* London: HMSO.
Department of Health (1991a) *The Children Act 1989, Guidance and Regulations, Vol. 2: family support, daycare and educational provision for young children.* London: HMSO.
Department of Health (1991b) *An Introduction to the Children Act.* London: HMSO.
Desforges, C. (1989) 'Teachers' Perspectives on Classroom Interaction', in C. Desforges (Ed) *Early Childhood Education*, The British Journal of Educational Psychology, Monograph Series No. 4, Scottish Academic Press.
Desforges, C. and Cockburn, A. (1987) Understanding the Mathematics Teacher. London: Falmer Press.
Dixon, A. (1989) 'Deliver us from Eagles', in G. Barrett (Ed) op. cit., pp.13–23.
Docking, J. (1990a) *Managing Behaviour in the Primary School.* London: David Fulton Publishers.
Docking, J. (1990b) *Primary Schools and Parents.* London: Hodder & Stoughton.
Donaldson, M. (1978) *Children's Minds.* London: Fontana.
Donaldson, M. (1985) 'The Mismatch Between School and Children's Minds' in N. Entwhistle (Ed) *New Directions in Educational Psychology.* London: Falmer Press.
Dowling, M. (1992) (2nd edn) *Education 3–5.* London: Paul Chapman.
Drummond, M.J. (1993) *Assessing Children's Learning.* London: David Fulton Publishers.
Drummond, M.J., Rouse, D. and Pugh, G. (1992) *Making Assessment Work: values and principles in assessing young children's learning.* London: NES Arnold in association with the National Children's Bureau.
Duckworth, E. (1987) *The Having of Wonderful Ideas and other Essays on Teaching and Learning.* New York: Teachers College Press.
Dunn, J. (1987) 'Understanding Feelings: the early stages', in J. Bruner and H. Haste (Eds) op. cit.
Dunn, J. (1988) *The Beginnings of Social Understanding.* Oxford: Basil Blackwell.
Dunn, J. (1993) *Young Children's Close Relationships: beyond attachment.* Newbury Park: Sage.
Durant, J. (1988) 'Racism and the Under Fives', A. Cohen and L. Cohen (Eds) *Early Education. The pre-school years.* London: Paul Chapman.
Edwards, A. and Knight, P. (1994) *Effective Early Years Education.* Buckingham: Open University Press.
Edwards, C., Gandini, L. and Foreman, G. (Eds) (1995) *The One Hundred Languages of Children.* New Jersey: Ablex Publishing Corporation.
Edwards, G. and Rose, J. (1994) 'Promoting a Quality Curriculum in the Early Years Through Action Research: a case study', *Early Years,* **15**(1), pp.42–7.
Eisner, E.W. (1990) 'The Role of Art and Play in Children's Cognitive Development', in E. Klugman and S. Smilansky (Eds) *The Importance of Play in Young Children's Learning*, pp.43–56. Colombia University, New York: Teachers College Press.
Elkind, D. (1981) (revised edn) *The Hurried Child.* Wokingham: Addison Wesley.
Equal Opportunities Commission (1992) *An Equal Start. Guidelines on equal treatment for the under-eights.* Manchester: Equal Opportunities Commission.
Evans, R. (1995) 'Culture and Curriculum: tensions and dilemmas for early childhood specialists in England and Wales'. Paper presented at AERA Conference, San Fransisco. April Symposium, Culture and Curriculum.
Everard, K.B. and Morris, G. (1985) *Effective School Management.* London: Harper & Row.
Evetts, J. (1990) *Women in Primary Teaching, Career Contexts and Strategies.* London: Unwin Hyman.
Faust, H. (1998) 'Multicultural Curriculum in Early Childhood Education', in G.M. Blenkin and A.V. Kelly (Eds) *Early Childhood Education: a developmental curriculum.* London: Paul Chapman.
France, P. (1985) 'The Beginnings of Sex Stereotyping', in N. Browne and P. France (Eds) *Untying the Apron Strings. Anti-sexist provision for the under fives.* Milton Keynes: Open University Press.
Freeman, D. (1968) *Corduroy.* Auckland, New Zealand: Penguin.
Froebel Blockplay Research Group (1992) 'Children being scientific and solving problems', in P. Gura (Ed) op. cit.

Fullan, M. and Hargreaves, A. (1994) 'The Teacher as a Person', in A. Pollard and Bourne (Eds) *Teaching and Learning in the Primary School.* London: Routledge in association with the Open University.

Galton, M. and Williamson, J. (1992) *Group Work in the Primary Classroom.* London: Routledge.

Galton, M., Simon, B. and Croll, P. (1980) *Inside the Primary Classroom.* London: Routledge and Kegan Paul.

Gardner, H. (1993) *The Unschooled Mind.* London: Fontana (first published, 1991, Basic Books).

Garvey, C. (1977) *Play.* London: Fontana/Open Books.

Garvey, C. (1983) 'Some Properties of Social Play', in M. Donaldson, R. Grieve and C. Pratt (Eds) *Early Childhood Development and Education.* Oxford: Basil Blackwell.

Garvey, C. (1991) *Play.* London: Fontana.

Geertz, C. (1973) *The Interpretation of Cultures.* New York: Basic Books.

Ghaye, A. and Pascal, C. (1988) 'Four-year-old Children in Reception Classrooms: participant perceptions and practice', *Educational Studies,* **14**(2), pp.187–208.

Gifford, S. (1995) 'Number in Early Childhood', *Early Child Development and Care,* **109**, pp.95–119.

Giroux, H.A. (1989) *Schooling for Democracy: critical pedagogy in the modern age.* London: Routledge.

Goldschmied, E. and Jackson, S. (1994) *People Under Three: young children in day care.* London: Routledge.

Goldsmiths' Association for Early Childhood (1994) *Focus on Maths, Science and Technology,* Newsletter, no. 7.

Goodson, I. (1992a) 'School Subjects: patterns of stability', *Educational Research and Perspectives,* **19**(1) pp.52–4.

Goodson, I.F. (Ed) (1992b) *Studying Teachers' Lives.* London: Routledge.

Goodson, I. (1995) 'Ignore research at our peril' in *TES,* 31 March.

Gordon, I.J. (1966) *Studying the Child in School.* New York: John Wiley and Sons.

Gracie, M. (1977) 'The Role of Play', *Forum for the Discussion of New Trends,* **19**(3) pp.83–6.

Graham, A. (1993) 'Storytelling and Equal Opportunities', *Early Years,* **13**(2) pp.28–33.

Griffiths, A. and Hamilton, D. (1984) *Parent, Teacher, Child: Working Together in Children's Learning.* London: Methuen.

Guha, M. (1988) 'Play in School', in G.M. Blenkin and A.V. Kelly (Eds) *Early Childhood Education: a developmental curriculum.* London: Paul Chapman, pp.61–7.

Gumpertz, C.J.C. (1991) 'Children's Construction of Childness', in B. Scales *et al.,* op. cit.

Gura, P. (1994) 'Scientific and Technological Development in the early years', in G.M. Blenkin and A.V. Kelly (1994a) op. cit., pp.127–47.

Gura, P. (Ed) with the Froebel Blockplay Research Group Directed by Bruce, T. (1992) *Exploring Learning: young children and blockplay.* London: Paul Chapman.

Hannon, P. (1987) 'Parental involvement – a no-score draw?', *Times Educational Supplement,* 3.4.87.

Hannon, P. and Jackson, A. (1987) *The Belfield Reading Project: final report.* London: Belfield Community Council/National Children's Bureau.

Hannon, P. and James, S. (1990) 'Parents' and Teachers' Perspectives on Pre-school Literacy Development', *British Educational Research Journal,* **16**(3), pp.259–71.

Hannon, P. and Welch, J. (1993) 'Tuning in to the home service', *Times Educational Supplement,* 12.11, p.13.

Hargreaves, A. (1994) *Changing Teachers, Changing Times.* London: Cassell.

Hargreaves, A. (1995) 'Kentucky Fried Schooling' in *TES,* 31 March.

Harms, T. and Clifford, R.M. (1980) *Early Childhood Environment Rating Scale.* New York: Teachers College Press.

Hartley, D. (1987) 'The Time of Their Lives: bureaucracy and the nursery school', in A. Pollard (Ed) *Children and Their Primary Schools.* Lewes: Falmer Press.

Hartley, D. (1993) *Understanding the Nursery School.* London: Cassell.

Haste, H. (1987) 'Growing into Rules', in J. Bruner and H. Haste (Eds) (1987a) op. cit., pp.163–95.

Haviland, J. (Ed) (1988) *Take Care Mr Baker.* London: Fourth Estate.

Heath, S.B. (1983) *Ways With Words, Language, Life and Work in Communities and Classrooms.* Cambridge; New York: Cambridge University Press.

Henry, M. (1990) 'More Than Just Play: the significance of mutually directed adult–child activity', *Early Child Development and Care,* **60**, pp.35–51.

HMI (1989a) *The Implementation of the National Curriculum in Primary Schools.* London: HMSO.

HMI (1989b) *The Education of Children Under Five.* London: HMSO.

Hohmann, M., Banet, B. and Weikart, D.P. (1979) *Young Children in Action: a manual for preschool educators.* Ypsilanti: High/Scope Press.

Holdaway, D. (1979) *The Foundations of Literacy.* Auckland, New Zealand: Ashton Scholastic.

Holt, J. (1984) (revised edn) *How Children Fail.* Harmondsworth: Penguin.

Honig, A. (1990) 'Working with Young Children'. Lecture presented at Froebel College, Roehampton Institute, 10 February.

Hood, L. (1988) *Sylvia: the biography of Sylvia Ashton Warner.* Auckland, New Zealand: Penguin.

Hughes, M. (1986) *Children and Number.* Oxford: Basil Blackwell.

Hughes, M. (1989) 'The Child as a Learner: the contrasting views of developmental psychology and early education', in C. Desforges (Ed) *Early Childhood Education.* British Journal of Educational Psychology, Monograph Series No. 4, Scottish Academic Press.

Hughes, M., Wikeley, F. and Nash, T. (1994) *Parents and their Children's Schools.* Oxford: Basil Blackwell.

Hunt, F. (Ed) (1987) *Lessons for Life. The schooling of girls and women 1850–1950.* Oxford: Basil Blackwell.

Hutt, S.J., Tyler, S., Hutt, C. and Christopherson, H. (1989) *Play, Exploration and Learning: a natural history of the pre-school.* London: Routledge.

Inagaki, K. (1992) 'Piagetian and Post Piagetian Conceptions of Development and their Implications for Science Education', *Early Childhood Research Quarterly,* **7**(1), pp.116–33.

Irwin, D. and Bushnell, M. (1980) *Observational Strategies for Child Study.* USA: Holt, Reinhart and Winston.

Isaacs, N. (1967) *What is Required of the Nursery-Infant Teacher in this Country Today?* London: National Froebel Foundation.

Isaacs, S. (1930) *Intellectual Growth in Children.* London: Routledge & Kegan Paul.

Isaacs, S. (1951) (abridged edn) *Social Development in Young Children.* London: Routledge & Kegan Paul.

Jackson, M. (1987) 'Making Sense of School', in A. Pollard (Ed) *Children and Their Primary Schools.* Lewes: Falmer Press.

Jones, A. and Glenn, S.M. (1991) 'Gender Differences in Pretend Play in a Primary School Group' *Early Child Development and Care,* **72**, pp.61–7.

Jones, E. and Reynolds, G. (1992) *The Play's the Thing: teacher roles in children's play,* New York: Teacher's College, Colombia University.

Jowett, S., Baginsky, M. and MacNeil, M.M. (1991) *Building Bridges.* Windsor, Berks: NFER-Nelson.

Judd, R. (1988) 'A Study into How Gender is Reinforced and Reproduced in the Nursery in Relation to Large Blockplay'. Unpublished essay, Certificate in Early Childhood Education, Froebel Institute College, Roehampton Institute London.

Kamii, C. (1975) 'Pedagogical Principles Derived from Piaget's Theory: relevance for educational practice', in M. Golby, J. Greenwald and R. West (Eds) *Curriculum Design.* Milton Keynes: Open University, pp.82–93.

Karrby, G. and Giota, J. (1994) 'Dimensions of Quality in Swedish Day Care Centres – an Analysis of the Early Childhood Environment Rating Scale', *Early Child Development and Care,* **104**, pp.1–22.

Katz, L.G. (1971) 'Sentimentality in Preschool Teachers', *Peabody Journal of Education,* **48**, pp.96–105.

Katz, L.G. (1977) *Talks with Teachers.* Washington DC: National Association for the Education of the Young Child.

Katz, L. (1984) *More Talks With Teachers.* ERIC Clearing House on Elementary and Early Childhood Education, University of Illinois, USA.

Katz, L. (1987) 'The Nature of Professions: where is early childhood education?', in L. Katz, (Ed) *Current Topics in Early Childhood Education.* New Jersey: Ablex Publishing.

Katz, L.G. and Chard, S.C. (1989) *Engaging Children's Minds: the project approach.* New Jersey: Ablex Publishing.

Kelly, A.V. (1994) 'Beyond the rhetoric and the discourse', in G.M. Blenkin and A.V. Kelly (Eds) (1994a) op. cit, pp.1–23.

Kidner, J. (1988) 'Under-Fives', in A. Cohen, and L. Cohen, (Eds) *Early Education. the pre-school years.* London: Paul Chapman.

La Fontaine, J. (1991) *Bullying: the child's view.* London: Calouste Gulbenkian Foundation.

Lally, M. (1991) *The Nursery Teacher in Action.* London: Paul Chapman.

Langsted, O. (1994) 'Looking at Quality From the Child's Perspective', in P. Moss and A. Pence (Eds) *Valuing Quality in Early Childhood Services.* London: Paul Chapman.

Larner, M. and Phillips, D. (1994) 'Defining and Valuing Quality as a Parent', in P. Moss and A. Pence (Eds) *Valuing Quality in Early Childhood Services.* London: Paul Chapman.

Lawlor, S. (1990) *Teachers Mistaught, Training in Theories or Education in Subjects?* London: Centre for Policy Studies.

Leach, P. (1994) 'Starting Points: how early are the early years', *Child Development Society Newsletter,* No. 43, p.11.

Lee, J. (1987) 'Pride and Prejudice: teachers, class and an inner-city infants school', in M. Lawn and G. Grace (Eds) *Teachers: the culture and politics of work.* London: Falmer Press.

Lee, V. and Lee, J. with Pearson, M. (1987) 'The Stories Children Tell', in A. Pollard (Ed) (1987a) op. cit.

Lindon, J. (1993) *Child Development from Birth to Eight: a practical focus.* London: National Children's Bureau.

Lloyd, B. (1987) 'Social Representations of Gender', in J. Bruner and H. Haste (Eds) (1987a) op. cit., pp.147–62.

MacGilchrist, B. (1992) *Managing Access and Entitlement in Primary Education.* London: Trentham Books.

Maclure, S. (1988) 'Introduction', in J. Haviland (Ed) op. cit., pp.xi–xii.

Macpherson, A. (1993) 'Parent–Professional Partnerships: a review and discussion of issues', *Early Child Development and Care,* **86**, pp.61–77.

Maher, F.A. and Rathbone, C.H. (1986) 'Teacher Education and Feminist Theory: some implications for practice', *American Journal of Education,* **9**(2).

Malaguzzi, L. (1995) 'No Way. The hundred is there' (poem, trans. Lella Gandini) in C. Edwards *et al.* (Eds), op.cit.

Malaguzzi, L. with Gandini, L. (1995) 'History, ideas and basic philosophy', in C. Edwards *et al.* (Eds), op. cit.

Massey, I. (1991) *More Than Skin Deep: developing anti-racist multicultural education in schools.* London: Hodder & Stoughton.

McAuley, H. and Jackson, P. (1992) *Educating Young Children. A structural approach.* London: David Fulton Publishers.

McLean, S.V. (1991) *The Human Encounter: teachers and children living together in preschools.* London: Falmer Press.

McMillan, M. (1930) *The Nursery School.* London: J.M. Dent.

McNeish, D. and Roberts, H. (1995) *Playing it safe.* Ilford, Essex: Barnardo's.

Meek, M. (1985a) 'Play and Paradoxes: some considerations of imagination and language', in G. Wells and J. Nicholls (Eds) *Language and Learning: an interactional perspective.* London: Falmer Press.

Meek, M. (1985b) 'A Stimulating and Rewarding Career', in F. Slater (Ed) *The Quality Controllers: a critique of the white paper 'Teaching Quality'.* London: Bedford Way Papers, Institute of Education, University of London.

Meek, M., Warlow, A. and Barton, G. (1977) *The Cool Web.* London: Bodley Head.

Merttens, R. and Vass, J. (1987) 'Parents in School: raising money or raising standards?', *Education 3–13,* **15**(2), pp.23–7.

Miller, J. (1992) *More Has Meant Women: the feminisation of education.* London: Tufnell Press.

Milner, D. (1983) *Children and Race, Ten Years On.* London: Ward Lock Educational.

Ministry of Education (New Zealand) (1993) *Te Whariki: national early childhood curriculum guidelines.* Wellington Learning Media.

Mortimore, P., Sammons, P., Stoll, L., Lewis, D. and Ecob, R. (1988) *School Matters: the junior years.* Wells: Open Books.

Mosely, J. (1993) *Turn Your School Around.* Wisbech: LDA.

Moyles, J.R. (1992) *Organizing for Learning in the Primary Classroom.* Buckingham: Open University Press.

Moyles, J.R. (1994) *Classroom Management.* Leamington Spa: Scholastic.

Murray, M. (1988) 'Negotiation and Collaboration in Problem Solving Groups', *Education 3–13,* **16**(2) pp.48–52.

Nash, B.C. (1981) 'The Effects of Classroom Spatial Organisation on Four- and Five-Year-Old Children's Learning', *British Journal of Educational Psychology,* **51**, pp.144–55.

National Association of Headteachers (1989a) *National Curriculum Helpline Guidance Note Six: a baseline profile for pupils at 5 years old.* Haywards Heath, Sussex: NAHT Publications, June.

National Association of Headteachers (1989b) *Bulletin No. 15 September 1989.* Haywards Heath, Sussex: NAHT Publications.

National Children's Bureau (1991) *Young Children in Group Day Care. Guidelines for good practice.* London: NCB.

National Commission on Education (1993) *Learning to Succeed.* London: Heinemann.

Navarra, J.G. (1955) *The Development of Scientific Concepts in a Young Child.* New York: Teachers College Press, Columbia University.

Nelson, K. (1986) *Event Knowledge.* Hillsdale, NJ: Erlbaum.

Nelson, K. and Seidman, S. (1984) 'Playing with Scripts', in I. Bretherton (Ed) *Symbolic Play: the development of social understanding.* New York: Academic Press.

Nias, J. (1989) *Primary Teachers Talking.* London: Routledge.

Nias, J., Southworth, G. and Yeomans, R. (1989) *Staff Relationships in the Primary School.* London: Cassell Educational.

Nutbrown, C. (1994) *Threads of Thinking.* London: Paul Chapman.

O'Connor, M. (1994) 'Listen to the Mamas and the Papas', *Times Educational Supplement,* 25.2, p.13.

Office for Standards in Education (1993a) *First Class: the standards and quality of education in reception classes.* London: HMSO.

Office for Standards in Education (1993b) *Framework for the Inspection of Schools.* London: HMSO.

Office for Standards in Education (1994) 'Annex A Inspection Issues and the Early Years: a consultative paper' *Update Ninth Issue September 1994.* London: OFSTED.

Ollis, J. (1990) 'Parent Held Development Diaries in Practice', *Early Years,* **10**(2), pp.20–7.

Paley, V.G. (1979) *White Teacher.* Chicago: University of Chicago Press.

Paley, V.G. (1981) *Wally's Stories.* Cambridge, Mass.; London: Harvard University Press.

Paley, V.G. (1984) *Boys and Girls: superheroes in the doll corner.* Chicago; London: University of Chicago Press.

Paley, V.G. (1986a) *Mollie is Three.* Chicago: University of Chicago Press.

Paley, V.G. (1986b) 'On Listening to What Children Say', *Harvard Educational Review,* **56**(2), pp.122–31.

Paley, V.G. (1988) *Bad Guys Don't Have Birthdays.* Chicago: University of Chicago Press.

Paley, V.G. (1989) *Must Teachers Also be Writers?* Occasional Paper no. 13, Centre for the Study of Writing, Berkeley: University of California.

Paley, V.G.(1990) *The Boy Who Would Be a Helicopter.* Cambridge, Mass.: Harvard University Press.

Paley, V.G. (1992) *You Can't Say You Can't Play.* Cambridge, Mass.: Harvard University Press.

Paley, V.G. (1995a) *Kwanzaa and Me. A teacher's story.* Cambridge, Mass.; London: Harvard University Press.

Paley, V.G. (1995b) 'On Listening to What Children Say.' Lecture given at Froebel Institute College, Roehampton Institute, London.

Papatheodorou, T. and Ramasut, A. (1994) 'Environmental Effects on Teacher': perceptions of behaviour problems in nursery school children', *European Early Childhood Education Research Journal,* **2**.

Pascal, C. (1990) *Under-Fives in the Infant Classroom.* Stoke-on-Trent: Trentham Books.

Play for Tomorrow (1991) BBC Horizon Programme.

Pollard, A. (1985) *The Social World of the Primary School.* London: Holt, Reinhart & Winston.

Pollard, A. (Ed) (1987a) *Children and Their Primary Schools: a new perspective.* London: Falmer Press.

Pollard, A. (1987b) 'Goodies, Jokers and Gangs', in A. Pollard (Ed) op. cit.

Pollard, A. and Tann, S. (1978) *Reflective Teaching in the Primary School.* London: Cassell.

Pollard, A., Broadfoot, P., Croll, P., Osborn, M. and Abbott, D. (1994) *Changing English Primary Schools? The impact of the Education Reform Act at Key Stage One.* London: Cassell.

Pound, L. (1988) 'Equality in a Child-centred Curriculum', *TACTYC,* **9**(1), pp.64–72.

Raven, J. (1980) *Parents, Teachers and Children.* Sevenoaks: Hodder & Stoughton, for the Scottish Council for Research in Education.

Reifel, S. and Yeatman, J. (1991) 'Action, Talk and Thought in Blockplay', in B. Scales *et al.* (Eds) op. cit.

Riches, C. and Morgan, C. (1989) *Human Resource Management in Education.* Milton Keynes: Open University Press.

Rieser, R. and Mason, M. (1990) *Disability, Equality in the Classroom: a human rights issue.* London: ILEA.

Roaf, C. and Bines, H. (1994) 'Learner Needs or Learner Rights?' in A. Pollard and J. Bourne (Eds) *Teaching and Learning in the Primary School.* London: Routledge in Association with the Open University.

Robinson, H.A. (1994) *The Ethnography of Empowerment: the transformative power of classroom interaction.* London: Falmer Press.

Robson, B. (1989) *Special Needs in Ordinary Schools: pre-school provision for children with special needs.* London: Cassell Educational.

Robson, S. (1992) 'How can Autonomy be Achieved in School?', *Early Child Development and Care,* **79**, pp.73–88.

Robson, S. (1993) '"Best of all I like choosing time": talking with children about play and work', *Early Child Development and Care,* **92**, pp.37–51.

Rodd, J. (1994) *Leadership in Early Childhood.* Buckingham: Open University Press.

Roehampton Institute (1995) *Initial Teacher Education Primary Programmes, Students in School, A Profile of Professional Development.* London: Roehampton Institute.

Rosen, H. (1984) *Stories and Meanings.* Sheffield: National Association for the Teaching of English.

Rouse, D. and Griffin, S. (1992) 'Quality for the Under Threes', in G. Pugh (Ed) *Contemporary Issues in the Early Years.* London: Paul Chapman/National Children's Bureau.

Rowe, D. and Newton, J. (1994) *You, Me and Us.* London: Citizenship Foundation.

Runnymede Trust (1993) *Equality Assurance in Schools: quality, identity, society.* Stoke-on-Trent: Trentham Books.

Salmon, P. (1988) *Psychology for Teachers: an alternative approach.* London: Hutchinson.

Scales, B., Almy, M., Nicopoulou, A. and Ervin-Tripp, S. (Eds) (1991) *Play and the Social Context of Development in Early Care and Education.* Columbia: Teachers College Press, Columbia University.

Seifert, K.L. (1988) 'The Culture of Early Education and the Preparation of Male Teachers', *Early Child Development and Care,* **38**, pp.69–90.

Sellers, S. (1989) 'Learning to Read the Feminine', in A. Thompson and H. Wilcox (Eds) *Teaching Women Feminism and English Studies.* Manchester: Manchester University Press.

Sherman, L. (1975) 'An Ecological Study of Glee in Small Groups of Preschool Children', *Child Development,* **46**, pp.53–61, cited in C. Garvey (1990) (2nd edn) *Play.* London: Fontana.

Singer, J. and Singer, D. (1979) 'The Values of the Imagination', in B. Sutton-Smith, *Play and Learning.* New York: Gardner Press.

Siraj-Blatchford, I. (1992) 'Why Understanding Cultural Differences is not Enough.' in G. Pugh (Ed) *Contemporary Issues in the Early Years.* London: Paul Chapman in Association with the NCB.

Siraj-Blatchford, I. (Ed) (1993a) *'Race', Gender and the Education of Teachers.* Buckingham: Open University Press.

Siraj-Blatchford, I. (1993b) 'Educational Research and Reform: some implications for the professional identity of early years teachers', *British Journal of Educational Studies,* **41**(4), 393–406.

Siraj-Blatchford, I. (1994a) 'Back to the Future?', *Times Educational Supplement,* 24. 6, p.19.

Siraj-Blatchford, I. (1994b) *The Early Years. Laying the Foundations for Racial Equality.* Stoke-on-Trent: Trentham Books.

Skelton, C. (1991) 'Study of the Career Perspectives of Male Teachers of Young Children', *Gender and Education,* **3**(3), 279–89.

Skelton, C. (1994) 'Sex, Male Teachers and Young Children', *Gender and Education,* **6**(1) pp.87–93.

Smedley, S. (1992) *Versions and Visions: women primary school teachers, their initial education and their work,* Unpublished MA dissertation, University of London Institute of Education.

Smedley, S. (1994) 'On Being a Primary School Teacher', *Early Child Development and Care,* **97**, pp.35–65.

Smedley, S. (1995) 'One Story Amongst Many', *Early Child Development and Care,* **110**, pp.101–12.

Smith, P.K. (1988) 'The Relevance of Fantasy Play for Development in Young Children', in A. Cohen and L. Cohen (Eds) *Early Education: the pre-school years.* London: Paul Chapman.

Smith, P.K. and Connelly, K.J. (1981) *The Ecology of Pre-School Behaviour.* London: Cambridge University Press.

Solity, J. (1995) 'Psychology, Teachers and the Early Years', in *International Journal of Early Years Education,* **3**(1), Spring.

Southworth, G. (Ed) (1987) *Readings in Primary School Management.* Lewes: Falmer Press.

Stallibrass, A. (1974) *The Self Respecting Child.* London: Thames & Hudson.

Stamford, G. and Stoate, P. (1990) *Developing Effective Classroom Groups: a practical guide for teachers.* Bristol: Acorn Books.

Steedman, C. (1985) 'The Mother Made Conscious': the historical development of a primary school pedagogy', *History Workshop Journal,* **20**, Autumn, pp.149–63.

Steedman, C. (1987) 'Prisonhouses' in M. Lawn and G. Grace (Eds) (1987) *Teachers: the culture and politics of work.* London: Falmer Press.

Steedman, C. (1990) *Childhood, Culture and Class in Britain: Margaret McMillan 1860–1931.* London: Virago.

Stenhouse, L. (1975) *Introduction to Curriculum Research and Development.* London: Heinemann Educational.

Stephen, C. and Wilkinson, J.E. (1995) 'Assessing the Quality of Provision in Community Nurseries', *Early Child Development and Care,* **108**, pp.83–98.

Stevenson, C. (1987) 'The Four Year Old in Nursery and Infant Classes: challenges and constraints' in *Four Year Olds in School: Policy and Practice.* Slough: NFER/SCDC.

Stierer, B., Devereux, J., Gifford, S. Laycock, L. and Yerbury, J. (1993) *Profiling, Observing and Recording.* London: Routledge.

Stonehouse, A. and Woodrow, C. (1992) 'Professional Issues: a perspective on their place in pre-service education for early childhood.' *Early Child Development and Care,* **78**, 207–23.

Stubbs, D.R. (1985) *Assertiveness at Work.* London: Gower Publishing.

Suransky, V.P. (1982) *The Erosion of Childhood.* Chicago: University of Chicago Press.

Swann, S. and White, R. (1994) *The Thinking Books.* London: Falmer Press.

Sylva, K., Roy, C. and Painter, M. (1980) *Child Watching at Playgroup and Nursery School.* London: Grant McIntyre.

Szreter, R. (1964) 'The Origins of Full-time Compulsory Education at Five', *British Journal of Educational Studies,* **13**.

Tamburrini, J. (1981) 'Teaching Style in Relation to Play in the Nursery School' in M. Roberts and J. Tamburrini (Eds) *Child Development 0–5.* Holmes McDougal: Edinburgh.

Thacker, J., Stoate, P. and Feest, G. (1992) *Groupwork Skills: Using Group Work in Primary Classrooms.* Crediton: Southgate.

Titman, W. (1994) *Special Places, Special People.* Godalming, Surrey: WWF/Learning Through Landscapes.

Tizard, B. and Hughes, M. (1984) *Young Children Learning.* London: Fontana.

Tizard, B., Mortimore, J. and Burchell, B. (1981) *Involving Parents in Nursery and Infant Schools.* London: Grant McIntyre.

Tizard, B., Phelps, J.P. and Plewis, I. (1976) 'Play in Preschool Centres, Part 1', *Journal of Child Psychology and Psychiatry,* **17**, pp.251-64.

Tizard, B., Blatchford, P., Burke, J., Farquhar, C. and Plewis, I. (1988) *Young Children at School in the Inner City.* Hove: Lawrence Erlbaum.

Tizard, J., Schofield, W.N. and Hewison, J. (1982) 'Collaboration Between Teachers and Parents in Assisting Children's Reading', *British Journal of Educational Psychology,* **52**, pp.1–15.

Tobin, J.J., Wu, D.Y.H., Davidson, D.H. (1989) *Pre-School in Three Cultures: Japan, China and the United States.* New Haven: Yale University Press.

Tovey, H. (1994) *Young Children's Learning: a reappraisal of sand and water play.* Unpublished MA dissertation, University of Surrey.

Tucker, N. (1977) *What is a Child?* London: Fontana.

Tudor Hart, B. (1963) *Learning to Live.* London: Sphere Books.

Van der Eyken, W., Osborn, A. and Butler, N. (1984) 'Pre-Schooling in Britain: a national study of institutional provision for under-fives in England, Scotland and Wales' in *Early Child Development and Care Reading,* **17**, pp.79–122.

Vedel-Petersen, J. (1992) *Daycare for Children Under School Age in Denmark.* Copenhagen: Danish National Institute of Social Research.

Vicinus, M. (1985) *Independent Women, Work and Community for Single Women 1850–1920.* London: Virago.

Vygotsky, L. (1962) *Thought and Language.* Massachusetts: Massachusetts Institute of Technology.

Vygotsky, L. (1978) *Mind in Society.* Edited by Michael Cole. Cambridge, Mass.: Harvard University Press.

Vygotsky, L. (1986) *Thought and Language.* Revised and edited by Alex Kozulin. Cambridge, Mass.: MIT Press.

Walkerdine, V. (1983) 'It's Only Natural: rethinking child-centred pedagogy', in A. Wolpe and J. Donald (Eds) *Is There Anyone Here From Education?* London: Pluto Press.

Walkerdine, V. and the Girls from the Mathematics Unit (1989) *Counting Girls Out.* London: Virago.

Walkerdine, V. and Sinha, C. (1981) 'Developing Linguistic Strategies', in G. Wells (Ed) *Learning Through Interaction.* Cambridge: Cambridge University Press.

Wall, W.D. (1975) *Constructive Education for Children.* London: Harrap; Paris: Unesco Press.

Waterland, L, (1985) *Read With Me.* Stroud: Thimble Press.

Weber, S. and Mitchell, C. (1995) *'That's Funny, You Don't Look Like a Teacher!'* London: Falmer Press.

Webster, A. (1994) 'SEN Code of Practice', *Child Education,* September. Leamington Spa, Warwickshire: Scholastic Publications.

Weiler, K. (1988) *Women Teaching for Change: gender, class and power.* New York: Bergin and Garvey Publishers.

Weiner, G. (1985) 'Equal Opportunities, Feminism and Girls' Education: introduction', in G. Weiner (Ed) *Just a Bunch of Girls.* Milton Keynes: Open University Press.

Weis, D. and Worobey, J. (1991) 'Sex-roles and Family Scripts in Early Childhood', *Early Child Development and Care,* **77**, pp.109–14.

Wells, G. (1986) *The Meaning Makers.* London: Hodder & Stoughton.

Whalley, M. (1992) 'Working as a Team', in G. Pugh (Ed) *Contemporary Issues in the Early Years.* London: Paul Chapman and the National Children's Bureau.

Whalley, M. (1994) *Learning to be Strong.* London: Hodder & Stoughton.

Whitehead, M. (1990) *Language and Literacy in the Early Years: an approach for education students.* London: Paul Chapman.

Whitehead, M. (1992) 'Partnerships in Literacy', *Times Educational Supplement,* 6.11, p.7.

Whitehead, M. (1994) 'Stories from a Research Project: towards a narrative analysis of data', *Early Years,* **15**, pp.23–9.

Willes, M.J. (1983) *Children into Pupils: a study of language in early schooling.* London: Routledge & Kegan Paul.

Winnicott, D.W. (1964) *The Child, the Family and the Outside World.* Harmondsworth: Penguin.

Wolfendale, S. (1984) 'A Framework for Action: professionals and parents as partners', *Partnership Paper 1, Working Together: parents and professionals as partners,* National Children's Bureau, pp.3–11.

Wolfendale, S. (1989) *Parental Involvement.* London: Cassell.

Wolfendale, S. (1990) 'Assessment by Parents', *Portage at Pontins Conference Proceedings.* London: National Portage Association London and South East Region, November.

Wolfendale, S. and Wooster, J. (1992) 'Meeting Special Needs in the Early Years', in G. Pugh (Ed) *Contemporary Issues in the Early Years.* London: Paul Chapman and the National Children's Bureau.

Wood, D. (1988) *How Children Think and Learn.* Oxford: Blackwell.

Wood, D., Bruner, J. and Ross, G. (1976) 'The role of Play-tutoring in Problem-solving', *Journal of Child Psychology and Psychiatry,* **17**, pp.89–100.

Wood, D., McMahon, L. and Cranstoun, Y. (1980) *Working With Under Fives.* London: Grant McIntyre.

Woodhead, C. (1994) Letter, *Times Educational Supplement,* 15.7, p.14.

Woodhead, M. (1989) 'School Starts at Five...or Four Years Old? The rationale for changing admission policies in England and Wales', in G. Barrett (Ed) (1989a) op. cit.

Wright, C. (1992) *Race Relations in the Primary School.* London: David Fulton Publishers.

Index